# Books by Jean Rikhoff

## NOVELS

**The Timble Trilogy**
*Dear Ones All*
*Voyage In, Voyage Out*
*Rites of Passage*

**The Buttes-Raymond Trilogy**
*Buttes Landing*
*One of the Raymonds*
*The Sweetwater*

*Where Were You in '76?*

## YOUNG ADULT NOVELS

*Mark Twain: Writing About the Frontier*
*Robert E. Lee: Soldier of the South*

## ANTHOLOGIES

The Quixote Anthology
*The Adirondack Reader* (edited by Paul Jamieson)
*North Country* (with Joseph Bruchac, Craig
Hancock, and Alice Gilborn)

T0367279

# EARTH AIR FIRE AND WATER

*A Memoir*

## JEAN RIKHOFF

iUniverse, Inc.
Bloomington

Earth Air Fire and Water
A Memoir

iUniverse books may be ordered through booksellers or by contacting:

iUniverse
1663 Liberty Drive
Bloomington, IN 47403
www.iuniverse.com
1-800-Authors (1-800-288-4677)

ISBN: 978-1-4620-0936-7 (pbk)
ISBN: 978-1-4620-0937-4 (cloth)
ISBN: 978-1-4620-0938-1 (ebk)

Printed in the United States of America

iUniverse rev. date: 8/4/2011

This book is in memory of Walter Lape

The events described in this book come from my own experiences. Some names have been changed for purposes of privacy, some events rearranged or telescoped for purposes of unity, some people and places omitted for purposes of cohesion. I have fused some events and dates. A lot of people have been left out of the narrative because they were not an integral part of the four sections; that does not mean they were not important in my life. (See acknowledgments at the end of the book for many of those people.)

Memory has many levels and is selective; often, fact and fantasy are not far apart. All storytelling is in the end a weaving of experience and a writer's need to make myth and meaning out of the events of his or her life.

Memory is never accurate and always selective and/or embellished, but still we like to think our memories represent what actually took place. Our memories cannot always be trusted, and even when they are accurate, they exist on many levels. We do not think horizontally straight through an episode. We begin with one story, and another may interrupt it. In some sentence structures, I have attempted to show these different levels of memory by interrupted sentence structure, punctuation, and typography. For example, I have dealt with conversation in different patterns. When the conversation is that of blurred memory, there are no quotation marks. When the conversation is as I believe it actually took place, there are quotation marks. Some sentences try to capture the mind's stream of consciousness and its tendency to be interrupted and wander by allowing more complicated sentence structure. Our brain works on many levels; so then should the sentence structures.

I have used capitals, italics, and typography to suggest different activities of the mind. I am trying to convey directly by the composition how my mind is working. The only alternative is to use the traditional methods of narrative by *telling* the reader how several levels can go on at the same time. The first rule of writing is to show, not tell. Therefore, instead of telling the reader that there are interruptions and concurrent thoughts, I have interwoven the thought patterns together.

Twitter, Myspace, and Facebook have made acronyms a way of life: BFF, CU, EOD, and so forth. The younger generation is growing up on abbreviations that often flummox their parents. Memory does not shorten the thought line, but extends it. Memory does not work on abbreviations and acronyms and explanations of how it is working. Often it rambles.

The same word can have different meanings. For example, take the widely quoted (and obviously inaccurate) phrase, love means never having to say you're sorry. Now look at the difference in meaning one word—always—can have by the way you follow that sentence up with the typography you choose.

Always.

*Always.*

**Always.**

Always?

*Always?*

***ALWAYS?***

Imagine what the editor first reading an e.e. cummings poem must have thought. Hasn't this guy ever heard of capitalization or punctuation? Or maybe there is something the matter with his typewriter and the capital key doesn't work. André Gide, when he read the first volume of Marcel Proust's book *Remembrance of Things Past,* did not understand Proust's elaborate prose style and turned the book down. Proust finally had the book published himself. Later Gide called his rejection of *Swann's Way* one of the gravest errors of his life. My point is this: literature is always in a state of transition, and writers are always trying to translate those differences by the way the prose is constructed and punctuated, or the typography changed.

# WATER

The ocean is where the first speck of life emerged, some 3.8 billion years ago. The speck evolved into algae capable of photosynthesis, resulting in the first supply of oxygen. This oxygen, interacting with ultraviolet rays from the sun, encased the earth in a protective vale called the ozone layer

Then, some 420 million years ago, life took its first step out of the water, and fed itself from the depths of the ocean with the help of oxygen and the ozone layer.

Masaru Emoto, *The Hidden Messages in Water*
(New York: Simon & Schuster Atria Books, 2001), 59.

I remember someone grabbing me under water and hauling me up by the hair, but my father claims I came up on my own and that I splashed a few strokes toward him—he had swan dived directly after me from the ledge of the pool. From that time on, anything that had to do with large amounts of water was something I looked upon with suspicion. I grew up in Indiana, a landlocked state, so all I had to fear were lakes and large rivers, not the true terrors of dark oceans and black seas.

I had a hard time growing up. The only thing that seemed to give me respite from the violent world around me, which my father controlled, was finding a place to hide and then pulling out a book and reading. I lived in books. I thought the people who wrote them were gods. They could create and control whole worlds, and the thing I wanted most to be was one of them. From the time I was eight, I wanted to be a writer.

This is ironic, because I have dyslexia, a term not widely used until the '70s. At the time I was growing up, you were just labeled dumb or stubborn about not learning to write right, or you were a cutup for transferring your numbers around, as if you were setting up a code to test the teacher.

That I could read at all was a miracle. Lots of dyslexic people never figured out coping skills to be able to bury themselves in books. I *had* to teach myself so that I had an escape to worlds that were not so dangerous as the house I lived in. I read and I dreamed of a family like the one in *The Waltons* and *Little House on the Prairie.*

I think that's how I came to marry so young, while I was still in college. In those days—the late '40s—you had to have the permission of the president of the college (a stern man who belonged in the pulpit of a chastising church, who ruled with a male iron hand over the women's college Emily Dickinson had fled in consternation). My about-to-be husband's reminiscences of his family were straight out of the fantasies of The Best Families of All Time. As a young boy, he had spent every idyllic summer on an island off the coast of Connecticut. His grandfather was one of those '20s Fitzgerald tycoons; he couldn't find an island that suited him, so he had one constructed, which I believe he named Potato Island, but surely a man like that would have named it after himself or found a more romantic-sounding tribute to his ingenuity.

My husband's grandfather constructed the island, whatever it was called, by having rocks piled up and then cemented together until they formed the rudimentary outlines of an island. Then he sent barges out with good top soil to fill in the outline of the island, until he had earth rich enough to sustain vegetable and flower gardens he could plunder all summer.

On his man-made island, he also built a fourteen-room house, a seven-room bungalow, a tennis court, and a large boathouse next to a seven-hundred pound mushroom anchor. He equipped himself with a seventy-foot yawl, a forty-foot ketch, a Star Class boat, something I thought my husband said was a Weskit, two or three dinghies, and several motorboats. Then, with the same determination that he had exhibited in constructing his own island, he taught himself to sail.

Every year during the winter, the sea knocked part of his island's perimeter wall out, and the precious topsoil seeped away. Each spring, before the annual migration of the family to Potato Island began, barge after barge made the three-mile trip out to refill the island. It was on this man-made cement-and-soil oasis that my husband had spent all his summers from the time he was three or four until he was fourteen, sailing a small boat alone, much the same way, I thought as he told me about his adventures, as I had escaped between the covers of adventure books.

In 1938, The Big Hurricane put an end forever to the island, washing the bungalow away, smashing the big house in two as if it had been struck by a giant fist, depositing the seven-hundred pound anchor in the midst of the tennis court, and spilling the top soil back into Long Island Sound. From that time on, my husband never again set a sneaker on a small boat, but he had never stopped dreaming about getting another one so that he could relive the magic moments of those long-ago summers.

One weekend, when we were first dating, my boat-husband, as I now always think of him, and I drove up to Stony Creek and hired a boat. He rowed us out to see what was left of Potato Island. It was not a happy sight, and my husband said he never wanted to go back. So far as I know, he never did. But then, I haven't seen him in several decades, so I couldn't testify to that in court, and now that he's dead (in 2008, at Belfast, Maine, loyal to the water to the last), I will never know. I was not mentioned in the obituaries, nor was his second wife, who had helped him put together a book about contemporary fiction. Of course, the obituary was written by his third wife, also a writer. Make of this what you will (and there seems to be a lot).

Even after five decades, I still recall the stories my soon-to-be husband told about the cohesive lovingness of his family—how a group of mothers would get together the day after Thanksgiving to make Christmas fruitcakes, how in spring they planned the annual Easter egg hunts that were filled with excitement because whichever child found the golden egg collected a twenty-dollar bill. (In those days, twenty dollars was a fortune.) At the Fourth of July picnic—with all its splendid food, each part of the family vying to bring bigger and better dishes—the dark night would be splashed with the splendor of sparklers and fireworks. Most of all, the tales my soon-to-be-husband told centered around those memorable moments when he had been out all by himself in his small sailboat, exploring the nooks and crannies of Long Island Sound.

"They let you go alone when you were that young?" I asked, horrified. From the look on his face, I was missing the point. After we were married, it turned out I missed the point of most of what my husband tried to tell me. At the time, I put it down to a bad marriage; now, I wonder if men and women don't usually miss the point of what they are trying to tell each other.

I was envious of that island off the Connecticut shore, where a family went every summer and seemed, the way my boat-husband told it—I never think of him now as anything but my boat-husband, as if he were a species of a generic brand. This was a family that had *traditions* and got together to laugh, a family that seemed straight out of a child's primer, one I would have given anything to have had. My own family had been so filled with arguments, violence, rage.

The first time I was invited to one to one of my husband's family get-togethers (I see now I was being vetted), I was thrilled with how warmly affectionate everyone was, even toward me, the stranger. Well, there was one moment when I happened to mention that I had been brought up in the Catholic church. A deadly silence fell on the room, but everyone went back to smiling when I announced I had left the church when I was fifteen. It took me way too long to conclude that if these people were anti-Catholic, they were probably also anti-Semitic, plus against desegregation, women's rights, and equality for gays. They had such a polished façade—except for that brief chilling moment when the word Catholic swamped the family dinner table—that I mistook their good manners for good morals. A psychiatrist would probably have concluded I married my husband's family, not my husband.

My mother was the most helpless of all. Her looks were the thing she prized most, and they were the first thing my father went for. He quieted down when he saw the blood run from her nose or her lips begin to purple and swell. I hid under the bed or ran out of the house and down the street, my brother trailing behind. "One day I'm going to shoot him," my brother often said, and I hoped he would. It is no coincidence, I think, that he became a big-game hunter.

Because the man I was going out with was better looking than Brad Pitt (Razzle-dazzle Rust, I used to call him) and belonged to a picture-perfect family, I married him in a daze of delight. I couldn't wait for the first Thanksgiving and the day after, when I would be one of the makers of the Christmas fruitcakes. But holidays bring out sins and shortcomings. My husband's family, whom I thought never spoke a cross word to one another, let alone raised their hands in anger, turned out not to be like the Walton family I had worshipped on TV. During my first Christmas as a new wife, I found people banging pots and pans in the kitchens, slamming doors throughout the house, throwing clothes out an upstairs window, screaming at spouses, ignoring crying children, weeping in the bathroom, running out into the night with the car keys and disappearing from the tree trimming and the Christmas dinner, Christmas day itself. I didn't realize until it was too late how much I had created a Walton-family veneer. There was no way my husband was or ever would be John Boy. From that first day my husband had rowed me out and showed me the wrecked family island, I was hooked.

Now that the ring was on my finger, I noticed things about my husband that I had never seen before or had overlooked or had thought in the beginning were endearing that were now rapidly becoming major irritations. At first, while we were working our way through school, my husband and I had become stars of at least some luminance at our Ivy League schools. People thought we were very avant-garde to get married and still keep going to school. We both had scholarships and worked all the scut jobs we could find, because our parents seemed to feel that the day we wed, their financial responsibilities to us ended.

We graduated and went on for our masters', and then we were out to work and were no longer the trophy couple of the young and rebellious. Now we were just an average married duo in Manhattan looking for jobs that paid enough to afford food and rent and an occasional night out. My husband was looking for a career. Women looked for apartments and then jobs, or the kind of jobs women could get in 1949, not career jobs, but the peon work of low-wage earners. Women would just get pregnant and leave, so what was the point of training them? The first question I was asked at any job interview was how long I expected to stay before I started a family. I'm not planning on starting a family,

I would say, and that seemed such a bald-faced lie that the interview ended. No one wanted to hire a liar.

My husband landed a position selling trade books for Henry Holt. I went to every magazine whose name was familiar to me and filled out an application. After each application, I was told I had to take a typing test, no matter how much I protested that I did not want to be a secretary, that I did not take shorthand, that I had a master's degree in English and wanted to write. Those interviews did not go well. Finally, I ate humble pie and took the typing test. I could type, but not well. I never got any callbacks.

I finally got a job in the business department of *Gourmet* magazine for forty dollars a week, twenty-eight something after taxes and all the other deductions were taken out. *Gourmet* was publishing its first cookbook (ten bucks a book, which would be like a hundred dollars today). If you bought a book, you had the option of having your initials printed in gold on the spine. My job was to divide the people who wanted initials from those who didn't. Most everyone wanted initials. I then had to type up a list of those who wanted initials, which ones they wanted, and send it to the printer. When the books came back, I had to check the initials against the original order to be sure they matched. Hundreds and hundreds of names and initials a week. It was like counting paper clips.

The elevators at the Plaza Hotel where *Gourmet* had offices in the penthouse and the floor above let me out at the eighteenth floor, the last number on the elevator panel, which opened onto lavish editorial offices. There were stairs in back, where no one would see them, that went upstairs, where all the lowly people like me worked in the business office sweatshop. There I typed names and addresses and initials for over a year, all the time pleading for a job in the editorial division downstairs, where the posh offices were. Upstairs—as if we were in the attic—the peons who worked at entering subscriptions and taking calls from people whose bills or initials were mixed up, plus some lower-echelon factotums of advertising who were out on the road a lot, lived in cells painted gunmetal gray. It had all the glamour of an insecticide company instead of a posh culinary magazine.

I was finally, after a lot of lobbying, transferred to the editorial offices on the eighteenth floor just before Thanksgiving. No one (fortunately) asked me if I knew how to cook, because the only cooking I had ever done—and I don't know if it could even be classified as cooking—was making some Jello-and-marshmallow dish for Campfire Girls, for which I was awarded a badge. I was to work in the library—paneled in oak and lined with hundreds of cookbooks—which I would share with an associate editor, Ann Seranne—blonde, beautiful, and an authority on desserts.

My first day, she told me to answer the phone. It was the week before Thanksgiving, and I kept getting frantic requests for the best way to cook a turkey. I had absolutely no idea, but I grabbed what looked like an interesting recipe from the files and gave that out over the phone. It turned out that the dressing I recommended for stuffing the turkey used two hundred dollars of truffles (I had no idea what truffles were). When Ann found out, she took me off the phone and put me on answering letters, where people had been to such-and-such a restaurant and eaten such-and-such a dish in such-and-such a country and wanted the recipe.

The letters also contained samples of strange herbs and spices the subscribers couldn't identify that they had picked up in, say, Thailand or Madagascar. I opened the mail in the morning and put the recipes I thought I could trace or approximate in one pile, and those that I thought of as hopeless in the to-do-later stack. This pile increased exponentially, so that the area around my desk began to have a peculiar smell. Even the Oriental houseboy, whose main job was to take the two poodles to Central Park in the early morning, after lunch, and at closing time, complained. The dogs were not well trained. They often relieved themselves in the elevator, and some Plaza lackey was constantly being sent up to complain.

If I let more than two weeks go by without identifying an herb or spice or sending a recipe, a terrible vitriolic letter arrived demanding to know why the strawberries with that special sauce they had had in Milan—or was it Paris?—had not been sent to them. My big mistake came in the moments when I pulled myself up short and said to myself, Is this what you want to do with your life? Was knowledge of *Bifteck Haché à la Lyonnaise, Fricadelles Veau à la Niçoise,* or *Mousseline de Volaille* really going to make some significant statement to the world? This thinking was a grave error, I realized the day I got fired, because—I was told in no uncertain terms by the owner of the magazine—I had no

7

respect for the serious mission of the magazine. You think it's funny to write Don't let your beans be has beans? he thundered. Do you? You're through here, this man who couldn't toilet train his dogs yelled at me. Just clean out your desk and get the hell out. I had no idea where I was supposed to be going, but one thing was certain: *Gourmet* didn't want me anymore.

My husband had loved the *Gourmet* offices. There were all kinds of views of the ponds and lakes of Central Park and even, far out, the waves that pressed against the island of Manhattan. He might even have got on with the people there who were so entranced by special breeds of lettuce and pastries that puffed. I don't remember much about what he was really like in those days. So much of my life consisted of trying to write a novel, a thinly disguised exposé of what went on in those offices. Witty and revelatory, or so I thought. It was accepted by several publishing houses, but every time a literary lawyer went over the manuscript, he would shake his head and tell the publishing house that they'd be sued if they published the book. It was no use arguing; I was telling the truth (and toned down at that). There was only one food magazine on the market at the time, and everyone would immediately start fitting the "fictionalized" characters to the real people at *Gourmet,* and the fat would be in the fire, to use a culinary metaphor.

I took that book out the other day and looked at it. It was dated and, worse, dull. The workplace has evolved so much in the last thirty years that it's hard to believe the young women (we were really girls) were so shamelessly paid and that the "fictional" owner of the magazine could be so nescient that he served Scotch with the salad.

Who cares?

*I* don't even care anymore, and I can't even begin to understand the person I was back then who wasted a year of her life and destroyed perhaps an entire forest of trees for the paper needed for the various drafts of that book. I thought I was doing the world a favor to reveal the shallowness of some of our civilization, to say nothing of the fact that I thought people would love all the sex I manufactured out of a relatively untutored mind and of a view of a glamorous—if marginal world—that took itself so seriously that its inhabitants actually believed a life's worth could be held in balance by the difference between sauces. I remember going to a blender party where every single one of the five courses was puréed and at least a dozen people had gathered with great solemnity to write about them. Duh.

In the Brooklyn Heights apartment where we lived because we couldn't afford anything even halfway decent in Manhattan, I stood at the window looking down at all the people going about their ordinary day. They would not have to say at its end, I was let go today. I lost my job. Or, I got fired. Most people can't stand to hear the truth in plain language, so I was not fired, I was let go. The dead aren't dead. They've passed over. Passed over what?

My husband took the news as if he had known it would only be a matter of time before I blew it. The main thing that concerned him was the twenty-eight something that wouldn't be coming in. How were we going to pay the bills? Unemployment insurance would only cover part of my missing salary, and I could see by his face he was reviewing in his mind the way I felt about taking government money. That money was for the poor. I've been poor several times, but I've never *felt* poor. I could get a job somewhere, maybe even make more money than I had been making. That's a young mind cogitating, not someone who's reached fifty or over and knows there's no comparable job out there to replace the one he or she has just lost. I was some thirty years away from those apprehensions. I was still someone eager to embrace the excitement of doing different things, of seeing different places, of leading a new, different kind of life. I said, Let's go overseas.

That sounds crazy when you just read it off the page in a book the way you are now. Someone says, Where's the rent coming from? And you say back, Let's go abroad. But I remembered, a couple of parties back, someone talking about the University of Maryland hiring people to teach on the American bases in Europe so that men who had been in The War (World War II was The War then) could work toward getting a college degree at the same time they were fulfilling their military duty. The army didn't need bombers anymore; they needed bureaucrats. After the party, I remember saying to my husband, Wouldn't that be fun, to go abroad? And my husband had said, Why throw away what you've got for something you know nothing about?

Both of us could qualify, I argued. We've both got master's degrees.

We just got the apartment fixed up.

We could sublet it. Maybe we could even make some money on it, if we sublet it furnished.

Absentee landlords always get screwed. People don't pay their rent. They trash everything. What do they care? The place isn't theirs.

We could sublet the apartment to someone we know. But I couldn't think of anyone I knew who would want to move to Brooklyn Heights, so I said, It wouldn't hurt just to find out if there are any jobs abroad.

Going abroad would be—there were no words for me to describe the whole Hemingway-Fitzgerald-Picasso soirees that had taken place at Gertrude Stein's atelier at 17 rue de Fleurus in Paris that had created a legendary world of writers and artists that I wanted to be a part of.

Maybe we could find the kind of people we've been looking for over there.

What do you mean, the kind of people we've been looking for? We have lots of friends here.

They're mainly the people we knew in college or the ones we've met at work—

Well, you don't come to Brooklyn Heights and expect to run into Dylan Thomas or Saul Bellow at the corner drugstore.

What harm can it do just to ask?

You ask. You're the one who got canned. Anyway, they say I'm getting ready to go on the executive track if I keep up the kind of work I've been doing.

The unidentified *they* is always the purveyor of information you don't want to hear. *My husband thought he was in line to get on the executive track. End of discussion.*

What's for dinner? he asked.

I didn't know what we were going to have for dinner, and I didn't care. I thought I was at the crossroads of one of those paths Robert Frost had talked about—

*Two roads diverged in a wood, and I—*

*I took the one less traveled by,*
*And that has made all the difference.*

I wasn't going to be allowed to make a choice about which path to take. My husband would make that choice. *The Feminine Mystique* wouldn't be written for years; before Betty Friedan, the idea of a woman being autonomous didn't exist. Well, there was Amelia Earhart, but look what happened to her.

My husband and my father interlocked in my mind. Both of them had the right to hold me a prisoner without any means of escape. I couldn't open a bank account or buy a house or car without a father or husband cosigning. The land of the free was the land of the free for men. I was never going to be able to do what I wanted unless I was *permitted* to do it.

There was no mistaking the look on my husband's face, the one that delighted in reminding me how Faulkner had choked to death on his own vomit, Tennessee Williams on the cap of a pill bottle. The cap of a pill bottle killed one of the great playwrights of the twentieth century, he would say, eyes gleaming. Perhaps it had occurred to him that one day I might go into the bathroom and screw around with an aspirin cap and, since lust no longer ruled our lives and I wasn't even going to be bringing in twenty-eight something a week, I might myself repeat the same kind of accident and he would be rid of me. I didn't see him crying over the loss. Men didn't cry.

I myself considered tears an exhibition of one of the weaknesses of women. When I was down in the basement being beaten and my father was screaming, I'm going to make you cry, goddamn it, if it's the last thing I ever do, I would bite my lips until they bled rather than give my father the satisfaction of seeing me cry. Now, my husband said, It's too bad you can't take shorthand. You wouldn't have any trouble finding a job if you took shorthand. I stood in front of my husband gasping and choking with the violence of all the despair of someone who has just seen herself locked up in a life that was going nowhere.

My husband looked astounded. All right, *all right!* I'll go with you if it means that much to you, but it'll mean I'll have to take a day off. That won't look good for my chances to get on the executive track.

My husband was tall and handsome as a movie star. When he went across the room and firmly shook the hand of the man who was in charge of hiring the University of Maryland professors for work overseas, I could see right away that providing references and submitting a résumé would be a mere formality. Here were two alpha males who dwelled on the Olympian heights of superiority. My husband gave the impression that he held little need for the job he had come to interview for—not wanting something someone else could give you if you groveled hard to get it is always a winner. My husband sat down, smiling but not speaking, remembering no doubt the old rule that he who speaks first loses.

There began a discussion about the perks of the job: you worked nine weeks and then got a week off; you were usually provided with housing and a chauffeur if you had to teach at two places; and the salary—well, when that amount came up, I saw my husband's face light up the way it had the first time he had looked across the room at me (at least as I remember it). He saw me with my head thrown back, my face filled with laughter, and the look on his face said, You're the kind who smokes too much and drinks too much. You probably have questionable morals, and you're everything I've ever wanted. I had looked back at him to see this incredibly handsome Ivy League man—the point then of a girl getting into one of the Seven Sister colleges was that it was a great base for husband trolling. Every girl wanted an acceptance from one of the prestigious Seven Sisters; the hunting ground for husbands was better than at state universities. I only got into Mt. Holyoke because the college had decided to try an experimental "creative" class, giving more emphasis to artistic flair than academic merit, an experiment that they never tried again. This class, as every single administrator reminded us over and over, gave them more trouble than any class they had ever had. That was true: we gave the administration and the professors lip; we organized picketing parties against what we considered unfair practices at the college (such as compulsory chapel); we were always having to be disciplined because we stayed out past the rigid ten-o'clock weeknight curfew.

I looked over at my handsome husband bent forward and talking intensely to the man who was explaining the University of Maryland overseas program. I realized I wasn't even in the room so far as those two men were concerned. I could see that my husband was starting to understand how lucrative the job was and how it might make his résumé seem as if he were one of those involved in an innovative enterprise like this that had taken place *overseas*. No trouble at all to jump back on the executive track when he got back.

There was only one opening in English. "Maybe you can pick up something part-time when you get over there," the man who was interviewing us said dismissively to me. "Occasionally we get a big enrollment and have to split a class in half and need another teacher." It never occurred to me that I should be upset—women didn't stand up and yell, I got better grades than he did! You should give me the job! I was still full of magazine and movie fantasies about how women were the preservers of heart and hearth. Instead of seething with resentment, I told myself, Everything is going to be better when we get overseas.

When, in '54 or '55 (I am terrible with dates), we got on a rusty old bucket that had carried troops during The War, my husband and I were still "we." My husband had the job, so "we" were fine.

I had no steady teaching job that I could count on, but there was always a section, sometimes two, that needed to be filled and a limousine to ferry me the fifty or sixty miles to some small outskirt base where the part-timer teachers got assigned. Between the two of us, we made good money: we had access to the PX, we were living rent-free in a Quonset hut with a maid who came in once a week to clean (a maid coming to clean a Quonset hut!); we were on the Burtonwood base outside Warrington, one of those ugly industrial cities in the British midlands that are black with soot and filled with people who had been pasty-faced even before they were whittled down by The War and the scanty post-war rations that came after. The British were eating whale burgers while we American gorged on steaks and had access to all kinds of fresh fruits and vegetables, cheap liquor and cigarettes, even cars, household appliances, and clothes, all of which could be purchased at the PX, where there was no tax.

We had been given officer ratings, so we used the Officers Club—oh, what a feeling of entitlement our green passports bestowed on us Americans, especially those amongst the grand vizier classes. That Officers Club had enormous buffets and live music and people who seemed to be celebrating something or other every Saturday. Huge planes full of food were sent over on American holidays. Before the Fourth of July, the government sent a transport bomber across the Atlantic filled with nothing but hot dogs and buns. We got turkeys and cranberries on Thanksgiving, and too many things to list at Christmas. Everything on those bases was cheap and prodigal, and I had twinges of guilt as I looked at the barren stores in Warrington and knew that the British were only getting one egg a week and a small ration of meat about the size of the palm of my hand, maybe a cup of sugar. The store windows in London were filled with cashmere sweaters and Burberry raincoats and other finery—and also signs that said "For Export Only," and nobody threw a rock through them.

We got temporary ration cards, and once, in some kind of snit thanks to my husband, I pranced off the bus and left my purse, which had my life in it—my passport, my American and British money, my travelers checks, my temporary rations cards, our guide books (of course I carried those), my *makeup*—everything basic to my life. Nearly half an hour passed before I missed it, though how this is possible I don't know. Every purse I have ever carried as an adult weighed somewhere near twenty pounds, as if I were waiting to take off for a life I wanted and in my purse had everything essential I would need.

When I discovered I didn't have my purse, I let out a shriek. We went back to the bus company, and they called the end of the line we had been on. Someone had turned it in. Is there any money left? I asked. I think everything is intact, the underfed man behind the bus counter said. *Everything* is in the purse? I asked, enumerating all the items that any sensible person, especially in England during those trying days, could have filched.

Of course everything is intact, Madam. There was a pause. We usually charge a 10 percent fee for the finder, but if we did that, it would be an enormous amount. We're only going to count the British money. That's how it was in those days. Not now. The last time I was in London, I could hardly understand the regional dialects people were speaking;

it was as if I were listening to foreign languages that had evolved over the past twenty or thirty years into odd new patterns of patois. If I left my purse on a bus now, there would be nothing left inside, not even a broken pencil, when it was dumped in an ashcan.

People like that who had so little and were so honest made the excesses on the American air bases seem twice as deplorable. I felt guilty all the time. Couldn't we Americans go anywhere in the world without bringing Coke and hamburgers and air conditioning and mammoth cars. (Most of the people on the base had American cars. Gas was rationed for the British, but there was plenty on the base for Americans at a ridiculously small price.)

My husband said, What do you want to do? Not use the Officers Club, the PX, the base facilities? I want you to feel guilty, too, I said. He gave me what I had come to think of as *that* look. He had three courses to teach compared to my two, and he complained so often about all the papers he had to grade that I soon found it made life easier to take part of his papers and grade them myself. He found reasons to hand me more and more—he had more preparations than I did (*one* more), he had to go to a base that was farther than the one I went to (by *ten* miles), I didn't mind doing it as much as he did (I don't know where he got that idea). I thought, We don't want any tantrums around here, do we? Grade the goddamn papers and don't make a scene. Things will be better in the spring. It's just the endless rain and gloom that's getting you down. Soon, I had something worse to worry about. I thought I was pregnant.

I remember trying to remind myself every other minute that there was a one-in-two-billion chance of a sperm achieving its goal, probably because it wouldn't, like most men, ask directions. One sperm may be just one sperm, and it may only have a one-in-two-billion chance to reach its destination if something went awry with the protective methods you were taking to forestall any arrival, but there were maybe millions of swimmers spawning their way up the channel, and one of them should certainly have had the endurance to succeed. I took quinine and drank hot gin and jumped off desktops when my husband wasn't around and prayed to a god whose existence I had quit believing in when I was fifteen. Examining the matter pragmatically, it seemed far more operative to go for a multitude of deities rather than putting all your gods in one basket and think God the Father (and I knew what fathers were like).

A one-basket god doesn't give you options and certainly not as much pleasure as seeing gods all around you. I liked syllogisms and preferred to adopt as my own a world having a diversity of many deities, as in that river has a god, that tree has its own god, that mountain has a really big god. I could have said that I believed in a pantheon of gods. Why should one god be any better than a lot of gods? Which god was it that drove the tadpole sperm to its home port?

I would get an abortion. Down some dirty back alley and up rickety stairs to some second-floor butcher who might kill me, but I was not going to have a baby. Nothing on earth could have persuaded me at that moment in my life that I would find it entrancing to change dirty nappies and spoon strained fruits into some infant's gaping mouth.

I had all the excuses of women who don't want to have a baby: I was too young, my husband and I hadn't resolved our "difficulties," which is to say that I was beginning to look at him with new eyes. His handsomeness didn't erase a lot of what I considered his deficiencies. If I had a baby, we would probably have to go back home, and that was the last thing in the world I wanted. It's possible to find plausible excuses for anything that doesn't fit into your plans.

The pill didn't exist in those days. Women wore diaphragms, and there were diaphragm babies that couples would make a joke about. "He's our little surprise, our diaphragm baby." But it was the best birth control then, much more reliable than using rubbers. You went to Planned Parenthood to get fitted. The one I remember was gritty, the waiting room crowded with boxes and embarrassed or petrified girls. I had to wait over an hour for my name to be called. I went into this cluttered room with open boxes everywhere and huge dead gray eyes looking at me (the different sizes of the diaphragms). I was put up on a table, and this bored woman came over, her hands covered with flesh-colored rubber gloves, one of which she poked up inside me. She had some kind of metal measuring tool. Then she gave me a number. That's the size you need, she said. You should get refitted at least once a year and after you have a baby—sounding as if having a baby was a hopeless business at best. You pay for the diaphragm at the desk when you give them your number. Use jelly with it. Be careful when you insert it, or it won't work and you'll get pregnant. For some unaccountable reason, she laughed.

Having a diaphragm baby was no joke to me. I was frantic, but I said nothing to my husband, all the time smiling, smiling, as if life couldn't be better. Then one day I went to the bathroom and something like a small pebble seemed to slide down the inside of me, and when I looked in the toilet bowl there was a small knob of whatever, baby beginnings probably, and blood began to pour down the sides of the toilet bowl.

Some god or other had taken pity on me.

I began thinking about the kinds of gods who might be monitoring us as my husband and I motored through the British countryside. We had bought a small, British Morris Minor convertible, cheap like you wouldn't believe because we didn't have to pay taxes, monumental taxes, the way any Brit purchasing an automobile would have had to do. On weekends and our one-week vacations, we tootled over the landscape crossing off items in an old Michelin guide we had found in a second-hand bookstore.

The car was so small that it was hard for both of us, who were tall, to fold ourselves into the two miniscule front seats. There were also two back seats suitable only for midgets or a small picnic hamper and a blanket to sit on, take your choice. On steep hills, I had to get out and walk. If the hill was really steep, we both had to get out and, pushing behind the open doors of each side of the car, strain to get the car to the top of the rise.

We had a lot of money compared to the British around us. We had a car, and we went on vacations on our week off between the nine-week courses. We were living the life of Riley, whoever he is, so why weren't we happy? I found out how bad things could get on a vacation in Venice when we were in a bar and I heard this voice that I was sure I recognized saying, "The passion of my life has been to sail the Adriatic in a small boat." When I turned around, there was the movie star Errol Flynn, throwing his arms out expansively as if he were taking in the whole Mediterranean. When I turned back to my husband, his eyes were glazed with delight. To this day, I blame Errol Flynn for breaking up my marriage.

I wanted to save money until we had enough to go someplace cheap and take a year or so to write. I would write a novel. My husband said he would write a play. A play didn't take as long to write as a novel, he said. This inferred that his play would immediately be produced, and we would be on Big Buck$ Boulevard with all the money he'd make. It was one of the reasons I should be doing more grading than he was so that he could think about his play. Now my husband evinced no interest in anything but a small boat to sail the Mediterranean. He said the Adriatic was part of the Mediterranean. He didn't say that Errol Flynn might only want to do the Adriatic, but he wanted to do the whole Mediterranean. He wanted to go back to the summers of his youth, I thought, and be better than Errol Flynn.

"We can sell the car and use that money to buy a boat," he explained in a reasonable tone of voice. "We've got some money in the bank. Mostly my money," he added. Though he did make more money than I did, I graded more papers than he did. I thought that should even things out, but it didn't. When I wanted to withdraw money, even for basic household expenses, I had to give a rationale for every single item. Since I had not had a model family growing up, I didn't really have a template for how husbands and wives ought to act in matters of finance. Perhaps this was the way things worked: the husband kept his hand on the finances and vetoed anything he didn't find favor with. But part of that money was mine, I had earned it, and I didn't want that part going to buy a boat.

My husband was in fact rapidly becoming a man I did not know. His fascination for the bad things that happened to people, especially people who didn't want to sail the Mediterranean in small boats, increased. He couldn't wait to tell me about Ruskin, who on his wedding night saw his wife had pubic hair and was so horrified that he ran (I like to think screaming) from the room and never went back; Charles Lamb, whose sense of family responsibility kept him from ever having a real life because he had to take care of his sister, who in a moment of insanity (or perhaps not, I used to think, remembering my family), had stabbed her mother to death and wounded her father. Lamb himself spent a year in a booby hatch.

After he read *The Seven Pillars of Wisdom,* my husband spent hours scouting out facts about Lawrence of Arabia. The one he liked best was that Lawrence had paid to have himself beaten with birches on the buttocks until he bled. But the book that really held my husband in thrall was *A Passage to India.* E.M. Forster was over thirty, my husband informed me, before he allowed himself his first sexual adventure—with an Egyptian tram driver, my husband said, pleased that the fastidious Forster had given way to base proletarian impulses.

What was Forster doing in Egypt? I said. I thought he went to India.

He was posted there during the war. The Levant liberated him. He didn't get to India until later. Forster found the answer to everything, my husband said.

What is that? I asked.

"Only connect," my husband said.

I looked at him. He was perfectly serious. "Only connect," I said to my husband. "That's the answer to everything, even to what God does when He gets depressed, what He does about not having friends, or the fact He can't have friends because He's out in a loop all on His own?"

Then a warning bell went off in my head. What my husband was really saying was that we weren't connecting anymore. He didn't care what I thought. He was going to have his boat.

"I don't think I can write a novel on a boat," I finally said to him.

"You can write anywhere if you really want to and, besides, writers need experiences. You'd get lots of new experiences to write about on a boat."

"I'm not writing here. I hardly have any time, what with teaching and grading all those papers, and when I do, I'm too exhausted to try. Writers need time to reflect, they need solitude, they need peace and quiet."

"That's just the point. You'd have plenty of time and peace and quiet on a boat. I'd be up top sailing, and you'd be down below writing. You can write anywhere, but this is the only chance I'm ever going to have to get a boat. *I want to do this."*

When people talk to you in italics, you know you haven't got a chance. I also saw that he believed that you could hoard memories the way a miser hoards money, that there were banks for both, the money bank and the memory bank. He had the money bank, and I could have the memory bank. He said a second time that it would be an once-in-a-lifetime experience. EXPERIENCE came out in capital letters.

Why didn't I say, Let's divide up the money and go our separate ways. The shine is off The Golden Couple. That epoch is over.

I thought, Maybe I *can* write on a boat. Deep down, I think I just didn't want to face making a life-altering decision, as that worn saying goes. Later, when I should have, I faltered again, which can be almost as destructive as making the wrong decision, which in time I learned I had a penchant for.

Still, I had arguments. We would have to deal with the Irish Sea if we bought a boat here in a boatyard near Warrington—

We could buy a boat on the east coast of England. We could go across the English Channel—

"That's worse than the Irish Sea. The weather there is violent and unpredictable."

"We'd wait for a calm day. It's hardly any distance at all from the end of England across to Boulogne—" he'd obviously been consulting maps "—and then we'll go on to Le Havre, have the mast unstepped there, and it will be easy once we get to the canals and waterways of France. We can go all the way through France by canals, and then exit in the Mediterranean. You could work on your novel while we lazed along the canals."

Get your rain gear out, I told myself, you're going to be visiting boatyards.

England in the winter scarcely resembles the sun-drenched advertisements of the come-to-Britain posters (and more frequently than not, in the summer as well). There are few places so cold, so damp, so muddy, so soul chilling as an English boatyard in February. Weekend after weekend, we crawled under damp, dripping, half-frozen canvas to look at mud-locked boats. Half of them were filled with dirty water on which floated potato skins, toothpaste tubes, rusty pliers, old milk cartons, a rotting soiled sneaker. In each one, my husband had a vision of sails, spray, sea, stirring voyages.

My enthusiasm was so noticeably lacking that my husband brought home book after book of personal reminiscences of small boatmen who had had exciting adventures on the waters of the world. These books fell into two classes: the ones in which the sailors had had horrible batterings by the elements and miserable months in cramped, foul cabins; and those in which all the plights of a small boat were enumerated and tossed off with great sangfroid. I still remember one book in particular—*Isabel and the Sea*—about an inexperienced young couple who had bought a fifty-two-foot motor boat and made approximately the same trip my husband had in mind. The entire account of 408 pages seemed to me one long description after another of murderous tides, ship-sinking gales, and hurricane-velocity winds. Fifty-two feet was huge compared to what my husband said we could afford. He was talking about half that size; moreover, he looked down his nose at people who only used motors. *Real* sea people used sails. It says sailors, doesn't it? You see sail in the word, don't you? You don't see motor.

Our kitchen table was littered with all manner of insurance pamphlets, some with extraordinarily suggestive titles—"A Beginner's Guide to Messing About in Boats," "Are You Properly Fitted Out?" and "Are You Properly Laid Up?" for example—the most appalling of which, "In Case of Emergency," I returned to again and again. This pamphlet, Gordon Chaplin's *Dark Wine, A Survivor's Tale of Love and Loss*, adopted a cheerful tone:

> Last year I dropped what I thought were useful hints about keeping out of trouble, and, bless my soul, the ink is hardly dry on paper when Boreas gets out his biggest trumpet and, with the aid of Neptune and a few huffs and puffs, blows down half the East Coast [where we were looking at boats] and a lot of the laid-up yacht that had not taken the precautions I advised are now no more of this mundane world.

Wrecks, floods, rammings, collisions, drownings, capsizing, explosions, fires, fumes, thieves, rot, worms, broken masts, dishonest boatyards, and inexperience could all be covered by insurance.

> For your friends are my friends, and my friends are your friends, and the more we are together the merrier we shall all be. There seems to be a growing feeling that the last line should be, The better you are insured the happier we shall be.

Uh, huh.

Gordon Chaplin's *Dark Wine: A Survivor's Tale of Love and Loss.* told me that

> Faith, in the religious sense of unquestioning belief, is necessary for any long ocean passage in a small vessel, now just as much as it was in Columbus's day. I knew we weren't going to sail off the edge of the world, but there were other things that could happen—and had happened over the years to other people. Columbus, being the first, was operating in blissful ignorance, whereas we had many well-documented accounts of real disasters: boats rammed and sunk by pilot whales, enormous rogue waves, unaccounted for groundings' (possibly on nuclear submarines), freak storms, piracy and STRANGE mechanical failures…

By the first of May, my husband began to get frantic, rising before dawn to pore over yachting magazines with advertisements for small boats. I was beginning to relax a little when Razzle-dazzle Rust laid eyes on an advertisement for a boat at Cowey Island, some seventy-five miles from where we were living, near Felixstowe on the North Sea, where the seas are so treacherous that even the United States Navy won't take their vessels anywhere near there.

21 foot British-built Bermudan (Marconi rig) sloop with
3-gear Stuart Turner P/55M, 8 horsepower, 2 stroke gasoline,
2 cylinder marine engine in perfect running order. Automatic
and hand bilge pump. Marine engine. Sails in fine condition.
Centerboard. Extremely comfortable for cruising.

Cabin has 3 berths, centerboard folding table, clothes
closet, fine brass and copper gimbal lamp, brass barometer,
more than adequate storage space, and galley with two-burner
kerosene stove, water tanks, sink, crockery for four, pots and
pans. Gear also includes pram dinghy, life preservers, tools,
fire extinguisher, three Lambretta fenders, spinnaker, spare
lines. Five hundred pounds.

There was a picture with the ad that had made my husband go wild
with joy.

He was dancing about in excitement. Here was a boat we could
afford that did not have dry rot or need extensive repairs and that had
lots of sail and a motor, the owner assured us over the phone, that never
failed. We went immediately to the boatyard where the *Blotto* had been
"wintering." I was looking at the boat in front of me in horror while the
owner was assuring my husband that of course the boat could only look
like the picture in the ad when it was on the water. "You know how it
is," he said to my husband, "when it's not in its own element."

Not being an old salt, I was plunged more into images of the
raptures of the deep, like the Wreck of the Hesperus. It had come to me
that I didn't look attractive in oily, wet boatyard clothes.

My husband was hooked. Of course, he said, a boat doesn't look like
itself on land; you have to see it in the water, you'll love it. Then and
there, he wrote out a check with all the flourish of Errol Flynn.

During the trip home, my husband could not stop talking about
how happy I would be after he had built bookcases under the bunks for
my books, how I would "just love" fitting out the galley, how we "just
must" bring the *Blotto* to the Felixstowe boatyard near us just as soon
as possible to get it completely checked over so that we were confident
it was seaworthy. "Next weekend," he said. I have never seen a more
beguiled individual in my life.

I said, I think that boat must have the world's tallest mast.

That next weekend, we took off from Benfleet to bring the *Blotto* up to Flexistowe for refitting in what I was later told was a southerly gale that even my husband seemed to consider perhaps not the greatest introduction to a rapturous life on the sublime seas. He started the motor, and we were thrown from wave to wave for about half an hour before the engine failed and the boat was at the mercy of the wind and waves. My husband hastily ran the jib up to try to keep some control; the jib line flew overboard and caught in the propeller. My husband frantically worked on the engine and, when he finally got it going, the jib line tangled so badly in the propeller blades that the motor began to smoke and then seized up. The rope that attached the dinghy to the boat snapped, and the dinghy was washed overboard.

My husband hysterically threw out an anchor, which held us just short of a sandbar; then he ran up his white nylon shirt as a distress signal. This attracted the attention of a small tanker, which unfortunately had to approach from the windward side because of the proximity of a sand bar. It drifted down across our anchor chain and overran it, nearly pulling our boat under. Before the tanker steered clear, it had bashed up the bow, snapped the forestays, broken a crosstree, ripped off the cabin rail, and parted a running backstay.

The Southend Lifeboat Association people came out to rescue us. It was at this moment that we made the second terrible error, the first having been (in my mind) to buy the boat. We got on board their boat and accepted mugs of hot tea. When we got on board their boat, we had done what is known as abandoning ship, which allowed the Southend Life Boat Association to file a salvage claim on our boat. Salvage money is not payable to the captain and crew of ships commissioned by a government specially for rescue operations, but the Southend Lifeboat Association was a volunteer organization—in other words, not commissioned by Her Majesty. We had abandoned our boat when we left it, so they owned it now, and they claimed that if we wanted it back, we would have to give the same amount as we had paid for it. We found this out three days later we received a registered letter from them. You can pretty much judge the kind of person I was then because I didn't say, *Let them keep it!*

My husband went down and talked to them, and they said, All right, they would take one third of the value, but if we didn't cough that up immediately, they would proceed with an arrest warrant. Arrest *a boat?*

My husband came back and lay in bed with his face turned to the wall. I taught his classes. I liked the one where a country boy, who had told me he wanted to be a doctor, after reading *Othello* and being asked on the exam to write a character portrait of Iago, wrote two words: *Plenty bad*. He had cut through to the heart of the matter. I had no idea what kind of grade to give him, so I wrote at the end of the exam, Passing. He apparently didn't compare his grade with any of the other students, who had As, Bs, Cs, Ds, and a couple of Fs, because he never came to see me about his mark. If he had, I don't know what I would have told him—perhaps that I admired his answer but that I was probably the only academic person on earth who would take a two-word answer as an essay, and maybe he should consider another profession besides the medical. Though who knows? He might have thrived in the sciences. It's pretty brilliant, actually, to have written an essay I remember to this day when all the others have been totally erased from my mind.

What I'm saying is that the situation we were in seemed to me plenty bad. I guess my husband did, too, because he was avoiding me. I thought it was because he had given the impression when we were scouting out the old family island that he was an accomplished boatman, and so far all I had seen was someone who didn't know what the hell he was doing. But wives have to make things go. That's their job. So I flung on a cheerful face when I tried to talk to him about our troubles with the Southend Lifeboat Association. I got nothing but a grunt. After two days of this, I went down to the rescue station myself and told them if they didn't cease and desist, I was going to the London newspapers and give them my story. I said it would be a dilly since they had "invited" us, poor innocent Yanks that we were, to come aboard and have a nice cuppa tea, and they had certainly said nothing about a salvage claim when they helped us find a boat repair place.

The Southend Lifeboat Association is sustained by voluntary contributions—there are little miniature Southend lifeboats on store counters that you can drop your money in—and, since little old ladies in trainers (what the Brits call sneakers) were the mainstay of the donations that kept them afloat, I didn't think that was the kind of publicity they would want. They backed off. Fast. We did end up paying them something; I can't remember what. Maybe fifty pounds, which in those days, when the pound was worth over four dollars, would have been over two hundred dollars.

Meanwhile, the boat was being held as a convalescent in a boatyard whose owner got a kick out of the whole story. (I'm glad someone did.) He fixed the damages and refitted the boat (more money—lots more money, as I remember) and we still hadn't got the *Blotto* even halfway near us, to say nothing of across the Channel, where our actual "summer adventure" was supposed to begin. But when my husband saw how spiffy the repaired *Blotto* looked, he was all elation and renewed faith.

"We'll take a trial run in better weather," he said. "It was a mistake to take you out when the wind was so bad. When the weather's nice, there's nothing in the world like being out on a small boat."


This time as we sailed out, we ran aground on Horse Sands in the Orford River. An eight-year-old named Malcolm rowed out and pulled us off with his rowboat. He wouldn't take any money. He said it had been fun. *Fun?*

The next time we went out, under full canvas, I kept hearing sloshing noises, but the day was bright, the wind just right, and my husband was in his element, where he had dreamed of being, here at sea. I never thought to look below. When I went down into the cockpit to make us a sandwich, I stood up to my knees in water. The boat seams had dried out during its winter on land, and the only thing that saved us from sinking was the combined effort of the two of us, with the anchor holding us more or less out of danger, bailing for all we were worth with pots and pans from the galley. When we got most of the water out, my husband went atop and tried to sail the boat toward what I had begun to think of as "our home port" while I continued bailing. I was frozen, and I had a long time to think while I was bailing down there in that cold, watery cabin. The conclusion I came to was that things would have to be better when we got across the Channel, and much better when we got to the canals and waterways, especially when we got to Paris, most especially when we just got to moor someplace for a while and I could get off this damn boat. We couldn't go on like this—at least I couldn't.

The boat had to be caulked, as I believe they called it—at any rate seamed up so that the water wouldn't pour in—and we went out two or three more cold, wet times when nothing too terrible happened. My husband said he thought we were ready to take the boat down the east coast and make the Channel crossing. "I don't think I can be any help to you if something goes wrong," I said. "I don't know that much about boats, and every time we get out of sight of land, I kind of panic, and—" The *ands* were endless.

My husband, making pointed remarks about unnecessary extra expenses if he had to hire a guide to get him through the treacherous shoals of the coast of East Anglia, waited for me to say, All right, I'll try it. I sat stubbornly at the kitchen table looking at the enormous distance on the map when I would have to be on that boat. I couldn't do it. I thought when we got to France and could see land—for some reason I assumed we would just sail along the coast, and if anything went wrong, I could dive overboard and swim for safety—I would be all right. But there was no way in the world I was going to go along the coast of East Anglia or across the Channel in a twenty-one-foot boat. My husband said he thought he had a *friend* who would go across the Channel with him. In other words, he could depend on *friends* more than he could count on his wife.

I hope he knows something about sailing, I said. I don't think you should go with someone who isn't familiar with the waters out there. They're really dangerous. The United States Navy doesn't even let its ships come into them. I think you should get someone with experience to get you down this coast. That definitely left me out.


Dougie, an old salt reputed to know the east coast like the back of his hand, did not look prepossessing when he came aboard. He had a square patch of mouth with a multitude of teeth missing; while he talked, he sucked air noisily, which made him sound drunker than he probably was. He was full of false cheer as he staggered around sails, petrol cans, blankets, crockery, ropes, galley supplies. My husband looked tired, old, and dispirited, but he stood up amidst the litter on the deck and held out his hand. "Good to have you aboard, Dougie," he said.

I went into town and bought eight gallons of petrol and four cans of oil to feed the engine; Dougie began to right the sails; my husband struggled to get the new dinghy on board. I had made fifty sandwiches and boiled two dozen eggs, and, at the last minute, somewhat doubtfully, stuck in a bottle of bourbon. Then I saw them off, feeling my husband had realized I was the kind of wife he should never have married.

Dougie and my husband would do the coast that day, and then Dougie would get off and my husband would wait for Roy Bongartz, a friend we had made from among the University of Maryland people working overseas, to come down to help him cross the Channel.

I, The Craven Coward, would take Roy's car on a *ship* across to Boulogne, where Roy would retrieve his car and start out on a camping trip across France. I envied him. It would be wonderful to lay curled up in a sleeping bag on hard, firm earth at night and think that when you got up in the morning you would see a car and hard, paved roads. Now I realize that to go camping in a country wrecked by war and whose people were still finding it hard to put food on the table was as quixotic an adventure as my husband and I were setting out on, but we were young. There you have it, the excuse for so many misguided misadventures and hare-brained schemes. We were young, and we were "finding" ourselves, the usual defenses for those under thirty who know they will be forgiven their excesses and misdemeanors until the big Three O, when they will be expected to become responsible citizens and wage earners, and maybe even, god forgive them, bring other little people into the world.

That night, my husband and Dougie slept aboard because they said they wanted an early start. There were high winds and intermittent rain with a flash of lightning every once in a while. At dawn, the wind grew stronger. If I had known what a big blow was, I would have surmised this was it. As it was, I was full of false confidence. Dougie would know if the weather was too bad to go out. But I did not sleep well. It has been my experience that drunks are not good judges of anything. Finally, I got up, washed my hair, and sat down to wait for Roy to come with his little Renault and whisk us to Folkestone-by-the Sea where we were to meet the *Blotto*.

Folkestone to Calais was the shortest route across the Channel, but that route presented too many problems if there was fog, and there usually was, which made crossing especially dangerous for a small boat because of the large ferries going back and forth where, in a fog, a ferry could smash into a boat like the *Blotto* and hardly realize what had happened.

Folkestone to Boulogne, on the other hand, was a good route, according to Dougie, because you went on a diagonal and made up a lot of unnecessary travel along the coast of France, and you were unlikely to meet many large ships that would be a danger to your well-being.

Neither my husband nor Dougie nor the *Blotto* arrived at Folkestone. Roy and I sat on a large bluff on top of the famous white chalk cliffs overlooking the English Channel and waited to spot the tallest mast in the world. Roy read to me a sequence from Beckett's *Molloy*:

> I took advantage of being at the seaside to lay in a store of sucking-stones. They were pebbles but I call them stones. Yes, on this occasion I laid in a considerable store. I distributed them equally between my four pockets, and sucked them and sucked them—

I couldn't, I couldn't stand it anymore. I wailed at him, "I don't care which pockets he puts the damn stones in. Please, can't we talk about something that goes somewhere?"

I had hurt his feelings. I always seemed to be hurting someone's feelings these days, mostly my husband's, but Roy had a cheerful nature. He said we could make bets about when the *Blotto* would come in. The weather looked really alarming. I said that if the boat wasn't there by 5:30, we should get the police. Roy said 6:30. Actually, it was the local police who found us (by the make of the car; there were not many Renaults in Britain at that time). They told us that word had come that the main sail had blown out in the wind, and Dougie and my husband were stranded in the Thames Estuary. They shouldna have been out, one of the policeman said disapprovingly. It was a gale-force wind, that, and nobody sensible goes out in a small craft in a gale-force wind.

Roy and I drove to where the boat lay stranded and waiting for the sail to be repaired. Dougie had been drunk when the mishap occurred and then had thrown up, fortunately over the side. He lay on the bottom of the cockpit moaning that he had never seen anything like this boat, and he hoped he never would again. Roy took him to the train station. My husband said there must be thirty sandwiches left, mostly tuna, but he thought they were all right because it was so cold. He said he was going to take the boat down to Folkestone himself.

Roy, engaging in noble behavior that I considered suicidal, said he would go with him. We could all sleep on the *Blotto* that night while the repairs were being made. The next day, I could take the Renault across on the ferry and wait for them in Boulogne.

The water all around us was filthy with oil, discarded plastic bottles, bubbling contraceptives. The *Blotto*, with the world's tallest mast, stood out amongst all the heroic boats around us that had years before plowed across the Channel to pick up the four hundred thousand defeated British soldiers standing waist-deep in water at Dunkirk when the Germans had overrun France during the Second World War.

A lot of these boats now looked derelict—it was obvious some of their owners hadn't the means to keep them up. The War had wiped out England and its once mighty empire, but not its people's spirit. I admired the way the English took their reduced circumstances, their rations, the reality of the world with the sangfroid that is the mark of real, everyday courage. Courage I considered, like Hemingway, to be one of the prime virtues. At that moment, I had none to draw on to make me volunteer to go on the *Blotto* with my husband across the Channel, which had turned out to be the grave of so many foolhardy men. Women, too, of course, but who ever mentioned them?

From the time my father had thrown me off the diving board and I had plunged deeper and deeper into the depths of its green baptism, water had always been something I had a very wary attitude toward. I would go into swimming pools, the shallower the end the better, and I would wade across thin ribbons of water in creeks, but oceans and channels and seas were on a list in the back of my mind that said Do Not Intrude. I saw myself as pusillanimous, while my husband and Roy were drinking beer and looking at the sea around them as if it were just some water they needed to take a boat through. I saw it an aqueous underworld, and I did not want to go anywhere on that water, but I was too craven to say so. This defect isn't an illness that can be cured or bad manners that can be eradicated; it is a character flaw that was beginning to define me. Beware, beware, the poison's in the glass, the wind's started singing, the organ's gone cancerous, the hounds are howling, the wolves are out, the guillotine's coming down.

I remember a British friend talking about Dunkirk. If the Channel hadn't been calm that night, he said, we would never have got out. He told me that after he watched the last small craft disappear, the French had run out and grabbed those they could, but they couldn't help all of them. The ones that were left stood waiting for what the Germans would do. Machine gun them probably, the man said. He had been transferred from attics to farm lofts to cubby holes the whole four years of the rest of the war. He had bad teeth and bad eyes, and he coughed a lot. I got saved because some Frenchies came down and grabbed me and dragged me into a hiding place—I was in a ditch all night and most of the next day. They threw some dirt over me to try to hide me. They would have been shot if the Germans had caught them.

I don't go near the sea, he said, not if I can help it. The wife wants to go to Blackpool on holiday, but I won't do it. We argue every year. What if I took her out so far she couldn't get back and left her out there helpless? Then maybe she'd have some idea how it feels never to want to go near water again.

We have a reunion every year, those of us who are left; every year there are less and less, and someone always says, The drink or the shakes got him. But it was Dunkirk that got them, standing waist-high in water with nothing but the sea ahead and the Germans behind. None of us who were there ever came back the same.

The sea gives off a strong smell—like the odor of a wet animal's fur, one of those first creatures who crawled out of the slime up onto land, breathed in the clear air for a brief instant, and sank back down into the muck. Each time, the stay in the good clean air grew longer, until that dark, coarse creature could no longer force itself to go back down into the black mud.

That smell still lives buried inside us. I smelled it strongly once in Africa as I was going out on safari in the dark moments before dawn. Suddenly there was this sickeningly strong scent that suffused the air all around me. It was wild dogs. Their smell precedes them, a warning they are coming. The prey will try to escape, but it has no chance. Wild dogs run in relays; when one tires, the next takes over, and then the next, until the running animal can no longer run. Then the dogs jump on it and tear it to pieces. That smell of the wild dogs, which is a residue of the odor of those first sea creatures who struggled up out of the primordial slime, remains to remind us where we came from. Aboard the *Blotto* that first night I was to sleep on the boat, I was conscious of breathing in that strong smell of sea mud and dark primitive creatures who had once lived there before rising to land and finally becoming man. The air was so thick with it that any of my exposed flesh became dark with a thin, oily coating of antediluvian ooze.

My husband and I slept below, and Roy, unpacking the sleeping bag he intended to use camping, lay on the deck with various rodents running over him. In the middle of the night, he came below and lay curled into a fetal position next to the centerboard that took up most of the space between the two small cots where my husband and I lay separate, as if we were strangers. When Roy got up the next morning, he was all crooked, like Father Time.

But he was game. He didn't repack his sleeping bag, grab his duffel, reclaim his Renault, and disappear. He handed me the keys to the car, and I stood on the pier watching them fiddle with sails as he and my husband started on their journey across an unpredictable body of water that had a reputation for suddenly turning turbulent, even though today it seemed smooth and gleaming as glass. The only navigating tools they had were an antiquated Michelin guide and a prewar picture map I had picked up at the French tourist bureau in London. I did not have great faith in these, but my husband said the compass was really all they needed to get from Folkestone to Boulogne.

The plan was for me to rendezvous with the boat in Boulogne. It never occurred to any of us the boat wouldn't be easy to spot, not with the world's tallest mast. In Boulogne, I drove the Renault surrounded by suitcases, cameras, and boxes of provisions amidst miles and miles of ocean-going vessels. I couldn't find a yacht basin; there were only berths for commercial ships and channel liners. I drove up and down the docks over and over, first disconcerted, then angry, and finally panicked.

The wind off the channel was freezing, darkness was coming on. I faced nothing but filthy fishing trawlers and large liners as I sat looking for the *Blotto*'s mast. Hours had passed. I was pretty sure something had gone wrong with the boat and it had gone down. I was sorry Roy had to lose his life, but I was so mad at my husband that I thought he deserved to be punished. Death just seemed a little stringent.

I decided that at eight o'clock, I would go to the building where a nautical-looking flag fluttered in the wind and tell them I thought my husband and his friend were lost at sea. At ten minutes to eight, my husband came loping along the quay as jubilant as if he had won the World Cup. The trip had been fairly uneventful, except that they had made the crossing in a dense fog and didn't really know where they were going. When they finally sighted land, they were only about a hundred yards off, proving the compass was reliable. He talked about the compass as if it were a son who had made him proud by winning a gold at the Olympics.

The whole time my husband and Roy had been trying to find their way through fog, they had thrown anything they were through using either on the deck or below in the small cabin. I have never seen a worse mess. There was no question of making a meal. Roy reclaimed his Renault and said he thought he'd be better off camping on land. He couldn't wait to get away from us.

My husband and I ate some leftover tuna salad sandwiches, threw the stuff on the cots onto the floor, and fell into a stupefied sleep, not even brushing our teeth. In the middle of the night, the boat suddenly lurched over, throwing us out of our cots. We both jumped up and scrambled outside to discover we were high and dry on a shelf of mud and tipped dangerously to one side. Although there must have been a good fifteen or twenty feet of water under us when we went to bed, there was now only gooey mud all around us. No one had warned us that there were fifteen- to twenty-foot tidal changes along the coast.

We hastily pulled the centerboard up and pushed everything we could find around the boat to try to level it. We brought blankets and books up and lay down on the sloping side, trying to preserve some kind of balance. The mosquitoes were persistent; unidentified animals paid us visits all night. At one point, something ran up my back and nearly sent me overboard. I sat up after that, swatting mosquitoes, watching rats the size of large cats run along the wharf.

The next morning, my husband stood looking around at the bleakness of the Boulogne seaport. Things will be better when we get to LeHavre, where we can get on the Tancarvillle Canal, my husband said. I would even be able to get off the boat and walk along side if I felt like it. He was joining the Things-Will-Be-Better-When Club.

Just stay close to shore till we get to LeHavre, I begged him. Don't go so far from shore that I can't see it. I felt that if I could see it, I could always swim for shore if the boat had to be abandoned. What could go wrong?

I realized what could go wrong almost immediately the next morning. The tide had come in and righted the boat, and my husband ran the sails up and breezed us out into the Channel. I was chilled to the bone by a relentless wind and sick to my stomach as the boat slapped and banged and rutted about in a sea churning with white-capped waves.

We passed Le Touquet, or so my husband said. How would I know where we were? He had the map, and he was careful that I didn't have access to it. Not that I cared at that moment. The boat pitched and bucked and throbbed, and I went from seasick to deathly ill. Finally my husband gave up and put in at Berck, irritated. "We could have made really good time in that wind," he said. I lay on a bunk and finally said, If you want something to eat, you're going to have to go into town and get it yourself.

He was supposed to sail. I was supposed to keep the cabin straight, buy and cook food, and generally run any errands. He didn't say, That's all right. I'll go get us something . Maybe in a little while you'll feel better. He didn't say, Can I make you some tea or anything? He sat on the other bunk and looked at me as if he wished I had died out there when I had been heaving over the side of the *Blotto*. He could have dumped the body over and gone on that wonderful wind all the way to Le Havre. I looked back at him thinking, It is terrible to wish someone dead—morally reprehensible didn't even cover such an idea— nevertheless, I wished him deader than I saw he wished me.

We waited in Berck four days for a decent wind. In those four days, we hardly spoke to one another except to issue some warning. At night we sat, drugged with despair, and ate cold baked beans out of a can. In the morning we got up, wet and cramped, and tried to take the boat out, but the wind would be too strong, the seas too high, and we would have to turn back. I had a moment when I thought that maybe my husband really wanted to see what it would be like to face death. He always said he wasn't afraid of dying (when you die, I thought, leave me out). I think he saw himself, after his final breath, as a silvery wraith conversing with other interesting silvery wraiths—Aristotle, Joyce, Dante, and of course Forester. They would connect. He might actually be looking forward to it.

I wasn't. I thought that once you were dead, that was it. You got one time around, and if you botched that, too bad. There wasn't going to be another chance. I didn't see myself in everlasting conversations with charming companions. My husband probably also envisioned some kind of Roman orgies now and again to relieve the tedium of too much talk.

When I happened to glance down at the tourist map, which my husband had guardedly positioned next to the compass, which I was *not* to touch, I saw it was a long way to go from Boulogne to Le Havre. Somehow I had imagined it would be a day's sail, and then we would be free of the Channel and safely near land. I would only have to jump off the boat to feel the good, solid earth under my feet. Now I saw the distance from Boulogne to Le Havre was much farther than the boat had already traveled (or not traveled, depending on its mood), a fact my husband had managed to conceal.

I had trusted my husband when he said, Once we get across the Channel, things will be a piece of cake, a variation on Once We Get to

*Fill in the Blank,* things will be better. I looked at my husband, hunkered over the engine doing something—who knew or cared what—and thought, You lied to me.

"I never realized it was such a long way to Le Havre," I said, pointedly looking at the tourist map.

My husband did not look up.

Try to be charitable, I told myself, you're going to be on this boat with him for a long time. Think of it more as his withholding the truth. Or, whatever floats this goddamn boat doesn't get *his* goat.

There are moments that are definitive. I think that was one of them, but then we had so many on the *Blotto* that, looking back, I can't be perfectly sure. I just know that at that moment, I put my husband in the category of people who presented a clear and present danger to anyone around them—like my parents.

My mother said her definitive moment with my father came on their honeymoon. He wanted to go camping. She was definitely *not* the camping type. She had been a great beauty when she was young, and she devoted the rest of her life to preserving herself. She thought I was too tall and would come into my bedroom while I was growing to wake me up and say, Scrunch up, scrunch up. You don't want to grow any more, do you? Looking back, I think the taller I got, the older that made her seem; often she tried to pass me off as her sister.

Her life had not been happy. On my mother's honeymoon, my father had his Ford jalopy piled high with camping equipment. They rode along through a blistering heat, the open windows offering no help at all. This was long before air conditioning. Finally they stopped at a mom-and-pop place to get gas. My father said, You wait here, I'll be right back. She waited and waited, steaming in the heat. She got worried and went to look for him. He was sitting at the soda counter, sipping a root beer float. I would label that a defining moment. My moment with the map I would call another.

The next day, the wind was "shallower," my husband's word, and we went less convulsively along the coast, passing Le Tréport, Dieppe (with its terrible war memories), all the way to Fécamp, where my husband looked less like a man planning to throw his wife overboard and more like one ready to gamble in marble halls, albeit nothing so grand as Monte Carlo. A chance to make a killing at the gambling tables would change his life. Someone had given him a sure system for beating the roulette wheel, and he was prepared to shoot for the moon.

The System went like this: one person played red or black, not back and forth; you chose either red or black and stuck to that no matter what; that was the key to the whole operation. A second person kept track of the amount of chips to bet. You wrote down 1, 2, 3, 5, 8, 13, 21, 34, in order to know how many chips to be bet. Your first bet was the first two numbers, one and two, which equaled three. If you lost the three chips, you bet the next number in the series, which was three and two, or five chips total, and if you lost that, you bet three and five, eight chips, on and on until you completed a series. I later learned this was called the Fibonacci system, after a thirteenth-century Italian mathematician.

The idea was that if you stuck with one color, you would eventually complete a series and win. In the middle of our losses, it came to me that even when you completed a series, what you would actually have won was only three chips. In other words, you might be betting staggering amounts of money in order to net three chips. I didn't grasp this until we were betting 144 chips. By that time, we were so far into the system that there seemed no way to extricate ourselves. Extricate ourselves for what, anyway? To go back on board that awful boat?

The casino was very small. We were the only two Americans there. My husband bought two thousand francs' worth of chips, and we went to the roulette table. He placed the first bet, three chips, on black. We lost the first bet. Then we bet three, and then five, and then eight chips. We lost four times in a row, but then we won once. I was writing for all I was worth, and my husband was sweating and betting. People began to crowd around us.

My husband lost the next three bets. It seemed impossible red could come up so many times. Our original two thousand francs were nearly gone. If we lost our next bet, we would have to cash a traveler's check to keep the series going. We decided to go outside and have a cigarette (people smoked with great relish in those days). My husband said it had been a mistake to choose black; we should switch to red. We went back and cashed a traveler's check, and he bet 144 chips on red, which we lost. Then we bet—I would have to work it out on paper and I haven't the strength, just say a lot of chips—which we won. We had at last completed a series. I just wanted to quit, but the three chips we had won were burning my husband's palms. Our luck's changed, my husband cried exultantly. We're going to make some real money now.

I tried to keep up with the figures my husband needed, but I soon realized it didn't make any difference: my husband had thrown caution to the wind and was betting either red or black on some hunch that came over him. He shouted when he won and moaned like one in need of an ambulance when he lost. A great crowd now encircled him. I sat slumped in a corner writing on a pad while my husband lost the next bet (34 chips) and then the next (55) and then won once, then lost again, and went on to lose. Then he bet 89 chips, which was *not* what I told him to bet. He had stopped even pretending he knew I was there.

There was no system anymore except for the amount of chips he felt like betting. When he won after a series of stinging losses and finally completed a series, I never knew how many chips we were ahead or behind. My husband was betting whatever he felt like on whatever color appealed to him at the moment. He had come to the conclusion three chips wasn't worth the worry and work. We had been at it two hours, and the crowd around us was enormous when a couple of large beefy men came over and stood behind me.

I really don't know what happened the next hour. I only know that after three-and-a-half hours, the roulette god must have thought, Shit, give these kids a break. My husband ended up with ten thousand francs' worth of chips—which equaled our original investment—and about ten pounds over, around fifty dollars. We had become so mixed up trying to convert dollars into pounds and pounds into francs or francs into dollars that we had decided to settle on using British pounds as our basic monetary system. We had been in England long enough to have mastered the pence, shillings, pounds, and quids that were in circulation those days. I miss that old system, which was based on a division of twelve. The new one is based (more logically, but less nostalgically) on units of ten. The money given us for our chips was in francs, and we seemed to have fistfuls. I like the sound of that: fistfuls of francs.

The two beefy men accompanied us to the cashier, where a man in a tux with a pencil-thin mustache came over as the money was being passed through the window. He told us it would give him great pleasure if we would depart and never come back. People were watching us instead of betting. And, *madame et monsieur,* when I say, don't ever come back, I mean that.

We emerged from the underworld of blind bargaining and came out into a sky of brilliant black that had millions of small slices where the stars had slit their way through. The moon governed the sea, and that strange, furry sea scent was in the air, but it was purring with pleasure. My husband, however, was engulfed in grief. He had been thinking of coming back to the casino the next night—and the next and the next, perhaps into infinity—the man who broke the bank, if not at Monte Carlo, at least at Fécamp. But some man in a thin mustache, some *Frenchman* in a ridiculous mustache, wasn't going to let him do that.

I watched a series of emotions play over his face—first despair, then disbelief, then the rebirth of enthusiasm. He had won *money*! He could win anything he set his heart on, and at this moment he said his heart told him to go put his hand on a glass and make good use of it, drink enough to have the time of his life, celebrating our fifty-some dollars of victory. With Calvados, my husband said triumphantly. In point of fact, Fécamp was renowned for its Benedictine liqueur, which the monks had invented in their still-standing splendid twelfth-century abbey. We had taken a few minutes to see it that afternoon. Fécamp had been the major port on the North Sea long before anyone had ever heard of Le Havre. At that moment, my husband cared nothing about architectural monuments or monks concocting potent brews or Roman ships braving the elements to reach this small nondescript town; what he was thinking was that all along he should have known things would be better when we got to Fécamp.

Calvados is distilled from the finest cider apples, for which the region is known, and after fermentation is completed, the liqueur is anywhere from 140 to 160 proof. It gets its name from where it was first made, the town of Calvados in Normandy. French Calvados remains in its wooden vats for ten years so that it mellows. I always thought of it as being like American moonshine, which is really made from corn mash, not apples, and is only aged two to five years. During the Depression, through the 1930s, there were all kinds of horror stories about people who went blind or crazy from drinking moonshine that hadn't been aged at all or had been tinkered with by adding pure alcohol to whatever came through the rusty copper pipes and passed itself off as booze.

What I most liked about Calvados was that in the midst of one of those rich French meals, a small glass would be put in front of you. For the *trou Normand*, the Normandy hole. You tipped the small glass and drank it in one shot. The Calvados burned through all that rich food and made a channel so that you could go on eating. At the end of the meal, you often got a small glass of Calvados again for the *digestif,* sometimes a second if you had had a really copious meal and sometimes, not very often, someone would take a cube of sugar and dip it in a glass of Calvados, a *canard,* it was called, and hand it to you and say, Put this in your mouth and suck your coffee through it, which was better than actually drinking the Calvados itself.

We found a small outdoor restaurant that was still open and sat down in the kind of white wire chairs they used to have at Walgreens and gazed out at the gentle sea. Before that, I had never drunk Calvados in my life. The *trou normand* and the *canard* I would learn about later. I was just tired, and figures were fighting one another inside my head. All I wanted to do was go back to the *Blotto* (something I had never before wanted to do, so I must have been really done in) so that I could lie down on my cot and die for a few hours.

A soft breeze floated over the sea into Fécamp, one free of the odor of fish, oil, gas, and garbage, those scents that seemed to me like the presentiment of death. I thought the air smelled of hyacinths. I didn't really know what hyacinths smelled like nor even what they looked like, but they contained a magic name, the way the nightingale did.

My husband, laughing, tilted his glass against mine. At that moment, I forgot how much he had probably wished I would die so he could dump me overboard. He became the most beautiful person on earth, and the trap that is often called love suddenly flew open and threw me, duped and enchanted, down its chute. Love will get through barred windows. It will cross oceans and scale mountains. It will send monsters to eat at your brain, dig down into your heart, gobble away any defenses you might put up. At that moment, it was Forster's "only connect."

That is the metaphysical side of the emotion. The more scientific (and probably more accurate) explanation is that the lactic acid levels in the blood are lowered, and the levels of endorphins in the brain give off a sensation much like morphine administered at an enormous rate; you become euphoric and unwise; the white blood cells react better and faster so that the chances even of catching a cold go down; the skin glows, the eyes look dazed. People in such a state are endowed with incredible amounts of energy, need less sleep, sometimes forget to eat, and to outsiders often appear like boneless wonders who have become utterly unhinged.

As the Calvados slipped down, for the first time since we'd set sight on the *Blotto,* I felt free from apprehension and dread. I saw what an extraordinary man I had married, how brilliant and witty he was. Metaphors and similes were flying inspirationally out of my mouth, and my husband was leaning forward, caressing my arm, smiling with that look of desire that can make a woman forget she has been seasick on a smelly boat for days at a time. I was like a goldfish who only has a memory span of three seconds.

I could not stop telling my husband how wonderful he was, what a perfect night it was, how lucky we were to be young and in love and in France. I could feel my eyebrows going up and down, my mouth opening and closing, my cheeks flushing with emotion, my face full of a million star-spangled expressions of love. The only problem was that from the neck down, the 206 bones in my body had turned to stone. My mouth worked, my eyes and ears worked; I could sing, oh, could I sing. I was singing at the top of my lungs, and my husband couldn't make me quiet down. "I have a head that works. I can talk and sing," I said, "but my body's gone dead."

My husband thought I was being witty. He "fed" me from his glass of Calvados sip by sip and kissed me in between. We staggered out of our ice-cream-parlor chairs—or rather, he did. I couldn't move. I was paralyzed from the neck down. He laughed. When I still didn't get up, he lost his smile. He was the kind who didn't like to call attention to himself (what did he think he had been doing in the casino?), one of those who believed "a gentleman"—yes, we had language and ideas like that in those days—could always be identified by how modest he was about all his talents.

I looked at him and thought, Someone in the Bible—or was it *The Odyssey?*—turned to stone. Or maybe I was thinking of Orpheus who went to the underworld to rescue his love (what was her name?), a great musician, and when his love—Eurydice, that was it—was bitten by a snake and died, Orpheus went to Hades to get her back. (So love could go to the underworld, could go anywhere it was so powerful?) Hades told Orpheus she would be his if he led her out but never looked back to make sure she was following. But of course he looked back. We always look back. She either turned to stone or vanished. Whatever, she was gone from him forever. This then was the metaphor for love. I wanted to tell my husband we couldn't look back—but I couldn't move, I could no longer even speak, I could hardly keep my lithodomous head from falling on the table.

Finally my husband grabbed me under the arms—the waiter came to give him a hand—and they got me upright and propelled me toward the door. Our dinghy was a few yards down. I could see the world's tallest mast gently bobbing at anchor out in the small bay. We had rowed in, and we would have to row back out. The waiter and my husband dragged me down the concrete walk and dropped me into the dinghy like a sack of cement.

I had behaved badly. My husband was mortified. He didn't love me anymore. He wished I had had been swallowed out at sea and found a watery grave. Disgusted, he got into the dinghy and began to row.

When we got to the *Blotto*, he crawled forward and tied a line to the side of the boat; then he tried to get me aboard. I would hang onto the side of the boat and pull myself up, and then I would slide back down into the dinghy and lie there and look up at him helplessly. Finally, with a great heave, he shoved me straight up in the dinghy. I stood stone still, propped up against the side of the *Blotto*.

All I had to do, I told myself, was climb up. I finally got my hands to go up in the air, and then I pulled my legs up and took a step toward the boat. Instead of stepping onto the *Blotto*, I stepped into the sea.

I was still hanging onto the big purse that held my whole life as it filled with water and drew me farther and farther down. It was as if the waters of the world were closing over me. I was a rigid rock going straight to the bottom of the sea. When my father had thrown me into the pool, the water had been a light, wavy green; this water was black as ebony and oily and could only be a baptism at the entrance to hell. A girl goes from her father to her husband, isn't that the way it's supposed to work? Isn't that the way it *had* worked? Grading more than my share of papers, the money going into an account my husband controlled, buying this boat—on and on, the list unraveled inside my head. Everything starts out so well; what makes it all go so wrong?

I felt someone yank my hair. The top of my head felt as if it were going to snap off the body to which it was attached.

My husband fished me up into the air, where, gasping and flailing— my arms had at last regained some feeling—I began spewing water and trying to bring some life back. Though my body was still numb from the waist down, my arms had life, though they didn't seem to be doing what I told them. They had minds of their own. One of them decided to hit my husband smack across the face.

He threw me against the side of the boat where I hung, with one thought only in my head: keep hold of my purse. It had my passport, my travelers checks, what French francs I had, my makeup, and other important items I couldn't remember at that moment but knew I couldn't live without. I think it was then that it dawned on me my purse was more important than my husband.

The next morning—oh, god, I would never ever drink or smoke again—I could hear the water whishing against the boat. We were underway. My husband had taken us out on his own. He didn't care that there was a high wind and water was slapping over the sides of the boat. He didn't care that I felt as if I would never be myself again. He knew a day or two would pass, I would feel better, there would be a bottle of *vin ordinaire*, so cheap and so good, because the wines of the countryside could not travel and had to be disposed of locally so they were sold for a pittance. Wine that cheap and that good was a sin not to drink. And what is good wine without a cigarette? I would be weak of will, I would discard my vow. I would once again embrace sinning with enthusiasm.

*Where was my purse?* I looked around the cabin and I didn't see it. My husband was busy up top, shouting down every once in a while that everything was fine, it was a great day to sail, we were practically in Le Havre, but he would need a hand.

He wanted me to get up and help him

Get up and help him. With the boat. This boat. This terrible boat.

For the first time, I saw that the name of the boat, the *Blotto*, was significant. I should have shied away from anything that had a name like that. Names are important. If you don't pay attention to them, you are inviting calamity.

"We have to motor in," he was saying. "You can't count on what the wind will do in a harbor, and it's a big harbor. We have to be careful not to get in the way of large ships."

*LARGE SHIPS?*

I pulled myself out of the cot and hauled myself over to the hatchway. We were at the mouth of a huge inlet of water. Humungous ships and long rows of barges and car-carrying ferries were plowing their way in and out. There was not another small boat in sight. "Can you just hold the tiller?" my husband shouted as he ran around getting ready to take down the mainsail and jib.

The sails were loose and flapping. Ropes were swirling about in the air. The stink of Le Havre harbor was terrible, and the entrance was maybe thirty feet wide at best. We were sitting, it seemed to me, right in the path of a huge ocean-going liner getting ready to run right over us and crush us so thoroughly that there would be no trace of boat or bodies left. *The last I saw of her, she was getting aboard this little boat with a huge mast, and then I never saw her again.*

The motor began to make strange noises. Then it made a spitting sound and died. My husband ran back and tried frantically to get it started. Then he said in a hysterical voice, "Take the tiller; I'll run up the jib. Maybe we can maneuver in with that."

The mainsail lay dead on the deck, wind ruffling its sides. If it rose, it would billow out and do god knew what. My husband had anchored it, I saw, with my purse. *MY PURSE!* To him my purse was just another piece of nautical equipment on this damn boat, which was all he really cared about. "What did you do to my purse?" I screamed at him, but he didn't care about anything except the wind, which was against us, the jib flapping back and forth. The *Blotto* zigzagged from one side to the other, totally out of control.

My husband shoved the dinghy over the side, climbed in, and started rowing for all he was worth, trying to pull the *Blotto* out of the way of the ocean liner bearing down on us, not to mention all the trawlers and enormous oil tankers in back waiting to take their turn running over us.

My husband rowed, his shoulders hunched, the oars flapping in the water. He strained as hard as he could to pull the *Blotto* out of the central channel into the port of Le Havre. Nothing happened. The *Blotto* wouldn't move. The tide was against him. In the meantime, the transatlantic steamer was so close that I could quite clearly see astonished faces staring down at us. My husband's adrenaline kicked in, he rowed as if demented, and the *Blotto* began to move very slowly out of the ship's path. From what looked like twenty stories up, someone waved.

Suddenly I heard a terrible scraping, and the boat stopped dead. We had run aground next to an enormous dredging machine. My husband looked up at me helplessly. I didn't know what to do. I wasn't the one who had sailed every summer of my life from the time I was five or six until I was fourteen.

I heard yelling. I turned and saw a huge ship with a bunch of sailors screaming at us. *And they were screaming in English.*

My husband got out of the dinghy and stood in water to his waist and pushed for all he was worth. "Go down below and pull up the centerboard," he said in a murderous voice. The centerboard is a moveable keel in the middle of the boat that in some boats, like the *Blotto*, can be hauled up. I hauled for all I was worth, my husband pushed, and we drifted off the sandbar. But my husband was still standing in water. I could see him out the porthole yelling and waving his arms. I ran up top and saw the dinghy drifting behind the boat, which was moving with the current, while my husband stood, stranded half in water, on the sandbar. "Swim!" I screamed, and he thrashed through the water until he could grab hold of the dinghy. A cheer went up from the boat with the American sailors. "Bring it over here," one of them shouted. My husband climbed into the dinghy, straining once more against the current, and somehow managed to swing the *Blotto* around and steer it toward the *American Reporter*. Some man up top threw a rope from at least fifty stories up, and I hung onto it while my husband got the dinghy next to the boat, tied it up close, and hoisted himself back aboard the *Blotto*. He did not say, as you are supposed to when you want to get on a boat, "Permission to board." He simply hauled himself into the cockpit and lay for a moment, spewing water and grinding his teeth. Then he sat up, took the rope, and wrapped it around one of the cleats. We were safe. We could rest against this huge ship, and maybe we would never have to leave.

But seven-eighths of the world is made up of water, so that hardly seemed possible.

A crowd of sailors gathered along the rail above us. My husband never looked up once. He was crouched over the engine trying to get it going. Since the very first day, he had been trying to figure out in liters how much petrol and oil we needed for one-third of a gallon of oil to two gallons of gas, an algebraic problem he never solved. People would scribble numbers on bits and pieces of paper and swear the problem was solved, but the Stuart-Turner motor never marched with any consistency *(il marche maintenant,* some Frenchman working on the damn thing would say when he finally got it going). My husband insisted that it was a choked exhaust. He had a series of things he did when the engine seized up—blow on the spark plugs, clean out the fuel line, just generally tinker around—but the real trick seemed to be to let the engine rest fifteen or twenty minutes, and then crank it for all it was worth. Sometimes the engine sprang to life, other times it didn't. Usually he would say, with a long sigh, "petrol starvation."

Now, none of his usual attempts to make the engine march were working. A lot of advice floated down, mostly concerning the carburetor, which my husband was leery of. A man up top the *American Reporter*, who said he was the chief electrician, began to shout emphatic directives down: since my husband had tried everything else—spark plugs, fuel line, clogged propeller—there was no alternative but to face the carburetor. "Compare it with the manual," the electrician shouted. My husband opened the Stuart-Turner manual and began resignedly to pull the engine apart. Pieces lay all over the cockpit floor. Meanwhile, members of the crew were pelting us with questions. "Where did we come from?" "In that boat?" "Where are you going?" "In *that* boat?" Soon oranges, soap, canned milk, corned beef sandwiches, and engine cleaner were lowered down in a bucket attached to a long rope. Two or three hours passed, the sailors lost interest; my husband started trying to put the pieces back together. Everything went in except one washer. What the hell was one washer in the bigger picture of life?

My husband took a big breath and then gave the starting cord an enormous pull; life flew back into the engine. We threw the line lose—I think "cast off" off is the term you're supposed to use, but I never mastered the nautical vocabulary of boat people, who have a language all their own, like those in other esoteric endeavors— psychiatry, astronomy, the culinary arts—that they insist on using to show their connection to some singular part of society. We began to motor down the thirty-foot passage to a mooring near shore where, exhausted, my husband tied the *Blotto* up then went below without a word and slammed the cabin door shut. I sat up top and cosseted all the grievances I had accumulated against him and tried to figure out what proper penalties he should pay.

I was trying to total them all up, but just as I hit the forties, a fishing boat came along and a big bearded man informed me in patois French we had taken his mooring. I pretended I didn't understand any French. I smiled, pointed to my mouth, shook my head, and shrugged my shoulders to indicate I had no idea what he was saying.

Then a brutish seaman in an enormous dory tried to cut us adrift; I fended him off with a wet mop and shouts of Anglo-Saxon abuse. My husband never stirred. I sat beside the motor and looked at the fishing boat circling about us. Finally I took the engine cord and gave it as big a pull as I could, and the Le Havre harbor god decided to let the motor march. My husband came up when he heard that sound. "We have to leave," I said. "We have their mooring." Razzle-dazzle Rust ran around the boat detaching lines as I put the engine in reverse and began trying to back out. My husband grabbed the tiller out of my hand and got our boat past the fishing boat, which was already reclaiming its rightful place in the harbor. We kept going for at least half an hour before the motor died again. My husband, with a sigh of resignation, pushed the dinghy over the side and began to row. "It's the damn fuel," he said. "We don't get the right proportions of oil and petrel, and the damned motor stalls. Things will be better when I finally get the ratio of gas to oil right." ·

Le Havre is the second largest port in France, some six hundred miles from the Mediterranean. Most guide books don't give it more than an inch, if that. I couldn't find it on the Internet encyclopedia, nor in my old Columbia encyclopedia in one volume. I could have tried the library, but it didn't seem worth the effort. Why look up something that is a nowhere place that you are going to warn people never to visit?

A seventeenth-century traveler (Edward Brown) wrote, "It is no unpleasant sight, to behold a new scene of the World, an unknown face of things…" but I don't believe he had ever been to Le Havre.

The *Blotto* motor marched fairly well as we worked our way down the long inlet—once or twice turning itself off just to show who was in charge—but we eventually got to what we thought was the Seine and the entrance to the Tancarvillle Canal. Frenchmen in blue work clothes with fishing poles lined the shores. They would look up when they heard the motor and frantically motion us away. Didn't want us to run over their lobster pots, I guess, the way we did somewhere along the way. I don't remember—or have deliberately suppressed—the village's name, the mutilated parts floating up as the motor churned over the lobsters' bodies and the lobstermen ran along the bank cursing us. I was at the helm at the time, and my husband screamed with them, You've just run over a fortune in lobster! Stop the damn boat! We have to pay for the damage *you've* done. Yes, I remember that scene quite well. Also the amount of money the lobstermen wanted. Highway robbery, my husband said, and we both knew whose fault that was.

At this moment, I was hailing the fishermen (You speak French better than I do, you talk to them. As in, You grade papers better than I do, so why can't you give me a hand?). Pardon me, sir, is this the Seine? A shake of the head. Do you know where the Seine is? Pointing. Next fisherman. Pardon me, sir, is this the Seine? Laughter. You have to go back. We go back. Excuse me, monsieur, is this the Seine? The Seine, for gods sake, I wanted to say, the most renowned river in France. Where the hell is the Seine?

The Seine is the longest inland navigational river in France. The Latin name for the Seine, *Sequana*, means snake; the Romans called the river snake because it wigwags in and out and around and back on itself. It often has broad branches of water that look like real rivers but are really camouflaged creeks that turn into little rivulets that meander back into swamps and bogs or grow so shallow we had to pull up the centerboard and get out and push, sometimes both of us, to get off some sandbar where we had run aground. I kept hoping that while we both stood on the sand bar pushing the boat, it would get away from us and speed over the water, never to be seen again.

When we finally found the Seine, I think it was blind luck. We had told each other that once we were actually on the Seine, everything would be better and, as a matter of fact, that first day on the Seine things did seem to be looking up. The engine marched. We had wonderful views of broken castles and small churches and sleepy river villages. Picturesque Frenchmen in blue shirts and pants fishing on the banks saluted us with their bamboo fishing poles. We motored along in a haze of happiness.

That night we drank lots of wine, and I think we might have made love. It is all rather hazy, that moment of having a happy time, because the next day there was no wind and the engine stopped and refused absolutely to start again. In was Sunday, and we were in Rouen, and the bank was closed, and we were out of money. Eventually I turned up a sympathetic hotelier who offered as a favor to change twenty pounds (for which we got less than fifteen dollars in francs). Armed with this, I stored in a good supply of food and hoped my husband had found someone to help us unstep the world's longest mast. Once the mast had been taken down, we would be able to pass under all those bridges that led to Paris—*Paris!*—and everything would be all right.

Coming down the quay, I saw my husband fiddling with the engine. Did you find someone to help with the mast? I asked.

I was waiting for you to come back. You're the one who speaks French.

I don't speak French. I listened to those records and learned some words, but I don't *speak* it.

Well, you speak it better than I do.

You wouldn't listen to the records—

I didn't have time for that kind of stuff.

Doing what? I wanted to ask. Not grading your papers. Not reading the manual on the motor.

He walked around with the boat manual clasped to his chest like it was the Holy Grail. I had a moment of insight: This trip was not to recover my husband's playful past; it was supposed to be his voyage of discovery, his way of giving his life meaning. He'd stay on this damn boat the rest of his life if he could.

The rest of my life on the *Blotto*.

I stood with the baguette, the wine and cheese, the tomatoes and pâté, unable to go on. I had been gone at least two- and-a-half hours, and he had just been waiting all that time for me to come back so that I could find someone to help unstep the mast. I was still standing there with my arms full—my husband had gone back to tinkering with whatever it was that had caught his attention—when a burly man with a pipe came over to me and said, *Difficulties?* I have always trusted pipe people. My woes began to pour out of me. Every time I came to the line *Things will be better when we get to …*, he would laugh so hard that he had to take his pipe out of his mouth.

It wasn't funny to me. *My* life did not take its meaning from this boat. I did not want to experience the raptures of the deep.

My husband's head suddenly shot up. Ask him if he can help us take the mast down, he said. Something in my face must have shown him that I had reached the limits of compliance. What happened to your wife? Oh, she went to buy a baguette in Rouen and I never saw her again, a French twist on the old, "He went out to buy a pack of cigarettes and I never saw him again."

My husband started gesturing and using what fractured French he had. I stood holding the things I'd bought for lunch. The Pipe shouted. A couple of other men came up from below a big barge's deck. The three Frenchmen looked at the world's tallest mast—which had to be at least a third again as long as the boat, which was twenty-one feet, meaning that it was, like, thirty feet high. When it hung over the boat, I know the overhang was twelve feet because I measured it, and I hated every inch of it.

The Frenchmen hollered instructions to one another; they got back on the barge and dug out ropes and some strange tools I had never seen before. Then they went to work. *And they went to work with good humor.*

The men I had known all my life—my father and husband, my professors and various school administrators—were always bad tempered. I had never known a man, except maybe my stepfather (the exception that proves the rule), who did not expect a cascade of praise for the smallest thing he deigned to do. Even if he carried a dish from the table to the kitchen, this was supposed to be regarded as a work of wonder.

The men threw jokes (most of which I had a difficult time following) back and forth; they tossed tools about with abandon and laughed when someone dropped one (instead of banging it in rage against some surface in punishment for its bad behavior, the way my father would have done). They handled the huge mast as if it were a long kind of toothpick that Frenchmen were well acquainted with, maneuvering it out of its central post hole and laying it down across the deck as gently as if they had been taking the long, slim arm of a woman, ready to press it to their lips in tribute to its soft skin.

These men took the unstepping of the mast as if it were a challenge that might end up as a section in a long Chaucerian poem that would one day give people a pause of pleasure amongst the mundane movements of their lives. From the moment they started handling the mast, they began reminiscing about other jobs they had done. Each job held the kernel of a story that ended in some lesson the man telling the story had learned, usually at his own expense.

They loved their mistakes because they defined a way to wisdom. Without failing, how could you become better?

I had a chance, while my husband and the two helpers were tying the mast along the top of the boat, to chat for a moment with The Pipe. He was horrified to discover we were navigating by a French Michelin road map. I explained we had had no choice, as new charts were not available and no one seemed to have any of the old ones. He shook his head, went over to his barge, and came back with a thick, tattered, sea-stained paper. This will get you to Paris, he said, and maybe you can get something there for the rest of your trip.

The Pipe badly needed a shave. He was missing a bottom tooth. He needed a bath. Yet he seemed to me one of the most wonderful men I had ever met.

This wasn't the kind of situation where you offer someone *money* for kindness, and I didn't have anything I could think of to give him.

If I'd had a novel, I would have taken a copy and written a grateful inscription. Even if he couldn't read the book, he would have had it. But of course I didn't have a novel. I didn't even have many notes for a novel. All I had were a few bits and pieces of ideas on paper—remember Lake Wawasee, don't forget the dark underground basement at Aunt Mabel's that was used in the Underground Railroad, show how Genevieve would never go out of the house and had everything delivered, most especially gin, show one of the scenes where your father throws his birthday cake against the wall, be sure to remember Aunt Ruth's box that was labeled "String Too Small to Save," which was filled with just that. Bits and pieces of paper, not even a general outline. That was all I was ever going to have, unless I had blocks of time and silence to shape these bits and pieces into a whole. *That* was what would give *my* life meaning.

So I leaned over and planted a quick kiss next to the bristly skin on the face of The Pipe and said, my heart brimming with gratitude, Thank you, thank you so much for everything. At least share some lunch with us. What I think he said in French was, Well, that would be mighty nice.

The mast hung twelve feet over the end of the boat, I thought, and wasn't that an awful lot? Wouldn't we run into things, especially in a lock?

Don't worry, my husband said irritably—what did women know about things like this?—everything will be fine.

I was the only woman at the centerboard table inside our cabin, and some of the men breaking bread with us looked away from me uneasily. I was bad luck. All women were bad luck on boats.

Sailors thrive on superstitions. You can never start a voyage on Friday. You *must* never step on board a boat with your left foot first. You must *never* bring a pet aboard. Flowers and bananas are taboo (*bananas?*). You must never cut your hair or nails on board. You must never say the word *drowned*. You must never look back when you leave (or, worse, look back longingly, as I did every time we put out from port). You must never use a black traveling bag to bring your things on board. Flat-footed people should never be allowed on board.

But the clincher is that a woman on board is bad luck. There is one exception: a naked woman, which explains why there were so many bare-breasted figures on the bows of boats, especially whalers. At that moment, looking at my handsome husband spreading camembert on his bread, I knew that he blamed me for every single mishap that had taken place and that he would have liked to nail me braless to the bow, though (thinking it over), I realized my weight would have dragged the front of the *Blotto* down, maybe even to the ocean floor.

I was sitting paralyzed with this epiphany when suddenly the tide changed and the *Blotto* violently swung around. I heard the stern line snap. The Pipe and his friends ran up on deck, jumped off the boat, and cast off our bow line. We went rushing with the current down the river and were out of sight before I had time to wave or my husband could get the engine going. The boat was cascading from one bank of the river to the other. I gave a shriek. "Rust, there's a dam ahead. We're going to go over the dam!"

Then the dam was almost on us. I ran inside and did the only thing I knew that might help. I raised the centerboard. Then I ran back up on deck and threw my arms around a post near where we were supposed to detour to go into a lock, but I didn't have the strength to hold on and, before the astonished eyes of the woman at the lock wheel and the people on the barges inside the lock, the *Blotto* was flung over the dam. The picnic lunch, along with all the pots and pans and books and anything else that wasn't lashed down, was tossed all over the cabin, crockery crashing against anything it hit. The boat was tilted forward, and everything slid into a heap at the end of the cabin. The boat scrapped across some rocks and plowed through a barricade of weeds. The tall overhanging mast snatched fishing poles out of Frenchmen's hands as we plowed on, and as they ran down the path beside us shouting and shaking their fists and howling imprecations, we tried to get the *Blotto* under control.

A decent person owns up to injurious failures and deleterious deeds. Instead, I threw the fishing poles over the side—some hit the bank, some floated along side us downstream—then threw myself below deck, where I hid so that I did not have to confront the enraged faces disappearing into a blur as we motored with full horsepower (for the first time I could remember) away from the scene of our iniquity.

The galley was strewn with food and wine and books lay amidst puddles of water that must have cascaded off the dam as we went over. I couldn't see one single cup or saucer, plate or glass that was intact. I sat down on the outer edge of one of the cots. The rest of it was soaked in olive oil.

Things would be better when we got to Paris. How could they not? Everything is better in Paris.

Yeah, yeah, but what about after Paris? And how long is it to Paris?

It's 367 kilometers (229 miles), as well as nine locks to go through before we get there and, with the mast unstepped, all there was to count on was the feckless motor. Well, actually there were two things you could count on for the *Blotto*: the motor breaking down and the cabin always being a mess. There was no time during the day to tend to all the things that got thrown down into the cabin, and by night I was so tired that I just threw things aside and usually fed us something leftover from noon before laying down on my olive-oil stained cot and staring up at the slatted ceiling. Make love? You've got to be kidding. Talk to one another? What was there to say? Read? You must be out of your mind. Anyway, read how? By a small, smoky kerosene lamp or a flickering candle stuck in an old wine bottle? As for working on a novel—let's just say that on a boat like the *Blotto,* some dreams best be deferred.

Somewhere after the dam, we were flagged to a stop and some officials came alongside. I thought, Oh, god, they've heard about our going over the dam and snatching all those fishing poles and whatever other damage we did, and now they are going to make us pay up. It's the French Southend Lifeboat Association.

What they demanded were papers. We had a bill of sale, that was it. That, apparently, would not do. It was still Sunday—a Sunday that seemed to go on forever—therefore the regular office was not open. We would have to pay an extra seven hundred francs to open the office and get the papers (or, rather, paper, a *laissez-passez*), and then we would be allowed to pass on. This absolutely necessary paper looked like some scribblings you do while you're on the telephone getting directions to a place you begin to realize you are never going to find.

I never did make out what the *laissez-passez* indicated that was so important. But we needed it, I had been told that by officials, *French* officials, so I knew better than not to comply. No matter; no one ever asked us about it again. We paid, we got the paper, and pass on we did, the sleepy river villages flowing by us as we chugged—the motor actually marching. We glided past landscapes out of Monet paintings, hay fields like ribbons of gold running over the landscape and willow trees bent acrobatically over the river. On every bank, a man in the ubiquitous French blue shirt and baggy pants rapturously fished away. In all the time I was on the waterways of France, I never saw one catch a fish.

Small birds sang. The bulrushes at the side of the river quivered in the wind. My husband was actually humming. He had a glass of wine beside the tiller, and every once in a while, he would lift it up to show it was empty. I would go below and get one of the bottles of wine that hadn't been smashed when we went over the dam and bring it up. If it had to be opened, I got out the corkscrew and liberated the contents for my happy husband, who looked the way he had looked when he had rowed me out to his family's island, like a man in possession of everything he had ever wanted in life. And me? Optimist that I am, I thought the past disasters were behind us, and we were going to be given golden days ahead.

We motored the final twenty kilometers to Paris in a daze of delight, chugging past the Eiffel Tower, the Palais du Chaillot, under the *ponts*, steering the *Blotto* to the Île de la Cité and putting the boat to rest under the shadow of the cathedral of Notre Dame. My husband found a cleat embedded in a concrete promenade across from the church; they were situated at various intervals along the river walk, and every once in a while, there were steps leading up from the Seine to a sidewalk. All I had to do was a make a small leap and I was on *land*, ready to conquer Paris.

I cleaned up most of the cabin. The olive oil stains on the cots I could not get out, so I just flipped the mattresses over and pretended I had taken care of the problem. I was learning, one way or another, to hide problems I couldn't or wouldn't deal with. I went clamoring up the steps of the bank, glanced across the *Blotto* at Notre Dame in the background, and went in search of provisions and some plates and cups.

We ate an enormous lunch of that wonderful French bread no one ever seems able to duplicate in the United States. We put slices of a coarse country pâté on it, or a soft Camembert, sliced tomatoes in oil, and finished with the puff pastry I had splurged on at a *patisserie*. We washed our lunch down with lots of wine. Drowsy and carefree, we slid the hatch all the way back, locked the doors to the cabin, pulled the curtains to the windows so that no one could see us, and lay down in one another's arms.

I don't suppose you can do that anymore—moor or make love under the shadow of Notre Dame. Every morning, when we came up from the cockpit, the first things we saw were the great spires of Notre Dame. The last things we saw at night were the shadowy flying buttresses like great, gray hands holding the walls up. I never thought of French churches being Catholic. They seemed more like museums.

If you're young and in Paris and moored across from the cathedral of Notre Dame and believe you have reclaimed the man you thought you loved, how can you not be happy? The past meant nothing—none of those terrible times we had had getting the boat to Paris spoiled our walks through the gardens, the dreamy moments in the museums, the sauntering down the wide boulevards, the visits (in the cheap seats) to the opera—and I felt no connection to the future. I was living in the light of the moment, and all my laughter sounded silvery. I didn't care about writing a novel and being rich and famous. I only wanted to be walking alongside my handsome husband, waiting for him to look down at me and smile. I hoped our time in Paris would never come to an end, but at last we had to leave. One of the laws of life is that you have to leave. Actually, it's the final one.

We started off lighthearted in what we now thought of as our "official" journey through the canals and waterways of France. Paris was hard for me to leave. I had come to see the *Blotto* as being in thrall of an evil god. As if to confirm these suspicions, as soon as we reached our first lock and I scrambled up the bank to see what information I could find about how many locks there were ahead of us, I ran into an old man who was fiddling with the large, metal wheel that controlled the flow of water in and out of the lock. I made the mistake of asking him if he knew how many locks there were between here and Lyon.

I think my husband and I had both assumed there would be picturesque countryside with charming, small villages along our way with a lock now and again, but far apart; however, when I scrambled up the side of the canal at the first lock and asked the old man fiddling with the large, metal wheel if he knew how many locks there were to the Mediterranean, he stopped what he was doing and shook his head in great distress. *Beaucoup*, he said. But *beaucoup* could mean a lot to one person and not too many to another. He gestured that he had a schedule inside he could show me, and we went into the little hut where he kept his canal entries. He opened a book and pointed to two open pages. I looked at them in disbelief.

There had only been nine locks in the whole of the Tancarvillle Canal, and that had covered 367 klicks (slang for kilometers; five miles equaling eight kilometers or, as we would say, eight klicks). Just nine locks to cover. That would mean somewhere in the neighborhood of 225 miles from Le Havre to Paris.

Now I read with increasing anguish

| | | |
|---|---|---|
| *Paris to Montreau* | 10 locks | 221 klicks |
| *Montereau (Yonne) to La Roche* | 17 locks | 212 klicks |
| *La Roche to Lyon* | 168 locks | 310 klicks |
| *Lyon to Port St. Louis* | 4 locks | 331 klicks |

What worried me most was that the 168 locks from La Roche to Lyon only covered 310 klicks, which came out to approximately to two kilometers between locks (or like a half a mile between locks). All the locks would not be equidistant, but at an average of two kilometers between locks, we would be doing nothing but getting on and off the *Blotto,* dealing with locks. Lyon was only about two-thirds of the way to the Mediterranean.

A lock is a long, rectangular body of water enclosed by a gate at each end that allows boats to move up or down when there are radical changes in the elevation of the land. You can't take a barge over a drop of twenty feet. You can't climb twenty feet up with a boat without help. A lock boosts you up or lets you down.

At the time of our trip in the late 50s, these locks were manned—a poor word choice, considering they were mostly operated by old, angry women or by sad, crippled men who had been wounded in the First World War, or sometimes it seemed anyone who still had a pulse to brag about.

Lock life was hard and dreary and monotonous, and the lock keepers were constantly irritated, especially when our motor died and we had to try to pull the *Blotto* out by ropes or by using the dinghy, which we kept on deck because we couldn't take up the space both the *Blotto* and a trailing dinghy would occupy in a crowded lock.

Sometimes no one was at the lock at all. I would have to jump off the boat and look for the lock keeper, often in back gardening or gone to the village five klicks away for groceries. Most of the time, I also had to bypass huge, snarling dogs nipping at my heels.

Every lock presented problems. First of all, we were usually the only small boat gong into the lock. The other vessels were big barges, and they looked upon us with scorn. We were obviously just some brainless Americans out for a lark. (We had a small American flag fluttering from the rear.) Secondly, when the water rushed in, the *Blotto* with its long overhanging mast bobbed dangerously about, and I always thought we were going to crash up against one of those barges and snap the mast off. This was such a frequent hazard that we were constantly jumping about trying to fend off disaster. At least half the time, if the motor got us in, it would not get us out. In one lock, a bargemen took pity on us and threw us a rope to pull us out. He said something in French neither of us understood, but we were so grateful we must have looked like lunatics as we jumped up and down, pummeling our fists in the air. My husband and I learned that when the water started to rush in, we should both try to steady the boat by standing on the side of the lock, holding the lines and moving them back and forth and up and down to keep the boat away from the side of the lock or from any of the barges that were near us. The water flooded in so wildly that this was a Herculean task that required both great strength and great grit.

A lot of times when we got to a lock, it was closed because traffic was coming the other way. We had to wait until those boats had been taken up or down, sometimes as long as an hour, sometimes overnight because the locks closed down at dark. While we were waiting at a lock, I would often go over the side and try to get clean. If I wore a light-colored swimsuit, it was stained brown when I got out. My hair stuck to my head from the oil in the water and gave off fumes of gas. I finally cut it and hoped I could get it cleaner now that there was not so much of it.

While I would soap myself and go for a swim, my husband tinkered with the motor. He seemed to have this feeling that if he turned his back on it, the motor would take umbrage and behave even worse than it usually did. He went overboard at least once a day, cleaning weeds from the propeller, so he stayed washed, if not clean.

Safe time, I used to think for just a minute as we sat still in the water and waited in line for the lock doors to open and let us in. Once we were in, the boat rose (or fell, depending on the water level compensation) and the barges—and once in a while a fancy motor cruiser—came at us like monsters bent on smashing us to bits.

Normally, however, we were squashed between two large barges. If the motor didn't go, my husband would get out and try to row the *Blotto* out of the lock with the dinghy. There wasn't time to pull it out. Pulling was a hard, slow business.

A lot of families lived on those barges—mother, father, rascally children. There was always washing hanging out. A few had flowerbeds and herb gardens in big tins, hopeless attempts to brighten up the dreary, greasy, sooty boats on which the women lived. The men were in the main grimy and cross, but then, it cannot have been inspiring to go up and down constantly one way and then back the other, year after year. Sartre had probably spent time on a barge before he wrote *No Exit.*

I didn't think my husband had any idea there were going to be so many locks. I don't believe he would have concealed this from me, but all things considered, I am more apt to convict him of crimes against our marriage now than I was then. I am older now, and it has occurred to me that if you know anything about sailing, even from only dealing with a small boat that you sailed summers on Long Island, surely you would know that if you were navigating from England to France by a Michelin road map, you haven't done your preparations properly.

Our lives, every day, day after day, involved dealing with locks. That was bad enough, but we were also living together in small, cramped, claustrophobic quarters where things were always going wrong. I had given up telling myself things would be better when we got to wherever it was that things might get better.

The motor god hated us and was never going to let us be happy and carefree. The shaft was *cassé*, the wheel was *dur*, the fuel line was clogged, the carburetor was on the blink, the exhaust was choked, the *bouges* were oiled up, the stern tube grease wouldn't melt, the gasoline had too much (or too little) oil, the cooling system had backed up, the pistons were worn out. When we had a good day, the boat god was just teasing us by letting us have hope. I don't think my husband ever comprehended there were deities you had to placate. He thought he was in charge, a mistake most of us make before we wake up to what life is all about.

The locks—all 228 of them— taught me even while you are sleeping and think you are safe in the land of deep darkness, the night gods are busily decaying your teeth, wrinkling your face, drying out your skin, inserting arthritis into your bones, turning your hair white and thinning it so that your scalp shows through the color of a flamingo. But this is only on a personal level. Globally, the gods are busily working on earthquakes, tornadoes, tidal waves, droughts, and fires; busily devaluing your money, rigging elections; the betrayal gods are planting the seeds of doubt about you at the IRS, revving up Christian fundamentalists to take away a woman's right to dictate what happens to her own body, and busily making changes in books to show that the earth was not as Darwin had shown but as they themselves believed it should be. There were businessmen happily orchestrating the defoliation of the great forests, supervising the operation of factories and machines that would make the ice at the poles melt so fast that in a few years whole cities would be inundated, men who were in cahoots with rapacious developers who were razing the green trees and bright bushes and replacing them with ugly row houses or huge ugly McMansions pressed up against one another; they were driving animals out of their natural habitats, species were disappearing at the rate of seventy a day minimum, tribal genocide was going on with machetes and spears and the guns we Americans had sold both sides, and evil geniuses were inventing new ways to massacre people into the millions. Even as you slept, the government (which never shuts down) moved on in thrall to the corporate rich, figuring out ways to get around the law to make even more profits, inventing lies to justify vast military expenditures and then making wars to provide a rationale for all that spending. There is one law in this life, and that is give to the rich and take from the poor so that the rich get richer and the poor get poorer. And what are you doing? You are sleeping.

By the time you awake in the morning, in the night millions of people will have died of starvation (but you don't know them, so too bad) or weapons of mass destruction (some petty regime the CIA helped put in place) and hired thugs are out bombing some hapless country to bits (never mind, we'll help reconstruct—so long as there's profit in it). And in some small, distant pocket of nearly useless land whose people are in such despair from poverty and disenfranchisement they don't even know what is meant by human rights, even there some form of extinction is taking place. Ninety percent of the world's largest fish have disappeared in the last half century.

Meanwhile, in the world inhabited by the *Blotto,* we were being visited by gales and rain. Day after day, the skies opened up and poured torrents down on us. Even in the midst of a deluge, my husband often felt he had to check on the engine. When he came into the cabin and sat down, scowling, he would tell me some terrible fact about some famous person I had always admired. Modigliani coughed up his lungs at thirty-five, an affliction aggravated by drug addiction and alcoholism. Hart Crane, who couldn't find anyone who wanted to publish his poems, was an alcoholic and homosexual and finally, in despair and in his pajamas, jumped off a ship he was taking from Mexico back to the United States. My husband even knew the name of the ship, the *S.S. Orizaba.* The last thing anyone saw of Crane was his hand coming out from the water. No one knew whether it was a salute goodbye or a mute cry for rescue.

Stephen Crane borrowed seven hundred dollars from his brother to get *Maggie, a Girl of the Street* published himself since no one else would take it. Most of the copies he burned to keep warm. He died at the age of twenty-nine from the ravages of what some idiot critic called "an arduous life." Roger Fry used to lick the dirt off Botticelli's *Primavera* when the museum custodian wasn't looking. What was he trying to do? Keep the painting in pristine condition?

These appalling stories were my husband's way, I thought, of reassuring himself that bad things happened to other people as well. Perhaps he suspected that I was having an interior dialogue adding up his sins. This is all *his* fault, I would tell myself. Then I would feel guilty and say to myself, Be fair. He didn't know the motor wouldn't work. He *would* have known if he'd taken the boat out more times before we started this trip. A *real* sailor knows his boat.

He's trying the best he can.

He wouldn't learn French. I don't want to be a translator. I don't want to be responsible for someone else's dream.

But the worst indictment I had against him was that he was like all the other men in the world who think that being born a man makes them better than women. When women fall in love, they always think the men they are in love with are different. I had come to that place where I now exempted my husband from that category. My husband wasn't different. He was just like all the other men who took their superiority for granted.

Sometimes when the motor wouldn't work and the lock was a tricky one, I had to get out with a rope and pull the boat.

More often than not, I bundled up in piles of bulky sweaters and a huge oil slicker and what looked like a sailor's knitted cap because it was always so cold in the mornings that my teeth chattered. By noon, I would be sweating. The temperature changes during a day varied by forty degrees. I started out piling one thick woolen sweater on top of another. Then when the sun came out—and it did do that sometimes—I would discard one after another until I was down to a tee shirt. Just as the sun began to warm my bones, clouds would suddenly boil overhead and the sun would go under, the day would start to die, and I would have to start piling the sweaters back on. At night, I slept in two or three layers of clothing, and I was still damp and cold.

I always look bedraggled, and the *Blotto* didn't look any better, with laundry hanging over the mast to dry and various ropes and cans thrown about the deck.

There wasn't a shred of sun in the sky, and at any moment a downpour was going to begin and drench everything—boat, laundry, people, anything on deck. But the fearsome sea was behind us. Now we just faced endless dark water punctuated by dangerous locks that went on into infinity.

Let me be absolutely clear about this trip. I hated the boat. I hated the small galley with its unpredictable Primus stove that often flared up for no reason and I had to beat the flames back so that the cabin wouldn't catch fire. Once in a fit of passion, I threw the stove overboard. My husband went over the side and retrieved it—wordlessly—and left it on the deck to dry out. Its immersion didn't improve it. Or, perhaps, like the motor, it was suffering from some kind of fuel deprivation, in this case kerosene. I would carefully fit the small spigot into the hole where the fuel went and pour the kerosene to a different level every day, experimenting to show the Primus god that I respected him and would do what he wanted. Like most gods, he didn't give a damn what I was doing to propitiate him. He didn't give a hoot in hell where I was or what I was doing. He had far more interesting clients to supervise.

The stove wouldn't light or, if it caught, flames would shoot five feet into the air. Once a barge going by saw the fire and frantically threw a bucket of water on it—but the flames burned on. The water drenched me.

I despised the smell below deck and the narrow cot, which made my back feel as if it needed a chiropractor. I hated the cockpit, which was a world unto itself where things that could went wrong and things I had never dreamed of broke down or refused to function. I was rapidly coming as well to hate the person I had become, this grimy, whiny woman who had, I am sure, a mean, tight look on her face all the time.

Because my husband had a vocabulary of maybe thirty words of French and didn't seem to want to learn any more or didn't have the strength to tackle two things at the same time—he couldn't do the boat *and* learn French—and we needed to find out so much information or directions or anything at all that had to do with the French, I had to try to figure out (with my compact dictionary that had no nautical terms, especially not specialized ones dealing with malfunctioning motors) and translate everything that was said to my husband and then what he said back to the person I had been talking to. Often after one of these marathon French-to-English encounters, I would be smoldering with rage. There are a lot of entries in my journal that say "I hate my husband."

Speaking and thinking and constructing sentences in another language is tiring, especially if you are tone deaf and do not have the ability to learn by ear. Sometimes by night I would have such a headache from trying to figure out verb tenses and from pantomiming what words I didn't know that I would think, Why can't he at least try to learn a few words?

Then there were the French kids who wanted to practice English, especially adolescent boys trying to show off. You have many things in cans in the United States? You have a car—a Cadillac? A Buick? You know Carmen Miranda? She dee-ed. Also Susan Ball. She dee-ed of cancer of the—how you call it, chest. My brother tolded me Susan Ball, she dee-ed yesterday.

There was the day, engraved forever on my mind, when the engine seized up and I trudged two or three klicks to a little town that seemed to have no name to look for a mechanic. There actually was a man who said he knew something about motors (it later turned out that this was not true) and a helper, who informed me he used to be a headwaiter at the Biltmore (which I don't think was true either, the *Biltmore?* Please). The so-called mechanic and his helper came to the *Blotto* and looked at the engine gravely, pulled on the cord to get it started, and nothing happened. Then they looked at one another, and the man who had been headwaiter at the Biltmore said a piston rod was broken. They would have to send to Paris for the part. Tomorrow was Sunday, and Monday was a holiday ("What holiday?" "Why,"—this said with great surprise—"August 15." August 15? What is celebrated on August 15? I asked, but I didn't really understand the answer. But I did understand, Yes, most certainly it was the piston rod.)

I kept saying, Don't you think you should take the engine apart to *see?*

No, most certainly it is the piston rod. You will be here until Wednesday at least.

Take the engine apart, I said.

I never saw so many pieces in my life. It was not the piston rod. ("Ah, very much better.") Only some ring inside the piston. Perhaps you will only have to wait until Tuesday. Can't someone make it? No, it is not possible.

I kept repeating, Why can't we go back to town and *see* if there is someone there who can make the part? I wore them down, and they shrugged their shoulders and said, *Et bien, allez.*

My husband stayed with the three hundred or so parts of the engine that were strewn on every available space on the deck, and the two men and I trudged back to town. There was a man who said he could come and take measurements and maybe he could make the part. I think he was the village blacksmith, but I didn't care what he was. He could have been Walter Mondale. I just wanted him to fabricate the piece we needed.

The fabricator came back to the *Blotto* with me, surveyed the parts flung all over the boat, bent down, picked up the piece that he said was *méchant,* and departed. He was gone two hours and returned, triumphant. The piece did not fit. He went back to town and got some tools, and he and the headwaiter from the Biltmore worked another hour filing and banging. The piece was inserted, and they spent another hour reassembling the engine and—of course—it didn't work. It wasn't the piston ring after all, but now nobody had any idea what it was. We went back to town—Walter Mondale, the headwaiter, his helper, and I— to try to duplicate the sounds the motor was making to a man who had, I was told, special tools. After I clucked and sputtered, he gave me a long, hollow instrument that looked like no tool I have ever seen before, and lo and behold, the flywheel was merely *loose.* With two turns of this magic tool, the motor turned over and began to purr.

It was too late go on, and anyway the laws of hospitality must be observed. I pulled up the two sides of the centerboard to make a table in the cabin and got out wine, and we all had a drink. My husband and the three men tried to figure out the bill. There was Walter Mondale working four and a half hours constructing a special part at his shop and then having to spend two more hours here and then having to go back and spend another hour and a half in his shop. Then there was the man with the magic wand that made the engine come to life as well as the headwaiter from the Biltmore, who had served as moral support. All were now late for dinner. The problem was, how much could they charge us for working on the wrong thing? They wrote figures on a piece of paper, and then erased some and wrote in others, and then erased those, and then talked to one another and wrote more numbers down, and then said we owed them three thousand francs, which at that time was $8.60.

If you live long enough, you come to love the French.

We had so many problems that it would be hard to list them all. We had the kerosene pump stove, not bottled gas, which I don't think existed then; at least, it didn't where we went. Water was always a problem. We didn't have a tank. No plastic bottles, but heavy, old-fashioned metal cans. We used gas and oil, not diesel, and had to carry those in fifteen-liter containers (a little over ten pounds each). There were no supermarkets in those days and no real general grocery stores. You bought each item—meat, vegetables, bread, wine, pastries, et cetera—at separate stores, all of which closed from noon to two for the traditional French lunch, making shopping difficult and often impossible. I had to jump off the boat, and while my husband tried to maneuver the *Blotto* through a lock by himself, I armed myself with the characteristic expandable French string shopping bags as well as heavy cans and baskets. I had to run to town, often a kilometer or two away from the lock, and then run back, trying to locate the boat. This was not as difficult as might have been, since the *Blotto* was often breaking down. The boat seemed to have an inner sensor that knew when it would be traumatic to have a crunch situation. Then the motor would sputter and die and lie dead for as long as it pleased. The boat god hates us, I said. My husband, a Presbyterian, looked at me as if I had lost my mind.

There were days when we found ourselves in totally unexpected pleasure and took one another's hands and were a husband and wife again. One of those days occurred in Courcelles, a very old and poor town where we went ashore to look for provisions. But there was nothing to be had—the butcher and baker made calls twice a week, and this was not one of their days. However, a very excitable and odd-looking woman took us into her home for some tomatoes. There she showered us with peas, beans, leek leaves, potatoes, onions, tons of clover (I don't know what she thought we would do with all that clover, graze like cows?), garlic, eggs—and didn't want to take any money. I thought of the old law of hospitality: that the traveler must be fed and kept safe and in return must not bring harm—not rob or steal or murder those who had taken the traveler in. The basis of the war against Troy occurred because Paris had stolen Helen when he was the guest of Agamemnon, had eaten

Agamemnon's food, drunk his wine, then run off with his wife. Being a good guest is a rule few of us know, but if you traveled on the *Blotto,* you learned that principle promptly. I will say this for that awful boat: it did teach me that learning how to be a good guest is a golden gift.

The husband in Courcelles gave us a glass of wine, and the wife put down rough bread and a dish of olive oil to soak it in. Their French was as bad as mine, but we were eager to share our lives with each other. They were refugees from the civil war in Spain, so the conversation often became a jumble of my one year of high-school Spanish and my bad fractured French. It wasn't the words that were important, though; it was the warmth of their dirt-floored house, more like a hovel, I suppose, but with what they had, their hospitality was limitless. My husband gave the other husband some American cigarettes, and he was as filled with joy as if he had won the lottery. That was a good day.

I remember two Hogarth-looking ladies who ran one of the locks and grew roses. They told us how they had tried to outwit the Germans by changing the water in a lock to the opposite direction just before boats with Germans on them arrived and how they tried to jam the locks. They had a wicked dog (*chien méchant,* my journal says) who was protecting, I discovered, her puppies. When we moved away from the small bush where she lay with her little ones, that dog turned out to be as amiable as anyone could wish once she realized her puppies were safe. That was part of a good day.

I remember St. Florentine—I will always remember St. Florentine. There were all these fishermen lined up along both sides of the banks of the canal as we came around a bend. They began shouting and screaming, so we pulled the *Blotto* in and moored above them. I needed to go up to town to revittle, as country people say, and my husband said he would come with me to carry the water. There was a town fête going on and a fishing contest. The streets were bedecked with paper flowers, cardboard figures of fishermen, and anchors fashioned out of paper flowers and ferns. It was not quite noon, and everyone was drinking and singing, so we figured we might as well join in. I don't know what time we got back to the *Blotto* or who won the fishing contest, but I do know that we carried on our shoes the smell of the fresh grass we had crushed as we walked back to the boat and held in our hands wildflowers that we had picked along the way. We had forgotten the containers for the water, and we hadn't bought any food, but we lay down on the embankment next to the boat and held one another and were happy for a time. I am thinking about that now. I can see us lying on the bank. I can see the *Blotto* moored under a tree in the canal. I can picture us embracing on the grass, the smothered wildflowers under our bodies. We were happy. I know we were happy there, at that moment. But we weren't happy on the boat.

At Montbard, there was a large open-air market where we bought all kinds of fresh fruits and vegetables, but what was best, we discovered, was that it was 35 klicks to the next lock, Port Royal, and then we would get what I had come to think of as "a lock rest."

We needed lock rests. We were both exhausted. At one point, we had to get through 56 locks in 30 klicks; going for water and provisions and gas and oil often entailed long walks (with empty cans, not so bad) and what seemed like longer walks back (with the cans full and heavy). Worry can wear you out as well. We were constantly listening to the motor to see what it was going to do.

The tunnel at Pouilly was so dark that we had to attach lamps on the deck so that no one would run into or over us. It was supposed to be about 3 klicks long, but it felt as if it went on forever. I remember somewhere after that seeing a lovely chateau and thinking how nice it must be to sit at a real table and get into a real bed and put on a real light and read a real book instead of a boat manual. Then we passed into a very primitive (at least then) and beautiful countryside, where there was a savage dog at every one of the locks. We passed a barge being pulled by two horses, and I was filled with envy.

We learned we had twenty-five more locks to Dijon when I got off the boat to walk up to a small village to buy bread and actually found some croissants, which we hadn't had since Paris. My husband pulled the boat along the bank, and we stopped for a second breakfast. He had had a Personal Appearance Hour the day before, and he was so handsome that I couldn't imagine why I was so angry with him so much of the time. We were just buttering our first croissant when it started to rain. It rained for the next five days. Perhaps you could say this was the story of a marriage, or of what happens in many marriages. They wore love away in ways they had never anticipated.

I had been looking forward to Dijon because we had told everyone to send us mail there care of Poste Restante, and we had agreed we would stop for a few days and get off to see what is usually called the mustard capital of the world. Dijon had once been the capital of Burgundy and there is a ducal palace, a thirteenth-century cathedral, museums, and thousands of stores with pots of mustard in their windows. The post office was closed. I don't know why. It would not open until the next day, either. (I don't know why, and I had ceased asking for rational explanations for why places were closed. I just accepted that the French had a lot more holidays that we did in America.) We did some sightseeing, and then treated ourselves to a real sit-down meal in a restaurant and drank carafes of wine. Somehow things had got to the point where, when we got up from the table, we were both looking at each other warily. It was hard to remember how we had held hands and stopped every once in a while to bring our lips together in Fécamp and Paris; it was hard to remember what love was like at all. It was hard to remember why I had married this man in the first place. True, he was very handsome. True, he came from a good family. True, I was desperate to get out of the Midwest. But I must have at least *imagined* myself in love.

How could intense feelings of love and hate be so closely related? When I thought about it, our relationship seemed more like an account in which each of us was running up debits and credits, and I was constantly checking to see what the final balance on my husband's side was. The cons were winning, way past the pros. Falling in or out of love is a full-time job, I thought as we went back to the boat and lay down on our separate bunks. I guess you could say that was the pivotal moment. There was still a long way to go, but it was like walking through a half-finished dream—you don't know whether you want to know how it ends or not. We lay on our backs staring at the slats in the ceiling; we did not speak to one another. It was as if we wanted a truce but did not know how to go about making one, and there was no one to mediate.

We did not talk the next day. I banged a lot of pots and pans around in the galley, though, to let him know my emotional temperature. When I came into the cockpit, he stared over my head out at that wonderful water he was so crazy about while all I could think of was that I wanted to go someplace where I could get away from water for the rest of my life. I would never even be able to go to the beach again in a beautiful bathing suit and anoint my body with sun lotion until it gleamed and I became one of those golden goddesses stretched out on a bright blanket while boys who almost looked like men were seized by such fits of desire they would make absolute fools of themselves trying to get my attention.

I hadn't looked—really looked—into a mirror in days. I never thought to put on makeup. My hair was matted with the oil the barges left in their trail, because the only water I could wash it in was canal water. I had come to the place where no sensible man would look at me with anything like admiration. Pity probably, and disgust maybe, and surely disapproval. All this I now counted in my husband's debit column. He had made me old and ugly at twenty-five.

In Lyon things certainly had to get better. We were required to hire a guide to take us down the Rhone. Its swift, dangerous current—from 8 to 23 kilometers per hour—made navigation so difficult that a pilot was obligatory. Someone else, someone *professional,* would be in charge. Surely things would be better then.

Unbeknownst to us, the French newspapers had been running human interest stories about us ever since we had been washed over the dam. They had interviewed the old woman who had made life so miserable for the Germans by raising and lowering the water in her lock so that the Germans were constantly held up. They had found the men who had charged us only $8.60 to repair our engine and, trying to translate their stories later, I didn't recognize either my husband or myself as having participated in these events. Almost all the papers described us as *beau* or *chic*, adjectives totally inaccurate. One paper called us *formidable.*

We found out we had become minor celebrities when we motored into Lyon. The quays on either side of the river rapidly filled with people shouting and waving. I thought they assumed from the little American flag we had attached to the rear of the boat that we had sailed the *Blotto* from the United States, but nobody it seemed to me could be that deranged. By the time we found a place to pull up along the quay and tie up the *Blotto,* a crowd had gathered and people were peppering us with questions so fast that I couldn't translate all of them. The word *maire* kept being repeated again and again.

My heart sank. We had done something wrong, and the mayor was going to come with gendarmes and throw us in the clink. *Maybe they will impound the boat,* I suddenly thought with elation.

My hopes were soon dashed when the *maire* appeared with a phalanx of journalists, all screaming and popping pictures. He made a speech, and then presented us with the flag of Lyon for outstanding bravery. They made us get off the boat for the presentation. None of them wanted to get on the *Blotto,* even to get pictures taken. Who knew what that boat would do?

Finally the little mayor asked both of us get back on the boat and hold the flag of Lyon between us, one on each side, since we couldn't run it up an unstepped mast, and it didn't seem respectful to hang the flag off an overhanging one. The small mayor was finally persuaded to get on. He gingerly came aboard but, as soon as he had his picture taken, he jumped off onto the solid concrete quay, where there was a table with wine and appetizers spread out.

We all gathered around it, smiling, and had more pictures taken, the small mayor squeezed between my husband and me. Nobody believes this story—they think I am spinning a fanciful tale—but I have faded yellow newspaper clippings with pictures of my husband and me smiling—*smiling!*—holding the flag between us, my husband as cocky as if he had been Caesar conquering Gaul. When we divided up our things, my husband took the flag and I took the running lights, which of course had never actually worked.

The guide, yes, yes, the guide for the Rhone. A man chock full of confidence came aboard, looked around disparagingly, shrugged his shoulders as if to say that he had seen it all in his time and been able to deal with every single problem without turning a hair. Then during the course of the run down the Rhone, he became so deranged by one narrow escape after another. The worst was when the motor died and the Rhone swept us along at a harrowing speed, the boat veering so close to land that it looked as if it were going to be thrown up on some woebegone track of weeds. As my husband frantically used his hands to push us away from the clump of rocks to the next, this peerless pilot plunged into the water and waded ashore and ran off into the weeds. That was the last we ever saw of him; he didn't even wait to get the other half of his fee.

You don't need more details of the things that went wrong. You would hardly be able to lift this book if I recounted them all. And a picture of how I looked says it all.

When we finally got to the south of France, we had the mast put back up. We should have been headed west on Homer's wine-dark seas to Greece, but the mistral, that cold vicious wind that rises out of Africa, had its own plans. It was fierce and unpredictable, changeable and treacherous, subject to sudden squalls, and it pushed us relentlessly toward Spain until finally, frantic that the wind was going to do us in, we washed up on the shores of Barcelona.

While General Franco remained in control, I had always vowed I would never spend a nickel in his fascist country. I wasn't happy about the Spanish Catholic church either, which for centuries had used its most draconian methods to keep the illiterate peasantry in medieval bondage. In parades, the soldiers of Franco marched, flaunting their guns alongside the cross of god.

The *Blotto* had brought us to Barcelona, and there I remained, waiting with my husband as the weather got worse and worse. Actually, I was lucky even to get in. If I had had WRITER on my passport under PROFESSION as I had wanted to—seeing it in print might make it a fact—I would never have been allowed to enter the country (would they even have let me stay on the boat if I promised not to get off?). Franco did not want foreign snoops poking around. I could have put down HOUSEWIFE, which would have been acceptable to the Spanish, but not to me, so I had ended up, taking the advice of the people sending us overseas, to enter TEACHER in the slot where it said OCCUPATION.

I was not a writer. I was a dreamer sitting in the run-down port of a beautiful Catalonian city, one with wide, leafy boulevards dotted with outdoor cafés where people went in the shadowy cool of the evening to be part of the *paseo*, the evening promenade where young men and women eyed each other and their parents checked them out for possible matrimonial matches. Arranged marriages, I was to learn to my own despair, still remained an integral part of Spanish life.

That was then, getting toward the late 1950s. I don't know about now. I don't know much about Spain anymore, except that I have heard Barcelona has become one of the places where thieves thrive on tourists and the splendid boulevards are filled with backpackers and bewildered people released from their cruise ships for eight hours of sightseeing and shopping.

My husband would go with me to one of the outdoor cafes on the Ramblas for wine and sit morosely watching people pass by. It wasn't cities he was interested in. It was water he wanted. We can leave in a day or two, he would say, when this awful wind dies down. He couldn't wait to get going and sail the whole Mediterranean. Errol Flynn wanted to sail the Adriatic, but *I* am going to sail the whole Mediterranean. That was what he wanted to do with his life.

We had had nothing but beautiful skies since we had arrived, but there was a terrible wind that tore at us all the time, and it was the wind he worried about. We have to wait for the wind to calm down before we take the *Blotto* out, he said. We? Look at what I had become, I thought, finally confronting myself in the mirror.

You cannot go back, you cannot go back: that was the cry inside my mind every day. No matter what people say, change is *not* necessarily for the better. I remember the light Spanish wine and the *tapas,* those small little plates with a bit of something to nibble while you drank your wine. We would go, my husband and I, to an outdoor café on the Ramblas, and I would always hope I'd get fried squid for my *tapa*. Once, in a café, I saw an enormous pile of jumbo shrimp on the counter, and I wanted a plate of those shrimp so much that I cried out in joy, but my husband said they were way too expensive. He advised me not to order them in the same kind of slow, venomous voice my mother would use when we went out to dinner and she said to me sotto voce, Look at the right side of the menu and order the cheapest thing you find. To this day, over fifty years later, I mourn not having those shrimp. I think they have become some kind of metaphor for how to use your life, or at least how I wanted to live my life. Like saying, To hell with it, let's have the shrimp, we're never going to be in Barcelona again, and I'm never going to want shrimp the way I do now.

But my husband controlled the purse strings and thus made decisions about who ate shrimp and who did not. Not being allowed to have the shrimp finally tipped the debits and credit columns, and nothing he could do after that would ever make him right in my eyes again.

No more seesawing back and forth, no more things are going to get better when we get whatever. I was resigning from The-Things-Will-Be-Better-When Club then and there. Those few moments of love under the shadow of Notre Dame, on the bank by the canal, didn't make up for everything else. That night, I sat down with my husband and said, I don't want to go on. I want to sell the boat and divide the money and each of us go our separate ways.

*What?*

I think we should sell the boat and split the money and go our separate ways. Hope is not a sound strategy. I wish we had never heard of Errol Flynn.

You're just tired. We'll take some time out and you can write.

*Write? I can't write on this boat. I'll never be able to write on this boat.*

Dante would have been better served to have used French locks to show the stages of hell in his *Inferno.* I can make one bet I am sure to win: In between circles, he wouldn't have been able to sit down and write.

We don't *connect* any more, I said. Weren't you the one who told me that "only connect" was the answer to everything?

My husband decided not to debate, that a superior strategy was to retreat into silence. Not an ordinary silence, you understand, but one that emanated disappointment, betrayal, and that smacked of reverting to what I would call hurtie feelings.

That was the first day. On the second, he tried to argue with me logically, coldly, patronizingly. In every love relationship, there is one partner who doesn't care as much as the other; that person is the one with the power. I might not have any money, I might not be able to make him sell the boat, but I wasn't going to live with him anymore in the way they mean when they make you take those vows at the altar to love, honor, and obey. I just stated that once, on the second day. From then on, he screamed at me, he pleaded with me, he even cried. What had he done to make me act like this? You wouldn't let me have the shrimp, I said, and he looked at me, dumbfounded. You make all the decisions. We do what *you* want, and if you want to sail to the Greek Islands, that's perfectly all right. But if I want some shrimp, I don't get them if you don't think I should have them. I want to be able to order shrimp when I want without your permission. I want to write. I want to be by myself.

But you're my wife.

That's not a good enough excuse.

Then he really went on a tear. I could not leave him because the boat was in his name, and there was no way in the world he was going to sell it.

That was the crux of the matter: In order for me to get free, the *Blotto* had to be sold, the money split between us, and there was no way my husband was going to agree to that. If he wouldn't sell the boat, what would I use for money to go my own way?

Then I had one of those inspired ideas that come to you unannounced but pure of purpose. We had some money left in our account in England—not much, but some. You can have the boat, I said, and I'll take the money from—

You're not taking any money out of that account. That's trip money.

*Trip money.*

It was at that moment that we heard someone shouting our names. Roy Bongartz had—god knows how—found us. Roy said he had seen our pictures in the paper. The Lyon paper? I asked. Nah, I forget what town I saw it in, but I couldn't believe my eyes when I saw you two on the front page.

Roy can sail with you, I said.

Roy said he didn't think he wanted to take all that time to go to Greece, and anyway he had a girl in the car he wanted us to meet. My husband said, How about as far as Italy? Roy said he thought he'd rather look around Spain. Cee wanted to do that. She wanted to go to some bullfights.

They torture those bulls before they kill them, my husband said. How can you want to go see animals tortured?

There followed one of those deadly moments of silence when everyone starts to see the next few hours are not going to be easy to get through. Roy went out to the car and came back with this gorgeous creature who had not been ruining her looks on the canals and waterways of France.

The four of us went up to the marina café and got a carafe of wine. I asked Roy how the camping trip had gone, and he shrugged his shoulders as if to say, Not what I expected. Then his face brightened. But I met Cee, and he leaned over and put his mouth on her bronzed cheek. I saw immediately he had entered the entrancement of love that my handsome husband and I had long ago left. Someone in publishing once told me that the end of a book was the end of a marriage. Maybe boats were like books.

There, in that dismal little café on the rundown waterfront, the four of us sat, silent. When my husband got up to go to the W.C., Roy said, What's up? I've had it, I said. I don't want to go on. Actually, I don't want to be married to him anymore. I don't in fact care if I ever see him or that boat again. Wow, Roy said.

But the trouble is, he has our bankbook, and he won't give me any of the money from it. He says that money is trip money.

Roy and Cee only stayed that one day. They had planned on staying on the boat with us for two or three days, but they couldn't wait to get off, and I didn't blame them.

I watched them go off in Roy's little Renault, envy scorching my heart. My husband said we were going on the next day, the wind was better. It wasn't any better. He just wanted me off land and out on the sea.

I'm not going. I'm going to the American consul—I'm going to tell them—

He took hold of my arm. You are not going anywhere.

I took my purse, which was probably heavier than a rock the same size, and swung it at him. He fell backward. I jumped off the boat and ran up the dock. I didn't know where I was going. I couldn't picture myself really going to the American consulate and telling them I was indigent because my husband wouldn't give me any money. Maybe they had even seen the picture of us holding up the Lyon flag (smiling, oh, so full of smiles) and knew all about the *Blotto*, though that seemed highly unlikely. They had been in the north part of Spain, and Franco used the Pyrenees as a wall to block the modern world out. It was doubtful any French newspapers had got through.

I went into the marina café and sat down. One of the waiters automatically brought me a glass of red wine. I probably had enough pesetas for a couple of glasses, but I certainly didn't have enough to rent a room or to go the telephone exchange and wait hours to make a call to my parents, who wouldn't send me money anyway. (You made your bed with him, now lie in it). So I just sat.

It got dark, and my husband didn't come for me. He was no doubt in the cabin of the *Blotto* working on a double cross-stick puzzle.

I had my engagement ring. It had been made out of a pair of earrings that had belonged to my husband's grandmother, two large diamonds surrounded by small diamonds. (Later I gave it to my daughter and said, If you're ever in a jam—remembering the marina café in Barcelona— and need money, you will always have this to fall back on. She gave me a funny look. *And then later she lost the ring.* She didn't even remember my giving it to her. Whenever I couldn't find anything, I used to tell myself, It's probably with the ring. The truth of the matter is that it was a very expensive but bad-luck ring. Something like the Hope diamond.)

Darkness was pulling night down over the bay. The sailors in the marina café had begun looking at me in a funny way. It was one thing to come in and have a glass of wine, another to stay hours sitting in a chair staring into space. And I was by myself. Women—correction, nice women—did not go anywhere by themselves, and never into a place like this. Well, I was an American, and everyone knew American women were difficult, that their men didn't know how to control them.

I got up and walked out of the café and tried to think what to do. I had no place to go except back to the boat. So I stood on the dock looking down into the cockpit and past that into the cabin. My husband was lying on his cot, asleep.

I climbed as quietly as I could down into the cockpit and was just getting ready to lower myself into the cabin when my husband opened his eyes and looked at me. *What the hell is it you really want?*

I want to write. And you're keeping me from doing that.

You could have written on the boat. He really sounded as if he thought I could have been down at the centerboard table writing my novel while we went through locks, over dams, down the thundering Rhone.

I need to be someplace where I can have peace and quiet, sit in a small room and think, where I can be alone. I can't write here, and I can't write with you around. You always need something.

If things stopped happening to you, how would you know you even existed? my logical, maddening husband asked. I had been reading *The Outsider,* and we both knew he had tried something like ten pages and thrown it aside with exasperation.

"You've fooling with Colin Wilson again," I said maliciously. "You'd never have come up with this on your own." Then a crack like an earthquake's fissure went through me. "You never come up with anything on your own. It's always something you read or I've read and told you about, or something you've borrowed from someone else. Like Errol Flynn." I had sunk to my lowest.

My husband, cornered, snarled, "You're the one who wants to be the writer. That's what you want, to be the writer, not to do the work— what you want is for people to know who you are, not to be someone ordinary—"

He's seen inside my skull, the terrible sense of wanting to be known, to be someone of value. Even Roy Bongartz wants that. Everyone wants that. But people are too intimidated to admit it. "I hate you," I said with all the energy I could muster. "I wish I had never married you."

We had come to that place all lovers arrive at after they have been closeted with one another too long and have to see the person they thought they worshipped with all his faults and fatal humanness.

My husband saw that I saw. His only strategy was to backtrack. "All right, all right, I'll sell the boat. We can get a car and drive to Greece. Maybe things will be better when we get to Greece."

He was willing to forsake his own dreams for me. The final gift of love. How could I turn that down?

He's trapped me, I thought. If he sells the boat because of me, I will owe him a debt that can never be repaid. The words I shouldn't have said came, unchecked, right out of my mouth on their own. "I don't want to go to Greece with you. I don't want to go anywhere with you."

"You don't want to be with me? What do you mean you don't want to be with me? You married me, didn't you?"

"I can't go with this boat, Rust. I just can't. Please sell the boat. Please just sell the boat, and we'll see."

Selling a boat in Barcelona was no easy job because, even if we could find a buyer, the buyer couldn't buy the boat. There was a law against Spaniards buying foreign boats. It was like the law against importing cars. Franco didn't want his country to have contact with the outside world, so he banned all imports that would have modernized the society and moved it into contemporary times. He wanted to preserve Spain in all its medieval splendor—at least for himself and a handful of the rich and privileged.

I did not know what to do if we couldn't sell the boat, which, I saw, was a happy turn of events for my husband, who believed we would *have* to sail for the Greek Islands. He watched me put up a sign that said **FOR SALE,** and underneath **SE VENDE**. People looked at the sign and laughed.

Every afternoon we went to the marina café, where we drank the local red wine and played Monopoly with fake British money since we were using a British set Roy had given me for my birthday. It had different streets—Mayfair, Oxford, Piccadilly, Baywater, Park Lane— than the American version. The Spanish were agog at our riches. We couldn't convince them that the money wasn't real. All Americans were rich. Look at all the money we were passing back and forth playing a *game*.

In desperation, I went to the American consular office in Barcelona. A tall, thin, disapproving Spaniard ushered me into the office of a young man, American, stylish, good looking, and, I found out later, unmarried. I saw a lot of him when he was transferred to Seville. He was very nice, but once when I said, What's under that calm exterior,

Sam? he said, Maybe nothing. Maybe whatever was there went in the war. I tried to figure out which war he meant and came up, finally, with the Korean one.

From that first day I met him, Sam was all sympathy as I sat nervously on the edge of a chair in front of this huge desk with the seal of the United States behind his head and explained my predicament.

You can't sell a boat here, he said, but what's the matter with renting it for a lifetime?

Fine, but I had to find someone who would want to rent it.

Well, you can post a notice on our bulletin board if you want. There might be someone here who'd be interested. So, god forgive me, I wrote up the following:

**FOR SALE:** 22 ft [this was half a foot off] Bermudian sloop (Marconi rig) with Stuart Turner reserve engine. Sails in good condition. Centerboard. Extremely comfortable for cruising. Has just completed two-month trip from England to Spain via French canals. The boat is completely outfitted and ready for immediate use. It was surveyed in June of this year, completely refitted with new running and standing rigging, taken out of the water and completely overhauled, mast restepped. Engine is three-gear Stuart-Turner P/55M, 8 horsepower, 2 stroke, gasoline, 2 cylinder marine engine in perfect [I took this out in a fit of conscience] running order. Automatic and hand bilge pump.

Cabin sleeps 2 to 3, others on deck. 3 berths, centerboard folding table, clothes closet, 7 ft bookshelf, fine brass and copper gimbal lamp, barometer, more than adequate storage space. Galley with 2 burner kerosene stove, sink, crockery for four, pots and pans.

Gear also includes pram dinghy, complete set of tools, life preservers, complete set of charts for Spanish coast from Sète to Gibraltar, completely accurate compass, binnacle, spinnaker, toilet, spare lines, etc.

Name: *Blotto* May be seen at Barcelona Yacht Club Price negotiable

I tacked this up on a bulletin board filled with notices about apartments and free kittens, used cars and share-a-car trips. I didn't say the toilet was a bucket that went into a small, square space in the front of the boat that had a separate hatch. When you went, you sat on the bucket, the top of your body plainly visible to anyone going by, who surely understood what you were doing sitting in such a strange place and position.

But it *was* a toilet. That part wasn't a lie. It just wasn't what you'd exactly think of if someone said, It has a toilet.

I came back feeling elated, but nothing happened. No one at the American Consulate wanted this wonder of a boat I had given them the opportunity of owning. I left the **FOR SALE** and **SE VENDE** signs up and prayed to the harbor god to send me someone who thought getting a boat for somewhere in the neighborhood of two thousand dollars was a bargain.

On Tuesdays and Thursday *Digame* and *El Ruedo*, the bullfighting chronicles, came out. I would walk up to town, buy them, go someplace my husband wouldn't think to find me, and sit over a tiny cup of café espresso while reading about places Ron Bongartz and Cee might be. Everywhere else—Seville, Madrid, Jerez, Valencia—exciting things were happening, and even in Barcelona there were bullfights on Saturday, but my husband wouldn't think of going to a bullfight, so it was as if nothing, nothing at all rippled our lives. We were becalmed.

Then we began to quarrel, small quarrels at first, almost as if to amuse ourselves. Then came serious, bitter altercations that we seemed unable to stop. We had taken to eating big meals in the middle of the day at the little harbor cafe that served really cheap food and where we drank so much wine that we were drugged into sullen apathy. After lunch, we often began flinging accusations at one another and the arguments would escalate until we walked toward the boat, our lips locked in silence, furious. There we sat on the gently bobbing boat, raging but silent, watching and waiting for the hour when the seamen on the Spanish fleet would parade out to lower the Spanish flag. They had some men with musical instruments who played what I took to be the national anthem. End of the day. My husband and I would light the kerosene lamps and lay down on our separate bunks and stare at the slatted ceiling. Even the quarrels seemed pointless.

Then one day, a nice Spanish man with three handsome sons came along and looked at the boat. I could see the boys were excited. I told the man the price, which was cheap by Spanish standards, and I told him in my bad Spanish that we couldn't actually sell him the boat, but we could rent it to him for a lifetime. The man at the American embassy would give him a paper, all stamped, that said that was legal. My husband took them out using the motor. I was watching from shore when the boat suddenly stopped and hung motionless on the water, and I thought, Well, that's that. Then I saw the sails go up, and my husband and the prospective buyer and his sons were swept so far out that that I could no longer even see the world's tallest mast.

He's going to buy the boat, I thought. Rent it for a lifetime, I corrected myself.

For years after, I used to wake up in a cold sweat because I had dreamed Señor Valenti had tracked me down and didn't want to rent the *Blotto* anymore. Come and get it, he would say. Come and get it right away. I never want to see that damn boat again as long as I live, and I would be back with the *Blotto* the way inside my head I am trudging along with empty cans that need water and gasoline that I can only get five or six klicks away, a woman whose whole future was bound by a boat getting ready to go down into Davy Jones's locker. Nobody I had ever heard of wrote under water. On the other hand, there might be mounds of shrimp to munch, and I would of course be accompanied by my purse, the lifeline of my existence, and I mustn't forget that handsome man who would always be there inside of my mind at the head of the line because he had been, any way you looked at it, my first love and it is a commonplace aphorism that you never forget (*get over* might be a better way to put it) your first love.

My handsome husband and I on board the ship to Europe

Our little Morris Minor convertible

The boat that brought joy to my husband's heart

My first glimpse of the *Blotto*

The *Blotto*'s mast

Roy Bongartz on the *Blotto*

The *Blotto* leaving England for France

The world's tallest mast in Boulogne

The *Blotto*'s mast being taken down
(unstepped I believe is the nautical word)

Mooring next to Notre Dame, the *Blotto* on the left

A typical lock along the canals and waterways of France

Entering a lock, the ever-ready dingy on board if needed to help

My husband working on the propeller

Resting up after going through a lock

I'm pulling the *Blotto* along

A lock rest for laundry

How I looked before we got on the *Blotto*

How I looked near the end of the *Blotto* voyage

Roy Bongartz, myself, and Roy's future wife Cee raising the flag of Lyon on the *Blotto* in Barcelona on the morning they left. (She should have been arrested by the Guardia Civil for wearing that bathing suit.)

# EARTH

Botanists say that of the ten thousand flowers known in Europe more than half are to be found only in Spain; navigators, that the scent of Spain is perceptible from the seas before her coasts are in sight. Such is the primitive fertility of the Peninsula, a fertility which is but a sign, a symbol of that quality which makes it one in its variety. Its quiet strength, its permanent vitality, is the source of that impression which the traveler finds everywhere as the Spanish essence under the Catalonian, Aragonese, Castilian and Andalusian forms. Rough, primitive, dry, but rich in spontaneous scent, in wild vegetation, in uncultivated grace, the Peninsula is, in itself, apart from the people who inhabit it, a great power and a great presence.

Salvador de Madariaga, *Spain*
[London:Jonathan Cape, 1961], 16.

My husband had decided he wanted to go back to the States. I did not say, I should go with you, or, Why don't you stay here after we've got the money from the boat and work on your play? It seemed perfectly clear to me that we needed a rest from each other. I thought that if my husband and I divided up the pesetas from selling the *Blotto,* I would have enough for a year in Spain to write my novel if I were frugal.

Unfortunately, the pesetas Señor Valenti had paid for the *Blotto* were not to be divided in half as I had assumed. My husband said the money was his.

How did you come to that conclusion? I put in half the money.

Oh, no, you never made as much as I did. The most you could have put in was a third, and you used all that up.

I used all that up how? You ate food, you rode on the boat, you drank more wine than I did.

I did not drink more wine than you did. *You're* the big wine drinker. *You're* the big eater. *You're* the one who wanted to buy the boat in the first place.

These endless rounds of wrangling went on until finally my husband agreed to give me half the pesetas we had sold the boat for, but not free and clear. I would have to sign a paper saying that I owed him a thousand dollars plus five percent interest until paid. I would have signed anything. All I wanted was for him to be *gone*. I was in a fever to say to him, Turtles breathe through their butts just like you, but discretion is the you know, and valor had nothing to do with it. I needed the pesetas in my hand before I made any definitive statement like that.

He composed a legal-looking document that said he was allowing me to keep one thousand dollars' worth of pesetas but that I owed him that money in dollars and with five percent interest per year. He went somewhere and had a document typed up, and then took me up to the marina bar, where we were going to get a couple of Spanish sailors to serve as witnesses. They wouldn't sign. They thought we were trying to put something over on them. So we took it to Sam at the American embassy, the man who had stamped my rent-a-boat-for-a-lifetime paper and had even, grinning, affixed a fancy wax seal with a ribbon so that it looked absolutely authentic.

Sam read the document. He sized up my husband. He picked up the phone and asked his secretary to come in and bring someone with her, and the two of them witnessed the document. My husband said he was pretty satisfied, but he had done some figuring again the night before after the paper had already been typed. I owed him seventy-five dollars more than the agreed upon amount in the document, and he wanted it *now*.

Sam was the kind who would stand in front of you looking perfectly affable, waiting to serve you; that was, after all, why he had been sent to this place. But I saw a spark fly into his eyes when my husband started talking about how was I going to get the seventy-five I owed him *now* because it was his seventy-five dollars, and he wasn't going to be cheated out of it; he had been cheated out of his trip through the Mediterranean, and he didn't see why he should be cheated out of anything else. He went on with this hissy fit in the middle of an elaborate office of the American consulate standing in front of Sam on a thick, blue rug like you see in pictures of the Oval Office and a large seal of the United States in back of Sam's head and framed honors and distinctions that the office had earned over the years on the walls and carried on, unstoppable.

That seventy-five dollars had come to represent his lost dream. I was the one who had taken that dream away from him, and, by god, seventy-five dollars was little enough to pay for a lost dream. He had forgotten, I could see, that I wasn't getting any pesetas for free, that I had had to sign a promissory note to pay him a thousand dollars for the pesetas he was letting me have, plus five percent interest per year, and he was giving me no credit for any of the American dollars in our joint account. That money belonged to him. I had no claim on it at all. The account was in his name.

He stood in the middle of Sam's office clutching the paper with the witnesses' signatures in his hand as if it were as important to him as my purse was to me and screamed that I was trying to take him for a ride.

I waited, mortified, for this outburst to come to an end, but apparently there was no end.

She owes me seventy-five dollars, and she's not going to get out of paying it because of some cockamamie Spanish law that says I can't trade my pesetas back into dollars. Why shouldn't I be able to trade pesetas back for good American dollars that were worth more than their miserable money?

It's the rule, Sam said.

What kind of cockamamie rule is that?

You'd have to ask General Franco. I don't have the privilege of his confidence.

She's not getting any money she's not entitled to. I want my seventy-five dollars.

Would you like me to have a new paper drawn up that says she owes you a thousand seventy-five dollars? Would that make it all right?

No, I want the seventy-five right now.

Sam looked at me. He looked at my husband. I thought, He's going to call for the security guards and have us both thrown out.

My husband was dancing around in his frustration. Then he stopped—an idea had come into his head. He turned to Sam and asked him if he knew someplace unofficial where he could trade pesetas for dollars. In other words, he was in an office of the Consulate of the United States asking for information from one of its representatives about how to trade on the black market. I couldn't believe my ears. But Sam said very pleasantly that he would buy the seventy-five dollars of pesetas that were in dispute from me, nothing wrong with friends exchanging money. I thought, I wish all men were like him.

Sam took hold of the telephone and asked someone at the other end what the official rate of exchange between pesetas and dollars was and then noted that on a piece of paper and multiplied it by seventy-five. He showed me the figures. That's fine with me, I said, but my problem was that I didn't have *any* pesetas. My husband was still hanging on to all the *Blotto* money, and I knew that if I didn't get my money now, I might never actually lay my hands on it. So long as he had the pesetas, he had me in the palm of his hand. I could see he was enjoying that sense of control more and more.

He won't give me the pesetas I just signed the paper for, I said, so I can't give you the seventy-five dollars for the pesetas. Ask him to give me the pesetas he owes me, and I'll get him his seventy-five dollars.

Sam didn't say then—he told me later—that my husband didn't really *have* to give me any money at all if he didn't want to. This is Spain, Sam said later. In Spain a woman has no rights.

But I'm not Spanish.

No, but the paper you signed that day has no validity in a Spanish court. Even if it were children you had that you were fighting to keep, you would have no rights. They would belong to the father.

I couldn't believe what he was telling me. You mean he could have refused to give me anything?

Yes, under Spanish law. But he didn't know that, and I didn't feel any obligation to tell him. I thought it would be better if he could be persuaded to honor the paper he signed in my office and give you the pesetas. I wasn't in any official position to make him, but then again, renting that boat wasn't "official" either.

If worse came to worst, I thought I could say that Señor Valenti should return the boat and get his money back because the Spanish government wouldn't have approved of the transaction he'd made with my husband, but then of course I would put this accommodating man in trouble. It never occurred to me to ask myself what I was doing deciding to stay in a country where women had no rights at all.

Back in Sam's office, my husband took out a huge roll of pesetas and counted out carefully a stack and counted them again. Reluctantly, he passed them across to me. Sam showed him the paper with the figures of pesetas changed into dollars. I counted out what would equal seventy-five dollars and handed them over to Sam. Sam gave me seventy-five American dollars. I handed those dollars to my husband. That should sink your ship, I thought.

Good, my husband said. He stomped to the door and flung it open. Sam and I watched him march out, head held high, shoulders set back. "I'm so sorry," I began. "I can't tell you how embarrassed I am. I'm just mortified—"

"He doesn't really care about the seventy-five dollars," Sam said.

"Oh, yes, he does."

"No, he's trying to keep you from leaving him. How do you suppose he's going to get the rest of all those pesetas changed into dollars?"

"I don't think you want to know," I said. I knew my husband would find some sleazy character who, at a really bad rate of exchange, would give him dollars for his pesetas. I thought perhaps that when this exchange took place—I pictured a back alley with hulking figures in the background—my husband might be whopped on the head and all his money taken. It was extraordinary how calm I was about the prospect of that happening.



In those days, Spain was like an Iberian Ultimo Thule. No one had heard of Torremolinos or the Costa del Sol. There were no fancy hotels, no tourists, few Americans except a cordon of foreign bullfight enthusiasts and a bunch of American engineers who were building bases in the south of Spain. I could live in a small pension where bed and board were ridiculously cheap. I wouldn't have any distractions. I would do nothing but write. At the end, I could leave because I could buy a ticket on a ship with pesetas.

Getting money out of my husband had been hard, but not half as hard as dealing with my mother when I told her over the crackling transatlantic phone that I was going to stay in Spain alone.

*Are you telling me that you're going to stay in that foreign fascist country and let your husband go home? How could you do such a thing? What will people say? What will the Pope think?*

The Pope? I had lost my faith at a young age when the priests and nuns beat you and you went to confession and reviewed your sins, were given penance, which you fulfilled, and then your soul was stamped Renewed, but it was never really clear for long because you were always going to commit some sin and blacken it again. Your life was a continual round of sin and repentance, with a high pitch of guilt in between.

At the Catholic school where I was sent, the nuns beat you on the back of your hands with the metal part of the ruler when you did something amiss. The students' names were listed alphabetically on the blackboard, and every time one of them blotted a writing paper, didn't remember to recite Bless me, Sister, for my mistakes, Bless me, Father, for I have sinned, a check was chalked beside the miscreant's name and the culprit had to recite, Dear god, help me to be disciplined.

When you didn't know an answer, talked out of turn, practiced any unacceptable behavior, you got a check against your name. At the end of the day, the class lined up, and the sister went down the line administering as many whacks with the ruler against the back of your outstretched hands as you had checks after your name. I always had a lot.

The metal edge of the ruler broke the skin on my knuckles one time and the knuckle got infected, but I hid it. I did not want my Protestant father to see it and fly into one of his rages. Eventually, there was a red line up to my elbow. My father discovered it by accident. He said, It's too hot for you to be wearing long sleeves. Why are you wearing long sleeves? Impatient, he came over and pushed up one of my sleeves. Oh, my god, he gasped. I thought he was going to strap me, but he took me to the doctor instead. I had blood poisoning. He made me tell him why I hadn't said something before, and I said it was because I was afraid of getting the sister in trouble and being punished some more.

That's it, Blanche, he said to my mother. She's not going back to that school. I don't care if I did promise to let you bring the children up Catholic. Those sisters are sadistic sons of bitches.

I loved going to public school where you only occasionally got a passing whack on the head, though I did miss my friend Roberta, still subject to the ruler at St. Mary's. Roberta once, after the confessions were all over and the priests had trotted off to the rectory, had slipped into a confessional to see if the priests could see through the lattice that separated them from the sinners. "They can see!" she shouted at me. "They told us they couldn't, but they can see plain as the light of day. They're all liars, the whole bunch of them."

I might have given up on The Church, but The Church had not given up on me. In their eyes, I hadn't departed; I had only lapsed. I could come back any time with the proper repentance. The Church certainly took some strange folks in, whether they wanted to be there or not, including—who can believe this?—my father, who had not only not been a Catholic, but had also had three wives and god knows how many other partners in sexual congress. His sister, a convert because her husband was Catholic, wanted him buried from the Church for reasons that passeth understanding. My brother and I wanted cremation and, if she insisted, on a service and a closed coffin, but she was intent on "a viewing" and high mass. There my father, my violent, Protestant father, lay in a satin-tufted coffin like a wax figure lent from Madame Tussauds's with a priest wafting incense over the embalmed body, chanting in Latin (it was Latin in those days) and telling us that my father was on his way to god and a peace beyond knowing. Everlasting. He said that, too, though what evidence he had for that, I have no idea.

After my husband left, I stayed in Barcelona, but Barcelona was neither quixotic nor, strictly speaking, Spanish, Sam the American Counsel Man told me somewhat dogmatically the first time he took me out to dinner. Barcelonans consider themselves Catalans, a separate society, with their own language and customs. NOT Basque, oh, no, never Basque. The Basques were a Pyrenees people—primarily fishermen, shepherds, and farmers—who inhabited the wild, mountainous area between France and Spain and were reputed to be the oldest surviving racial group in Europe. They spoke a language unrelated to any other. They had a fierce sense of independence, and they constantly made trouble for Franco. In 1959, they had formed the separatist group ETA—*Euzkadi Ta Azkatasuna*, roughly translated as Basque Fatherland and Freedom—with the explicit idea of using terrorist techniques to gain Basque independence.

The Basques waged constant guerilla warfare, but the Catalonians went on the assumption that eventually Franco would die, and then perhaps things might look up, or perhaps not. They were in the north of Spain, mainly out of sight of Madrid and Franco, and they assumed, incorrectly, that out of sight also meant out of Franco's mind. Franco didn't forget them; he prohibited both the language of the Basques and the Catalonians from being used either in print or in the schools. He made a proclamation that neither could speak their own language, not even in their own homes. That must have been impossible to monitor. Still, it had an insult value he probably relished.

When Franco did occasionally make a visit to Barcelona, the people of Barcelona found unpunishable ways to express their feelings of contempt. I remember a bullfight General Franco attended on one of his infrequent sorties to Barcelona. When the generalissimo entered his private box and raised his small, fat fists over his head, there was a mild spattering of applause; but when the bullfighters came out, the audience went wild, clapping and cheering, as if saying, We hate you, Franco, and this is the way we are going to tell you so. You can't arrest or shoot us for how we clap and cheer.

The uproar for the fighters lasted at least ten minutes while the judge frantically kept waving his white handkerchief, the signal for the fight to begin. Nobody paid any attention. People were whooping and jumping up and down creating absolute pandemonium. The trumpets for the fight to begin sounded and the crowd calmed down, but not before the Catalans had made their feelings for Franco clear.

I knew almost nothing of the Basques, the Catalonians, or the

Spanish in general. How could I? I had been living on the *Blotto*. Maybe by staying in Spain, I was trying to live out some kind of fantasy even I didn't understand. Maybe I was trying to be an updated American version of Lady Brett, only with a happy ending.

*Who?* asks the reader.

You know. Hemingway. *The Sun Also Rises*. The woman he describes as "built with curves like the hull of a racing yacht," the one who bewitches all the men who encounter her. She can't have the man she loves because he's suffered a wound in the war that makes normal sex impossible, and so the novel is about a great love affair that can never be consummated.

Oh, *that* Lady Brett. I always thought they could have come up with something to solve their problem if they had put their minds to it.

I think it's supposed to be a metaphor for the impotence of the generation after the war, I said.

My first dinner with Sam. Time takes away most of our memories, but that is one I refuse to let it have. After my husband had apparently gone back to the States (I did not check up, I did not care, I was free of him and that was all that I cared about), I found a small, cheap pension where I dragged my things and started trying to write without much success. I understood my husband pursuing his dream, but in return he had damaged mine. Maybe put it permanently out of commission. Did that make us even? No, in marriage there are no evens.

I liked being alone. I didn't have to try To Make Things Go, I didn't have to try to play the role of The Wife as Good Sport. I would stride along the streets of Barcelona ignoring the whistling from the men and the raunchy remarks and the slight brushings up against me, a hand put on my body. Let them insult me any way they wanted. They couldn't really *touch* me because I was living in a world of my own construction.

Lovers were everywhere, dreamily leaning up against one another—they must have been meeting in secret, and they couldn't embrace; the Guardia Civil would arrest them, but they could not keep from touching—lovers and carriages, which people often used instead of taxis even though they were more expensive. The rich had their own carriages, ornately elaborate, pulled by fine horses, often matched pairs. Sam explained to me that if you were in Seville for *feria,* you saw the finest horses and carriages in Spain.

Since no cars could be imported, every motor car on the street was a mishap waiting to happen. If you rode in one, the springs jabbed you, the seats slipped, the brakes didn't work, the driver's cigarette smoke choked out every ounce of air.

One night, one of the pension maids, all of whom seemed to be constantly on their knees scrubbing tile floors, rapped on the door. There was a señor downstairs who wanted to see me. I couldn't imagine how anyone knew where I was. I thought of myself as in hiding.

Perfectly simple, Sam said. All travelers have to turn in their passports when they register at a hotel or pension, and the information was transferred onto an official fiche and sent on to the proper authorities. I just shuffled through the fiches every day until I found yours. I thought you might like to go out to dinner.

I don't have any decent clothes. They're all back in England in a trunk I stored with Roy Bongartz, and he's camping in France.

In other words, I might have said, this is the way my life is, scattered all over, things in the States, things in England, the leftover junk from the *Blotto* in this room in Spain. To Sam I said, You don't bring nice things on a small boat when you think you are going to be gone months sailing the Adriatic. I never thought in a million years I'd end up staying in Barcelona.

You don't have a skirt packed somewhere?

Well, yes, an old black one, but it's not exactly fancy, and it's all wrinkled. And I don't have one shirt that isn't dyed brown from the canal waters.

Give me the skirt, Sam said. You shower and do whatever it is women do when they're going out.

He was back in maybe fifteen minutes with a pressed, starched skirt that looked almost brand new and something wrapped in a brown-paper package. Now, he said, if you wear this—and he handed over the skirt and the package—you'll look perfectly fine.

Inside the package was a plain, white Spanish version of a tee shirt and an elaborately embroidered shawl with shimmering rainbow colors against a black background, a beautiful piece of hand-done work that must have cost a fortune.

Where did you borrow this? I asked, holding up the shawl. It's gorgeous.

I didn't borrow it. I bought it.

Sam wasn't the kind of man who bought a woman a tee shirt and shawl so that he could lure her into a cradle of sheets. I tried to think of what his motive was. All I could come up with was kindness. It's beautiful, I said, shaking the shawl out so that we could both see the intricate rainbow embroidery. The material was light and soft as fleece. I threw it around my shoulders and felt as if I had been suddenly transported into becoming another kind of person. You can't imagine how it feels to be in something like this after all the months on those canals. Then I laughed. It cost seventy-five dollars, didn't it?

Not quite.

Near enough? And there's no way he's ever going to know.

But you do. Here, he said, handing me a jar of peanut butter.

How did you know I wanted peanut butter? All our conversations had been about getting rid of the *Blotto*—and of course the transfer of the pesetas into the seventy-five dollars.

You told your husband at one point if you couldn't have had the shrimp you would have settled for peanut butter—

I said *that*?

You don't remember shouting at him that he wouldn't let you buy shrimp and now he was asking an official of the United States government to lead him to the black market?

I had no recollection of anything like that at all. *Did I cry?* If I'd let my husband reduce me to tears, he would have won.

No, you were just mad, about as angry as anybody I've ever seen, and believe me—in my line of work, I see lots of people who are incensed. But I would say you win first prize.


I hadn't worn makeup since I'd left England. I had some in my lifeline purse (what woman goes anywhere without her makeup?), and now I wanted to go out in my magic shawl looking like someone of consequence, hanging on the arm of a man who had *official* status, someone not to be messed with, someone who had made good things happen in her life.

I wanted to feel beautiful and desirable, but the face reflected in the mirror did not say **glamorous like you wouldn't believe.** That was no Lady Brett looking back at me. The face I saw looked incredibly tired and miserably sad. However, with a foundation base and powder, plus a touch of rouge, mascara, and lipstick, I might create another woman. Maybe not. One look at me would say American, put together like an athlete (as opposed to the exotic, fragile, hothouse plant that was the ideal of so many Spanish women), with a mind of her own (absolutely unlike Spanish women). **In trouble with the Pope—how's that for refractory?**

Sam stood up when I came out to the entry where he was waiting. I had my shawl draped around my shoulders and even had on a pair of decent shoes I had found at the bottom of my knapsack. His eyes went wide. He didn't say a word. He just looked.

Well, was it worth the seventy-five dollars? I asked.

So worth it we'll take a horse and carriage instead of one of those old rickety cabs, but we'll have to walk to the square to get a carriage.

Sam chose the fanciest carriage. Real flowers had been braided into the horse's mane and red fringe tassels strung around the body of the carriage. We clopped over cobblestone streets, and there was the sweet smell of jasmine in the air. I felt like one of the nobility, sitting beside a man who thought I was worth a seventy-five dollar shawl and wanted me to ride in a fancy carriage and show me off to the world. He was an American, so why should the Spanish care if I was scandalously unchaperoned? We had no validity in their eyes.

At the entrance to the restaurant, a woman came up to Sam with a tray of flowers. He gave her some money and took a large, fragrant flower that might have been some kind of camellia or a gardenia. If I hadn't chopped all my hair off somewhere in the midst of all those canals, I could have put it behind my ear and fastened my hair around it. I had the shawl, but I didn't have the hair. I held it in my hand and later left it—forgotten—behind on the restaurant table, but I still remember the scent.

We walked down an enormous staircase into a fancy underground restaurant where small goats were roasting on open spits, thirty, forty of them slowly turning, and a man dressed like a gypsy was basting them from a big, copper bucket. When I picture that restaurant, I can still bring back the sound of the crackling flesh and see the crowds of fashionable people chatting and laughing, *having a good time.* It had been so long since I had seen Beautiful People and heard happy laughter that I stopped dead, absolutely enthralled.

A man in a tux (a Spanish version of the bouncer at the casino in Fécamp) led us to a table. Not just any old table. He said something in Spanish to Sam, and Sam said something back and tucked unobtrusively some money into his hand. When we sat down I said, What was that about?

He said we would have a good view of the dancers here.

They have dancers?

As close to real flamenco as you can get in a place like this—I guess real flamenco is only be found in the caves of Granada and in some of the back alleys of Seville and maybe a couple of places in Madrid if you know how to find them. It's like belonging to a secret society knowing where to go to find the real thing. Tourist flamenco is like something out of a Carmen Miranda movie. But it's not bad here. It's not completely authentic, but it's not completely tourist either. That's Sam's take on the matter.

We were handed menus, but Sam shook his head. He ordered what later turned out to be half of one of those goats (I couldn't think of it as a kid, though that would be the accurate way to describe those small bodies turning on the spits) and sangria and some strange dishes I liked but had never had before. Sometime around eleven—the Spanish dined late, beginning around ten, which I never got used to—while we sat having a brandy, the flamenco music and dancers started. Since I had been on water all that time, I had been parched for a place like this, where I didn't have to worry about going over dams or being run down by large ships or staying cramped up in a smelly cabin as the rain poured down and the kerosene lamps smoked and the man I was shut in with looked at me as if he had never understood what disgust and disappointment meant until he had been shut up in a small cabin on a boat on a canal with someone like me.

I knew few people in Barcelona, and it seemed that if Sam had friends, he never mentioned them. He talked about the people he worked with, but he never mentioned people he went out with the way you do with friends. He planned excursions—or I pestered him to take me to someplace I had heard of and had no business being, though I wouldn't have known it at the time, like the Chinese circus. I kept seeing posters all over Barcelona that advertised a Chinese circus, and I longed to see that Chinese circus the way I had wanted those shrimp. Sam got us tickets, fourth row center.

I thought it was very odd that only men seemed to be in the audience, but I was quickly learning that women were either decorations or chattels in Franco's Spain, so I just assumed that the men were out on the town and had left their wives and mistresses at home. I had on the shawl, so I felt I looked respectable enough, but something was the matter with the way the men looked at me. I couldn't place what it was.

When the curtain opened, I was expecting animals, acrobats, aerialists, clowns. What came out were a parade of women who had nothing on except hats and guns in holsters concealing private places or feathers and fringe, sequins and faded paper flowers.

It's not a circus, I said. Apparently not, Sam said. The two of us sat there—we didn't want to make a scene by getting up and walking down the length of the theater, the American embassy man and the unchaperoned American girl, neither one of whom should have been at a burlesque show.

Didn't you know? I said. Didn't anyone Spanish at the office say anything when you said you were coming here?

I never mentioned it. I mean, what was there to say? That we were coming to a circus and was that all right? I would never have thought about coming if you hadn't said you wanted to go.

Oh, this is awful, just awful. I should never have asked you to bring me here. But I thought it was a real circus, Sam.

Things are often not what they seem—but I don't think he said that, I think that's what I thought. Or am I thinking it now, when I know more about the world. I am remembering teaching my students that whenever they got a test question on literature, if they were stumped for an answer, they could always fall back on illusion versus reality. *Everything*, I would say, is about the difference between illusion and reality.

But at that moment in Barcelona, I was watching someone who was like a master of ceremonies (think Joel Grey in *Cabaret*) standing at one side of the stage leering at the women as they put on their performances. He made comments in rapid Spanish that made the male audience go wild with laughter. Sam and I sat like stones. We couldn't follow the Spanish and we didn't want to look at the naked women, but we were trapped in our seats until intermission. I figured an hour, maybe only forty-five minutes if we were lucky, until we could escape, but one after another, the women slid out on the stage and began to gyrate toward the audience, discarding anything there was to dispense with, which wasn't much.

They weren't young, and they were worse than not pretty—they looked soiled, an expression I remembered my Hoosier mother using. She's a soiled woman, my mother would say, meaning the woman had done something that set her outside the boundaries of polite society.

Dirty was fixable, dentists could have done something about their teeth, but no one on earth, not even the Pope, could have fixed the looks on their faces, which struck like weapons straight at my heart. All around me the audience was in enthusiastic pandemonium.

Sam had never once touched me except to help me in and out of chairs at restaurants or to put a protective hand around my arm as we were walking back to the pension where dark and suspicious (at least to my mind) characters lurked in doorways. Now he took one of my hands in both of his and held it very gently as if he were comforting a disquieted child.

He's a grownup, I thought. He's maybe the first real adult I've ever known.

Now, I'm not sure. Now I think it was something else. But I mistook everything in those days.

It was a long time before I discovered Sam had been an air ace in Korea, had been decorated time and again, had even been to the White House to meet the president, who undoubtedly said he was proud of the way Sam had served his country. Sam's American minute of fame. Probably TV didn't even cover the garden ceremony, there were so many of them in those days. There had no doubt been a picture taken of Sam and the president together. I tried to think back to all the pictures on the wall in Sam's office; surely, I would have remembered one with the President of the United States. But I didn't.

Sam a Korean war ace? He looked like one of those nice, wholesome Mormons who come to the door with their Bibles and wait patiently while you tell them, No, you do not want them to come in; no, you do not believe in god; if anything, you believe in lots of gods, a god for every single thing in the universe, and those gods were perverse and demanding and had to be placated at all cost. The Mormons nodded politely and said, If you would just give us a minute—

To do what?

Explain the golden tablets that only Joseph Smith saw? Who would swallow such a story? Don't take that personally. I don't buy any of the myths about religions. I'm an animist—a neo-animist, I would say for shock value, and watch their blank faces remain blank. They didn't know what a neo-animist was, probably had never heard the term before.

I wanted to shock Sam. I wanted to strike at the heart of his apathy, his acceptance of life as a bureaucratic routine of monotony. I wanted to explain what Colin Wilson meant by An Outsider.

Sam was a wall builder. That was how he had learned to survive. He had built a large vault where he had locked up all those things that had brought him to the White House Rose Garden and some man who gave him a metal for what had happened to him. He had become painstakingly exact in order to survive in a world of so much disorder and senselessness.

If he took his time and worked through an observation, that moment to make it have meaning had slipped past, especially with someone like me, who only talked in half sentences because my mouth couldn't keep up with my mind. I would start off and everything would be fine for maybe eight or ten words, and then the idea I had begun to dissect would split and expand and I would jump to the next level and go on for a time with that new ramification until another slant struck me and I would ... on and on, at least in English. In a foreign language, I had to slow down. It was easier to follow where I was going. But with people who spoke English, there was no need to finish up the beginning of a sentence because the end was already apparent and it was perfectly all right to go from A to K to M, leaving out all the steps in between.

Sam, in contrast, put his faith in the literal. If you told him it was a circus, it was supposed to be a circus. Then, faced with the discrepancy, I could see his mind trying to work out why it was called a circus if it wasn't a circus. I had already made the leap to these women being a kind of circus. They were all dressed up in costumes, they performed tricks (one woman spun the tassels on her nipples in opposite directions at the same time, and another smoked a cigarette out of her you know what), they moved about in those trashy kind of wagons that small-town circuses use. It was a circus and it wasn't, I was saying to Sam, as we ran for the exit, the Spanish men in the audience politely parting to make a small aisle for our escape.

Outside I said I needed a cigarette. Then I thought of the woman in there smoking her cigarette and said, On second, thought I think I'll skip it.

Sam was just standing there, waiting patiently for me to move from A to B to C to D. Perhaps the ability to make leaps in thought and language had been left behind in that foreign country where, for a time, he had been a genuine American hero. I think that's what he meant when one time I said to him, What's under that calm exterior? and he had said, Maybe nothing. Maybe what you see is all there is. I thought, He's given everything there was to give. Now he's left with the shell of that body that he's got to drag around until it finally lays down and dies. What he had to show for that lost life is a medal in a box stored in some drawer. The government had arranged a job for him that was safe, but one where he'd never get invited back to the White House again. He was like everyone else who grew up and recognized the world for what it is, numbed down to no expectations. What was needed to be really alive wasn't available anymore. He had used all that up in Korea.

I was perhaps a reminder of what he had once been, someone intent on experiencing life passionately, not someone who just stood by passively and reacted to what was happening. I wanted to *make* things happen. I wanted to have adventures. And—sadly, I am sorry to report—I wanted to make a mark. I didn't want to die without people knowing I'd passed through.

I looked at Sam as he stood beside me outside the Chinese circus, a

Knight of Woeful Countenance. Look at her, he was probably thinking, she's a born gambler in emotions. Stick with her and you may get back some of what you've lost.

I have often been accused of conjuring up complexities where none exist. Perhaps it was possible that Sam was just lonesome. His Spanish was worse than mine, though he took lessons on his noon hour, eating a sandwich while his Spanish teacher tried to instruct him in the rudiments of ordinary conversation. He also took classical guitar lessons twice a week in the late afternoon from a maestro who knew no English. Thus, Sam's Spanish conversation tended to rely on music and the mundane, while mine centered almost exclusively on the bullfights. What Spanish I was learning came from reading weekly copies of *Digame* and *El Ruedo*, the bullfighting periodicals that I devoured with the help of my pocket Spanish dictionary.

I knew twenty-four different words for the shape of the horns the bull had when it came into the ring, and which kind of horns were dangerous, and which were so perfect in conformation that they could provide the bullfighter with the fifteen minutes of glory he—and the audience—craved. All my life, I had rooted for the underdog, probably because I've always felt like one myself. So why wasn't I rooting for the bull? This is a question I am still unable to answer. There just came a time when I knew too much about how the bull could hurt the man, and I could see immediately when a bull came into the ring what the man was facing. I couldn't stand to see the goring or the near-goring that was at hand. I was always sitting with my hands over my eyes with little mews of fear coming out of my mouth. Why buy a ticket for that?

Today, I would probably be called a bullfight groupie. Neither the word *groupie* nor the concept existed in those days. We aficionados considered ourselves acolytes trying to be inculcated in an ancient ritual handed down from the Cretan acrobats who did leaps and tumbles over bulls in honor of their god Minos. In the king's palace at Knossos in Crete, there is a famous mural of a figure vaulting over the back of a bull. A female figure—males were depicted in red, females in white—stands in front of the horns and another stands in back of the bull waiting to catch the male vaulter. The vaulter has just gone through the "gates of horn," identified in later Greek mythology as the entrance to the kingdom of the dead, so that the act symbolized reaching for a life beyond death.

These ancient rites were both a religion and an art, and I identified with the gates of fear and the gates of death, though exactly how I couldn't have told you then—or now. What I knew is that to earn recognition, you had to learn how to deal with danger and make an art of it. In Spain, the art of bullfighting had skidded past secret religious rites in a dark cave below the surface of the earth and risen to a popular sport where thousands of people in an open area under a blazing sun watched one man taunt death and try to tame it.

There are several theories about where the present fighting bulls in Spain came from. Some believe they are offspring of those Cretan bulls, some say they are descended from the wild bulls of Europe and Asia, others say their origins come from ancient animals that had once inhabited the Iberian Peninsula and over the centuries had been bred specifically for bravery.

There are prehistoric pictures of bison on the walls of the caves of Altamira in northern Spain that date back at least twenty thousand years and have a remarkable resemblance to modern fighting bulls. Whatever their origin, the animals sent to the ring by the time the Roman legions had conquered Spain were bred solely for their fighting abilities; consignments of them were shipped back home to Italy for contests in the Coliseum with lions, elephants, and men who would play a game, tag dodging this way and that to get away from an enraged animal. There is a story that Caesar himself participated in some of the taurine games of Rome.

The Moors are said to have had regular competitions of men on horseback using lances against the bulls as they charged, a skill that still exists today in the art of the *rejoneador*, the man who fights with a long lance from the backs of several highly trained horses that the rider switches during the course of his encounter with the bull.

The few foreigners I saw in Barcelona were almost all, with the exception of Sam, bullfight *aficionados* who traipsed from one corrida to the next. One was a British major who had been wounded in WW I in some way that was never clear to me but that yielded him a modest pension, which he chose to use traveling from one bullfight to the next in a van he had rigged up with a cot, a rudimentary kitchen, and a bookshelf full of bullfighting books. He cured and dried the ears and tails of bulls that some of his bullfighting friends had thrown to him. After a bullfighting performance, if the fighter has done an exceptional job of dealing with the bull, he may be awarded an ear, or two ears if has executed his work with the bull in an outstanding way, or—in very rare cases—he may be given the two ears and the tail of the bull to show his triumphal talent.

The Major used these as decorations over the little crate that served as his larder. Each one had a small tag with the date of the corrida, the town, the name of the bullfighter, and the name of the bull printed neatly in a little column underneath the petrified ear or tail.

The Major had a Primus stove, much like the one I had struggled with on the *Blotto*, but he turned out fabulous food using it. He was so erudite that he knew the names of Greek and Roman gods and poets I had never heard of. Once, when the bullfighting season was over for the year, I visited him in London, where he went during Spain's rainy winter months. I have no idea why I was there, probably something to do with an Anglo-American literary magazine I helped put out called *Quixote*, but unless I kept careful track in my journal, there was no explaining sometimes how I happened to turn up in particular places.

The Major lived in a tiny flat that was almost an exact replica of the inside of his van. I think maybe he shuffled his stuff back and forth from the van to the flat. He had a trim military mustache and was given to what I guess could be called bacchanalias.

His closest friend, an English ex-ballerina, was so eccentric that people paid for her meals just to hear the outlandish things she would say and—if they were lucky—to witness one of the crazy stunts she would pull, like getting up on a table and dancing with swirling skirts and no pants on. Where she slept no one seemed to know, but I had my own ideas. Jail was one of them, because I remember one incident where she wrapped herself into a transparent Isadora Duncan-style costume and cavorted on the beach before she was carried away by the Guardia Civil while she kept on singing at the top of her lungs "Mad Dogs and Englishmen Go Out in the Midday Sun."

Like all the other expatriates I hung out with, she was corrida crazy. In her case, it was the fighters that fueled her enthusiasm. She gobbled up bullfighters the way some people pop peanuts. She bragged she had slept with all the major matadors and most of the *noverillos* (the young aspiring fighters who hadn't reached the rank of matador). To make sure I believed her, she showed me a little book with names and numbers. She used a one to ten system. Ten was The Big O and zero meant he couldn't even get it up.

*Death in the Afternoon* was our bible. I believed the rites Hemingway was talking about might teach me something about living life on the edge, about what the words *courage* and *honor* meant, though having been on the *Blotto,* any sensible person would have wondered how great living on the edge was.

I read everything I could get my hands on about Spain, though there was not much of accuracy because of heavy censorship. The 1936–1939 Spanish Civil War had been over almost twenty years, but you did not talk about that war, even though a lot of people, myself included, believed if Hitler and Mussolini had been prevented from helping Franco, World War II might have been averted.

When the Civil War was over, Spain was a broken country, a million bodies in ditches where they'd died fighting or in mass graves where they had been massacred; thousands of political prisoners detained in prisons where, even in the late 1950s, thirty to a hundred thousand men were said to still be incarcerated. The enormity of the destruction from the war was indescribable, and between 1940 and 1953, seven seasons of drought had reduced most of the population to a point of poverty unimaginable to people like me. The living wage of the average unskilled laborer was about five dollars a month. The shrimp I had craved in Barcelona would have cost the average Spaniard a week's wages, and I would have devoured them in, say, ten or fifteen minutes. Stop and think about the distinction money makes in the world where some people, a relative few in relation to the whole global population, can casually drop into their mouths for a few careless moments some form of pleasure, while others will never even be able to conceive of what that action in itself is. Eating shrimp. Some people will *never* even know that there are such things as shrimp. And you want to talk to me about believing in god.

The fascist dictatorship of Franco—*el Caudillo,* as he liked to be called—saw itself as benevolently paternalistic, and it was fervently, fanatically Catholic. Any dissent was brutally suppressed, not that there was much left. Those still alive were too worn out by the war and the years of famine to have any strength to protest anything, and even if they had, they would have been carted out to the huge prison camps where the "undesirables" were warehoused.

Everything was censored, from books to bathing suits, which I had discovered when I was almost arrested for wearing my two-piece bathing suit on the *Blotto.* I had to cover my arms and my head if I went into a church. I couldn't ride a bicycle or drive a car. No decent woman interrupted a man, or went anywhere with one without a chaperone. Women didn't need an elaborate education and if poor probably had none at all. Women, rich or poor, did not need opinions. Certainly shouldn't smoke. The crowning blow was that in Spain, all the angels had to be men.

*What?*

Women were so inferior that they couldn't be elevated to that celestial rank. What about all those angels who looked like women in the churches, reproduced in statues and paintings? Franco's piety police went to a great deal of trouble getting angels on church walls and in museums into the right gender. I would often look at a religious picture and think, Something is the matter. Closer observation would show that clumsy adjustments had altered the angel into the proper sex.

Art was for instruction, like the catechism. No one ever mentioned Spain's most famous painter, Pablo Picasso, because Franco considered his paintings decadent and immoral. Picasso had left Spain when he was twenty years old and had been living in Paris ever since. He could not return to his home country, even for a quick visit to see his family, because he would immediately be arrested for the evil, corrupting art he had produced.

For his part, Picasso always maintained that he would never go back to Spain so long as Franco was alive. He lived the next six decades in France, but he never became a French citizen. "I am a Spaniard, and I will die a Spaniard," he is quoted as saying. Franco outlived him by two years. Picasso painted a picture of the destruction of Guernica, a small Basque town in northern Spain bombed into extinction on a market day by planes that Franco got from Germany and Italy. Hitler wanted to test the effectiveness of civilian bombing to see how they destroyed the morale of a population, a technique he would pursue in World War II. Picasso's *Guernica* is a canvas filled with maimed and dead people, distorted and destroyed bulls and horses, demolished buildings, the whole town reduced to rubble, those trying to flee the incendiary bombs machine-gunned down as they ran to escape in the fields. It is, I think, one of the strongest pictorial statements ever made against war. It did not return to Spain until after Picasso's death. Today, it is in the Centro de Arte Reina Sofia in Madrid. The last statue of Franco (on a horse), also in Madrid, was pulled down in March 2005 amidst jeers and catcalls from the small crowd that had gathered to see its final moments of public display.

In the days when I was in Spain, however, there were slogans, pictures, and monuments to El Caudillo all over Spain, even in Barcelona, where the Catalonian population hated Franco. I would walk around the crowded quarters of the poor and think of the internecine fighting that had gone on between the Spanish Communists, who were supposed to be on the side of the legitimately elected government, and the other Spanish Republicans fighting for their democratic rights. The Communists would rather have seen Franco triumph than share power. They spent the last terrible days of the war killing the Republican forces who wouldn't capitulate to the Red Brigade's doctrines.

The British writer George Orwell fought on the Republican side in the Spanish Civil War. He was shot in the throat by a sniper and returned to England disillusioned by the ruthless murdering of his Loyalist comrades. His bitterness spills over on every page of *Homage to Catalonia*, which vividly described scenes of the Spanish Communists mowing down his compatriots. Orwell was young—forty-seven—and suffering from tuberculosis the last days of his life, gagging on his spit and blood, coughing his lungs out, a segment of literary history my boat-husband would have relished.

Ernest Hemingway went to Spain to report on the war and borrowed Emilio Mola's phrase Fifth Column for those who burrowed from within to provide information to the enemy. All his life, Hemingway remembered his early years as a reporter for the Spanish Civil War as some of the most defining of his life, and I think he always considered Spain his second home. He wrote that there is always another country beside the one you are born in that calls to you and something in your heart answers; it's as if you had two countries that owned you, the one you were born in and the one you found that answered to your heart. You find it accidentally. You are in this foreign country, and one day you look around and you know you're there, the place your heart embraces.

Hemingway also took the Spanish phrase *el momento de la verdad* and translated it into the English phrase *moment of truth*, which caught on to describe the final move the matador makes when he goes over the horns to drive his sword into the heart of the bull at the end of the bullfight. (Need I say that women were not allowed in the bullring in Spain? A few intrepid women did try their skills in South America, though.) At the moment that the man goes over the horns, he is completely exposed and has no way to protect himself. You throw your heart over first, bullfighters say, and then your body goes and you drive the sword in.

The moment of truth meant for Hemingway the test in a person's life that called for courage and constancy in the face of danger and possible death. Hemingway saw men defined by how they reacted at that moment. (I don't know what tests he considered for women, since I don't think he much thought of them as anything but conveniences for specific moments of pleasure, succor, and—possibly—heirs.) If a man failed his moment of truth, he was worthless. If he stood fast, even if he died, his life had value. For Hemingway, I think the moment of truth served as a substitute for religion. Courage was his god. I realized then that I made it mine, too. On the *Blotto,* I had failed that test.

Most of the corridas in Barcelona were fought with beginner bullfighters, the *noverillos.* They fought young three-year-old bulls. Matadors fought bulls five years or older, mature animals who had had the time to master deadly ways to use their horns as they sparred with other bulls on the range.

The *noverillo* had to fight on the junior level until he was considered good enough to earn the title of matador. He changed rank to matador in a formal ceremony known as the *alternativa,* where a recognized matador awarded him a sword that served as a symbol for his elevation in rank. That title had to be confirmed in a fight at Madrid's Plaza Monumental to have legitimacy, and most bullfighters never made the advancement in rank.

The best bulls in Spain came from the Conde de la Corte ranch and were so expensive that sometimes a cartel would only be able to afford four and have to fill out the mandatory six with two floaters from a less renowned ranch. Three fighters fought two bulls each. Fighters longed to fight a bull bred by the Conde de la Corte because they knew a Conde de la Corte bull would, as the bullfighters said, "run on railroad tracks." That meant the fighter could rely on the bull making a straight charge when the lure of the *muleta,* the red cloth that was used after the capes had been put away, was presented to him. Such a bull would not swerve and gore the man or throw its head and hook him, or turn and butt him and then try to gore and trample him.

Conde de la Corte bulls might be the most highly prized of all fighting bulls, but the most feared were Miuras. They had killed more fighters than any other bulls; it was a Miura bull that killed Manuel Rodriquez Sanchez, always called Manolete, the most famous bullfighter of the twentieth century.

He met his death in a small ring in Linares on August 27, 1947, gored by a Miura bull named Islero. Immediately Islero came into the ring it was apparent he had a tendency to hook with his right horn. Manolete's *cuadrilla* warned him the bull was dangerous, but Manolete had been making some poor showings that year and had been booed in his last fight. He insisted on going straight over the horns at the moment of truth. Islero lifted his head and drove his right horn into Manolete's groin. Then he lifted Manolete into the air, threw him to the ground, and spiked him twice while Manolete lay helpless before members of his cuadrilla could lure the bull away. Manolete's first words as he was put on the operating table were, "Did it die? Did they give me anything?" Manolete's *peón de confianza* took the matador's hand and said, "They gave you everything, both ears and the tail." At five o'clock the next morning *(a las cinco de la mañana,* as the refrain goes in the famous

Garcia Lorca poem about Manolete's death), Manolete said, I can't feel anything in my leg. A moment later he cried, I can't see! And then he was dead.

Everyone in Barcelona was obsessed with a young *noverillo* nicknamed Chamaco (The Kid), who now has a bullfighter son also called Chamaco. But the son does not have his father's valor—or craziness, as a lot of people said.

A lot of bullfight enthusiasts had begun to compare Chamaco to Manolete. Chamaco was so brave that when he was in the ring, you jumped to your feet and shouted *olé,* four times and then, on the fifth pass, gave one long, painful Ohhhhhh! as Chamaco was gored and carried out of the ring. People said he was *carne de toro* (meat for the bull), and that you had to hurry and see him before he got himself killed.

Chamaco had the dark, dangerous gypsy look of every woman's fantasy. He was so brave and beautiful that he set my teeth on edge. When he was not fighting, he would run for miles, trotting along with heavy weights in his hands.

Bullfighters needed strong hands to manage the sword when they went in for the kill. The sword had to go into a small spot about the size of a quarter to pierce the heart and kill the bull instantly. (It often staggered about for a moment, but it was essentially dead.) If the sword hit bone, it sprang back and could easily snap a man's wrist.

Chamaco was full of all kinds of arcane bits of information about the corrida—he told me that bullfighters always tried to spit just before they entered the ring because fear made a man's mouth so dry that he couldn't even moisten his lips. Spitting showed he had overcome that fear. He told me that when matadors got rich and were afraid of the bulls, they would send one of the members of their *cuadrilla* out in the middle of the night to saw an inch or two off the horns of the two bulls that had been allotted to them on the cartel the next day (they maneuvered a bull into a chute to perform this surgery) and would then cover the ends of the horns with black shoe polish.

He told me that the night before his last fight, some of Manolote's *cuadrilla* went out and shortened the horns of the bulls that Manolete was going to fight and made the usual disguise with black shoe polish, but it hadn't done any good. If a man was meant to be gored, he would be gored no matter what stratagems he tried to evade his fate.

I wanted to say, What about all that praying you guys do? If you think it's fated when you're going to be gored, why are you praying not to be gored? I thought I knew the answer: We are asking the Virgin to help. God was merciless, but His mother had pity in her heart and sometimes could be persuaded to intervene.

You want a woman to help you when you treat women like dirt?

I didn't say that. I probably didn't even think it at the time. I've had years to go over things that didn't make sense then to try to make sense of them now. I think it's called growing old.

Chamaco was slender as a reed, filled with grace and elegance; yet his hands were large and thickly knuckled, hands that came from generations of men who had worn themselves out on small, hard, cruel plots of Spanish soil. There were thousands of men like that who owned nothing and were willing to work for bread and soup and a place to put down their heads at night. Their lives were so worthless that you could rent one for thirty cents a day to follow after you and carry your purchases. All over Barcelona, I saw beautifully dressed women followed by ragged beggars who held in their hard, calloused hands thousands of pesetas' worth of merchandise the women had been out purchasing that day.

No matter how hard those earth hands were scrubbed, they would always carry a small dark rim around the edges of the fingernails, as if the nails were embroidered in black. The cuticles were thick, and the nails themselves as hard as a horse's hoof. I thought a man who had those kind of hands was a man who had trained himself to believe life might give him some gifts but would want a large payment in return, and that Chamaco, like Achilles, had made the choice between living a long life of anonymity or a short one that would win him fame and glory. He had opted for the same choice Achilles had made.

Chamaco fought his last corrida in 1967. He beat the odds and became rich and famous. Most of all, he had *lived*. Now his son carries the same name, but he is not *the* Chamaco. Who remembers the name of Achilles's son?

They were not restful people to be around, those bullfighters, but since I was crazy myself (I see that now; then, I would have said I was adventurous), I was intoxicated by the romance of their brief, brave lives.

Chamaco's main rival was El Litri (Miguel Baez), who was said to have a matched pair of everything so that he always had a backup—two houses that were exactly alike, two identical Hispano-Suiza cars—even, people said, twin mistresses who could not be told apart. The odd thing was that both Chamaco and El Litri came from the same small town, Huelva de la Frontera, and they had both learned to fight by sneaking into the fields of nearby ranches where there were herds of fighting bulls. They would separate one out from the others and practice making passes.

Bulls in a herd are quiescent. It is only when they are separated from other bulls and stand by themselves that they become dangerous. They are also so smart that they will discern the difference between a man and the piece of cloth he flashes before them in the space of twenty minutes. That is why the entire *faena* of a bullfight is limited to about fifteen minutes. Sometimes a bull will come into the ring and go right for the man instead of the cape that is flung out in the first part of the bullfight. Everyone in the stands understands this bull has probably been practiced on by some young, penniless boy who did not have money to go to a bullfighting school in Madrid, Seville, or Valencia, and had no way to get any experience unless he clandestinely practiced his craft illegally by going out at night to some ranch and separating a bull from the herd and trying to make some passes. Often the body of a young boy will be found badly gored and barely breathing or dead in the morning.

Often at a bullfight, you can also see an *espontáneo* jump over the rail into the ring, usually just as the bull has come in; he is hoping to make a few passes before being seized by the Guardia Civil and carted off to jail. Those boys are hoping some impresario will notice them and come bail them out and get them a place on a cartel in some small village that doesn't even have a ring. On the days of their fiesta, the men of small villages pull carts in a circle to form an oval where the bullfighters will perform. The bulls used in these small-town improvised rings are the cheapest that can be bought, and they are very often not killed at the end of the *faena* but sold to another small village to be used in their annual bullfighting festival.

The animals are removed from these makeshift rings by using castrated oxen to crowd around the bull. When the bull finds he is no longer on his own, he will go with the oxen placidly. Such an animal has learned the difference between the man and the lure. Those bulls maim or kill a lot of hopeful boys who, if they are lucky, get a small paragraph in the back pages of *Digame* and *El Ruedo*.

When an animal who has already been practiced upon comes into a real ring and pounds across the sand straight for the bullfighter, you hear a gasp go up because the audience knows there will be nothing the bullfighter can do but try to get through a few basic passes and go in for the kill any way he can without getting gored. Bulls in regular rings are always killed, then hauled out of the ring by the castrated oxen, who drag them through the *toril*, the gate from which the bull and the bullfighters have entered the ring, called "the gate of fear" by the fighters.

Once in a blue moon, a bull shows such bravery that it is pardoned and led out of the ring alive by the oxen. If the bull survives the wounds it has received from the *picadores*—those men on horseback with long poles who use the poles to make wounds in the *morillo* (the hump that contains the bulls' neck muscles) in order to tire the bull's neck so that it will lower its head and a man can get over the horns for the moment of truth—the pardoned bull will be returned to the ranch it came from and be used for breeding purposes. It will command enormous fees for its sperm (often cows are artificially inseminated, which is a lot easier on everyone concerned, men and animals). A pardon is so rare that it is unusual to see one even if you go a whole lifetime to the *corridas*.

At a fight in Malaga, Caesar Giron, a small, ugly little Venezuelan fighter full of valor, fought a bull so extraordinarily valiant that the crowd began to wave their handkerchiefs to ask the judge to pardon it. Giron looked up at the judge. The crowd screamed and kept waving their handkerchiefs. Finally the judge raised his own white handkerchief, granting the pardon. Giron went in over the horns with a small rosette in his hand instead of the sword with which he would normally have made the kill and pinned the rosette to the spot where the sword would have plunged in. The bull was led out of the ring amidst great applause, and Giron took a victory lap around the ring holding his hands high, as if he had been awarded both ears and the tails for his great performance.

There was a famous story, probably apocryphal, about a girl who took a bull whose mother had died giving birth to it and bottle fed it; she even taught it to follow her around and eat from her hand. When it grew to its full size, her father took it away from her and put it in with bulls destined for a *corrida*. The girl pleaded with her father not to send her bull to the arena, but he wouldn't listen. When that bull gave such a magnificent performance that the judge decided to pardon it, the girl ran down to the *barrera*, the wooden fence around the arena that separates the area of the fight from the aisle for the matador's helpers and the ring itself. The girl called to the bull and it came over to where she was standing. One of the *cuadrilla* helped her over the fence, and she put out her hand. The bull touched its nose to it. Here, the Spaniard telling me the story was often so reverential that his eyes teared up. Then the girl led the bull quietly across the ring and out through the Gates of Fear. The bull, one hoped, lived a long, good life after its wounds had healed.

Spaniards saw this story as some kind of tribute, but I couldn't figure out to whom. Why would her father have sent the bull to the ring in the first place if his daughter loved it so much? When I asked that question, I always got the same answer. It was a *fighting* bull.

Strict accounts were kept of how a ranch's cows behaved when they were taken into the owner's private ring and tested, because the mother's bravery was as important as that of the sire. The worst mortification a breeder could imagine was to have his animals turn out to be cowardly and to know his breeding ranch would be identified in the next week's editions of *Digame* and *El Ruedo* for its animals' bad performances.

For a foreigner to be invited to a *tienta* for a testing of the cows was considered a singular honor. My friend the Major had been to many, but his cohort, the ballerina, had never had the honor, because she was a woman, he said. He did not need to add that women had no business being where anything significant took place.

You have to know really rich people, the ex-ballerina said, to get an invitation. The *tiendas* are always held on the really big *fincas* where they have their own bullrings. The only men I know who ask me out are soldiers and sailors. She gave a laugh you could hear half a mile away. At least they're real men.

The Major was absolutely enraged. Why do you think only the poor can be real men?

Experience, she said, tossing her long, wild hair back.

I wanted to say that perhaps if she would behave herself for a while, she would get an invitation, but who was I to talk? I was spending the whole year like someone who had had a collapse of reason. I did nothing but go to bullfights; I talked of nothing but bullfighting. I was only interested in conversations about bullfights, about the fighters and the animals and the good rings and the bad ones, about the bribery amongst the bullfight critics, about the has-beens and the up-and-comings. I was barely literate on any of the things that made up everyday conversation. I didn't care. Everyday living meant nothing to me. I was only interested in the *corridas*, the ones I had just been to, the ones I was going to, the mythical ones I would never see and would feel forever cheated because I had missed. I was always looking forward to the next bullfight because that one might be one of those mythical encounters. I was also always fearful my favorite fighters would come back to the ring too soon after a goring in search of that one *faena* that would make them immortal in the annals of bullfighting. I spent considerable time at the Sanitorio de Toreros outside of Madrid, where my bullfighter friends who had had the misfortune of being gored lay pale and wretched, staring at the ceiling.

I met Luis in the middle of the Barcelona bullfighting season. A bunch of us were at an outdoor restaurant eating *arroz con pollo* and drinking from great pitchers of sangria after that afternoon's bullfight. The Major, who had become my principal mentor of the *corridas*, came up looking very pleased with himself and said, Here's someone you should know. Bulls from his ranch are going to be used in the fight on Saturday.

The Major was maybe five-seven, and the man standing next to him had to be at least six-three or -four. They looked like Mutt and Jeff. The man beside the Major had a face whose image I had been storing all my life in anticipation of the day I would encounter it. When Luis pulled up a chair beside me and sat down, I felt as if fire had sucked all the air out of my lungs.

To my immense relief, Luis began to speak in English, but I don't remember much of what he said. I sat stunned, as if the *Stockholm* and the *Andrea Doria* had collided, as they had in the cold dark waters off Nantucket the year before, and I was one of the passengers who wasn't going to make it to the lifeboats.

He had a large crescent scar near his right eye, chalk-white against his sunburned skin. I was trying to brand a calf, he explained to me once. It threw its head up, and one of its horns caught me under the eye. I was so surprised I let go, and then it spiked me in the arm. I never felt the arm at all, but the cheek hurt like hell. He had turned back a sleeve on his right arm to reveal the long, thick scar that was the result of that goring.

At one point, he tilted his head to one side in a way I was to learn was characteristic and said, "You must come to my next *tienta*—that is, if you'd like to."

*Like* to? Was he dimwitted?

He had earth hands like Chamaco. When he put his hand down on the table and I inched one of mine next to it, his hand was more than twice the size of mine. You would never have known from those hands that his family had a mansion in Madrid and a fancy hunting lodge with thousands of hectares of land near Seville. His hands made the opposite statement of one of those grand seigniors of Spanish aristocracy because *gentlemen* did not soil their hands. Their role model was Alfonso XIII— living in exile in Portugal—who had been perhaps the handsomest man in Spain and, without a doubt, the most impeccably groomed. His *whole* life had been consumed by nothing but hunting.

The oldest son, Alfonso, a hemophiliac, renounced his right to the throne to marry a commoner. At the age of thirty-one, he was in an auto accident where his injuries where minor but caused so much blood loss that he died. The next son, Don Jaime, was deaf and dumb as the result of a childhood operation and could not be considered for next in line.

Franco looked around for someone to follow him after his death, and finally he decided on the young grandson of Alfonso XIII, Juan Carlos, who was sent to Madrid at an impressionable age to learn how

Franco wanted the country run after his—heaven forbid anyone even think of it!—death, which did finally occur in the late 1950s. While I was in Spain, the idea of death had probably never occurred to Franco. Certainly the idea that Juan Carlos would one day lead his country into a constitutional monarchy was the farthest thing from anyone's mind. Nobody ever dreamed this meek lad who did everything he was told had a hidden will of iron. He had never forgotten the humiliations of his family. *Pundonor*, pride, Spanish pride, burned in his blood, and he bided his time.

Since Luis was the only boy in the family, the fortunes of the dynasty lay in his hands. His parents wanted him to stay in Madrid, where the father had some post in the government. Luis never told me what it was; I'm sure he knew I would have been horrified to think *anybody* would work for Franco. He said his family was not pleased he spent almost all his time in the country overseeing the breeding of brave bulls. They wanted him to be "like they are," he said so savagely that I took this to mean that he didn't want any part of that urban existence. When he spoke of the bulls he was breeding, his voice took on a lyrical tone and his eyes shone with pleasure. I'm sure all his parents saw was the scar on his face and thought how dangerous being around bulls could be.

Sitting next to me, he fizzed with energy and determination and, when he was amused, he threw back his head and laughed loud as a laborer. He took out a stained leather case from which he poured strong shag country tobacco and then, expertly, between thumb and index finger, rolled a cigarette, put it in his mouth, and lit it. The heavy scent filled the air, a smell that at the time I couldn't know would haunt me for the rest of my life. The gods might visit other countries, but the ones with any sense always went back to Spain.

At first, Luis and I tried to make conversation, but then we fell silent and stared at our wine glasses, afraid I think to look at each other. The eyes have a language all their own, and we were afraid of what our eyes would say to one another. I thought that if people came near us, they would go away with burns all over their bodies from the fire emanating from ours.

When it was time to leave, he asked me where I was staying. I said in a pension. I couldn't even remember the name. He took my hand and laid it in his palm. My hand felt as if it had been seared. "I would like very much for you to come to see my *finca* if you are ever in Andalusia," he said.

Then the Major came, and I found myself pushed back into the crowd. The ex-ballerina began to make one of her scenes, and I fled.

The next day I went out and bought a book, *Spanish for Dummies* or its 1950s equivalent, and began to study seriously. The trouble was, I was both tone deaf and dyslexic. Left on my own, I would never have picked up the language just from hearing it spoken all around me. I had to see it in print, memorize the words, then listen and try to connect what I heard with what I had seen in the book.

I was constantly making mistakes, and verb tenses seemed impossible to master. People around me were always bursting into laughter over some error I made. When I came out with I won't have any more, thank you, I'm full, someone, choking with laughter, explained to me what I had actually used was the word for pregnant when I meant full. A regular stand-up comedian.

I saw Luis again Saturday when his bulls were on the cartel. They performed with credit but were not spectacular. He was sitting up over the *toril* totally concentrating on making notes on how each animal behaved. I was in *sombra,* the expensive seats, with Sam from the American consulate. Luis didn't notice me until he looked up at the end of one fight when his bull was being dragged from the ring. He frowned, picked up a pair of binoculars, and looked straight at me. I looked right back into the binoculars, waiting for some response.

He put the binoculars down and concentrated on the last faena of the afternoon. After the fight, Sam and I got up and pushed our way through the enormous crowd and found Luis waiting near the exit when we came out. He asked Sam—he was a very correct man—if we'd like to go out for a drink.

When we got to the bar, Luis sat down next to me. It was as if someone had thrown the switch for the electric chair and both of us were being fried to a crisp. I don't think we said more than two sentences to each other, but the intensity of the touch of his trousered leg against my thin summer skirt made me lightheaded. Suddenly, I was happy.

People react in crazy ways when they are happy. Of course, they do so even more when they are unhappy, but I was at the point where everything was starting out so well that I refused to see how wrong things could turn out in the end. I upset my wine all over both of us.

I looked at my dress and thought, It's ruined. I panicked, because this was obviously the luckiest dress I would ever own, and I needed to keep it the rest of my life.

I tried dabbing at the wine stains with my napkin, which I had soaked in my water glass, certainly a breach of etiquette if ever there was one, but I was frantic to do something. "Water won't take a wine stain out," Luis said and took up the material and looked at it. "I'm afraid it's ruined," he said as if making a prediction about our future.

That was the last I saw or heard of him while I was in Barcelona. I thought, Well, that's one of those things that could have been and isn't going to be. I threw the wine-stained dress out.

The bullfighting season was over in Barcelona and the rainy season had started, when the air is so thick with moisture it feels as if you have to carry a cane to beat it apart to get through. I'm off to London, the Major said jauntily. And the ex-ballerina? Who knew. She had taken up with some Spanish fisherman and was living on his boat. She wants to get pregnant, the Major told me. She thinks she should have a child before it's too late. The kid she's with is about twenty, and she's at least in her forties. They look like mother and son walking down the street together. Wait till you see them. Why would I want to stay in Barcelona for that?

Why would I want to stay in Barcelona at all now? If the bullfighting season was over, Luis wouldn't be coming back to Barcelona. He could be in Madrid, or he could be at his *finca* in Andalusia. That's all I knew. Andalusia is a pretty big place, but Sam was being transferred to Seville, and Seville was in Andalusia.

Still, Luis knew I was in Barcelona. A man who wants a woman will come and get her. So I waited for Luis to come and get me. I wrote millions of words about the bullfights, which I feverishly mailed off to magazines in the United States, where no one was interested or, in those days, would not have published anything by a woman on a subject like bullfighting. I was too dumb to disguise my name by using my initials. I still have a library of bullfighting books that seem to me, looking at them now, to form an extraordinary collection. I spent *a hundred dollars*, when the dollar had buying power beyond belief and would have paid for my pension room for a couple of months at least, for a set of three volumes bound in fancy red leather of Cossio's *Los Toros*, that encyclopedia on everything and everyone who had ever been involved with bullfighting from the seventeenth century on.

A hundred dollars! Sam was so distressed when he discovered what I had done that he sat down (from weakness, I suppose) and simply stared at me. That was about the time he was being transferred to Seville, and he was upset with me anyway because I wouldn't commit myself to what I was going to do next. I wanted to go to Seville, but perversely I held onto the notion that Luis ought to come find me, that I shouldn't have to go claim him.

Maybe I'll go to Madrid, I said.

You won't like Madrid, Sam said. It's cold and damp now that it's winter, and Madrid isn't the real Spain. The real Spain is in the south. Everyone knows that. *Everyone?* He sounded like my mother.

My mother, yes, yes, okay, my mother. Well, the truth is I think she was relieved I was in a foreign land, for so many reasons they seemed limitless, but mainly because since I had grown up, I was living proof of how old she was. Actually, I don't think she ever really liked me. I mean, right from the start. She wasn't made to be a mother, but if you had to be one, it was better to have boys than girls. I never heard from my father, except when he got married and I got an announcement from the bride's family. He was on wife Number Three (I think; maybe it was Number Four). My brother was off hunting big game. He had trophies all over his house, including the leg of an elephant that held an ashtray in the scooped out top. There were bear and tiger skin rugs with glass eyes on his floors and big shellacked marlins on his walls.

Where I should be going was back to New York and my husband, but the longer I was away from him, the more I knew that was never going to happen, even if I hadn't met Luis. I had no family to claim back there in the States, neither my own nor my husband's.

Sam, I said, what about your family? It was the first time I had ever connected Sam to anything but the American embassy. That had been his family for me. I knew he had been in the Air Force. All those military people who went to war formed a family they never let go of. You never talk about your family, Sam.

I have a sister. My mother and father still live back in Idaho.

I waited. With Sam, you had to pull every piece of information out of him like a surgical procedure. What does your father do?

He runs a hardware store.

Well, that fit, I thought. And your sister, is she married?

She's married, with a boy.

Silence.

Do they ever come visit you here?

They don't like foreign places, he said.

So much for that.

When are you going?

In a week, he said. I was going to tell you sooner, but you had so many things on your mind—

Make a decision, I told myself. Grownups weigh the evidence of their choices and make a judicious decision. I wanted to go to Seville, so I went to Madrid, as if the *Blotto* had taught me to seek a safe haven in turbulent waters.

I didn't know anyone in Madrid, and I didn't let myself look up the address of Luis's family. I wanted to see his house and walk around and look at it carefully, as if it would give me clues about Luis. What would I do then? Stand at the door, knock, and wait like Little Orphan Annie come to call on Daddy Warbucks? What if Luis came by and caught me gaping up at his house? How would I explain that? So I deliberately did not go to where Luis's family lived. Instead, I slogged through streets surrounded by Fascists and tattered street vendors and old women who looked like witches in their long, black dresses and thick, black head coverings. I sloshed through parks, which were silvery with rain. I saw more Fascists, more Guardia Civil. The whole place was swarming with uniforms.

Sam was right. Madrid wasn't Spain, at least not the Spain I envisioned in my imagination. I despised the Guardia Civil, I hated fascism, I hated Franco, but I found the people extraordinarily warm and generous, sustained by the kind of sardonic humor they needed to survive the oppression they lived under.

I worked conscientiously on my novel every morning, but my brain was empty by noon and I walked, woozy with words. I obsessed on Luis. It was ridiculous. I knew it was ridiculous, but I couldn't stop the tyranny of my imagination. Sometimes, it was as if Luis were walking right beside me. I could feel him take my hand and put it in his.

At night, I lay on the lumpy bed in the cheap pension and listened to the voices from the street. Their Spanish had a magical sound. Sometimes, people played guitars and sang. Sometimes, I heard the rapid tapping of someone dancing. I remembered Sam saying that real flamenco could be found in some places in Madrid, if you knew where to look. Sam was in Seville. He would know where Luis's ranch was.

Seville was where I should be.


Spanish transportation in those days was terrible, whether you took the train or a bus, and there were almost no cars on the roads except ancient trucks held together with tape and wire and chewing gum. The big Hispano-Suiza cars that went at extraordinary speeds carrying the *cuadrillas* from one bullfight to the next had been put up on blocks and covered with tarps until spring, when the *corridas* started again.

I got on a train that looked as if it belonged in a museum devoted to the history of transportation. The car I was in was crowded with people holding screaming babies, toddlers wobbling down the aisles and falling into people's laps, men spitting, women parceling out food from baskets with stained white cloths covering them. Drunks, lots of drunks. No Americans. This was second class, but all the seats were falling apart, and the aisles were filthy with debris that dated back to the beginning of time. Everything was dilapidated, the toilets were clogged, and there was no place on the train where you could get food.

I had had enough sense not to go third class, though I was beginning to worry about my money. Worry isn't a powerful enough word; I was becoming obsessed. I sat on the train adding and subtracting figures and tried to figure out how much I could afford a week for a pension in Seville, while the train, which had no cushioning or stabilizers or whatever trains need to keep each shock from breaking your back or sending you flying without warning against the people on either side of you, jolted along as if it didn't know where it was going.

There were long, unexplained delays. Men came through the train and sold that rough Spanish tobacco that permanently scarred your lungs. Women hawked small, bitter oranges and sometimes *churros*, strips of dough deep-fried and powdered with sugar.

We passed towns that had been left devastated by the war, but mostly I looked out at long, empty earth where there was nothing, not even wind. The train would rattle into some little village falling down in despair with a railroad station pockmarked by bullets. We would sit for what seemed hours looking at these ruins. The trains didn't run on schedule. The engineer left when the mood hit him. Sometimes he didn't even stop where he was supposed to. I would see frantic people running along the side of the tracks, shouting and waving their arms for the train to stop.

Once the train stopped and we all had to get off and transfer to another train. The trip seemed to go on forever. It was purgatory with a different name. Finally we got to Seville, where I stood alone with the remnants of my life in two shabby suitcases and the beginnings of my novel clutched close to me in a thick, brown folder. Courage is the prime virtue, I reminded myself. I went over to a rickety cab and told the driver I was poor and needed someplace cheap but decent to live. I was hoping that I was so bedraggled from three days on the train that he couldn't even identify my nationality.

He took me to a huge house near the Alcázar Gardens, where I trudged up to the big, locked door and knocked. I would have stayed at a three-star hotel if that was where the cabbie had dumped me. I had used up all reserves.

I missed the Major and the crazy ex-ballerina, the bullfights and the familiarity of Barcelona, but from my rented rooms on the second floor of a once magnificent mansion, I saw nothing but sheets of rain. All my clothes began to mildew, and fungus grew on my shoes. The second day there, I heard a nightingale singing—once you hear the song, you know immediately what bird is making it—and I took this as a good sign.

I lived on "the good side" of the river in three large, airy rooms that cost twenty dollars a month, which included a maid, but the bathroom was down the hall and someone always seemed to be using it. I had no radio, no television, and my only books I had already read two or three times. I hadn't seen a movie in eight months, probably longer; there were no drive-ins, no fast food franchises (that was all still to come), but I had a maid, which seemed to me ridiculous for the three rooms I had rented. The woman who owned the huge house was so down on her luck that she had rented out rooms to "nice foreigners," whom she overcharged, but she threw in the maid because she wanted to be sure her rooms stayed in mint condition. She worked her maids from sunup to ten o'clock at night, worked them hard and screamed at them when something displeased her. I could hear her voice on and off all day. When I found out what my maid, Carmella, was being paid, I gave her money on the sly, which made all the other maids complain to the señora that they had to work harder for less money than Carmella. They were also enraged because I didn't make Carmella get down on her hands and knees every day to scrub the tile floors the way they had to. Carmella got to use a *mop*, which I had gone out and bought.

I kept what I considered a tidy place—you couldn't eat off my tile floors, but what kind of hostess would ask her guests to eat off the floor when there were a table and chairs? Then I learned that the señora had cut the pay she gave Carmella because she claimed that Carmella knew what she was going to get when she was hired, and that was what she was going to get, not her salary *and* a bonus from me. The señora, whom I was rapidly coming to dislike intensely, and I had a knock-down, drag-out screaming match. I said I was going to move. It was winter and there would be no other renters, so she said if I would stop giving Carmella money, she would return Carmella's pay to her regular salary. I kept on giving Carmella extra money, which both the señora and I ignored. In the end, each of us could pretend we had won the argument. I was rapidly learning that the Spanish were as fanatical about saving face as the Japanese. You never wanted to do anything to challenge their *pundonor*, or you were in for big trouble.

The señora hated me—her piercing black Spanish eyes would squeeze into slits of distaste every time she saw me—but she was greedy for the money I paid her. I thought she was one of the models, like my mother, of what a woman shouldn't aspire to emulate.

Carmella had once been a devout Catholic and still wore a small crucifix around her neck, but—like me—she distrusted the church and disliked the parading spectacle of the soldiers of Franco marching side by side with the guardians of god. She wore the crucifix because she didn't want any trouble. She had troubles enough in her life without being accused of not being a good Catholic. Both her father and her fiancé had fought on the side of the Republic, and both had been killed in the war—her father at the beginning, her fiancé sometime near the end. She would always be associated with them and their traitorous acts against Franco. No other man would marry her because she had had a fiancé once. She was off the marriage market. It didn't matter whether she had actually committed an act of fornication with her intended or not. Assumption was the operative law here.

She lived with her aged mother, who was bedridden, in one room across the river in the gypsy quarter, the Macarena. She was further tainted by working for me, an American who represented all the immoral forces foreigners exemplified. I lived alone, I didn't go to church, I smoked, I ran around barefooted, I went out unchaperoned with men. I obviously represented the threat of a woman being independent, which meant that I did what I wanted when I wanted and spent money in a reckless way. No proper Spanish lady ever let her servants get off easily or gave them money on the side.

It took the señora some time to discover I didn't go to church, that actually I was violently opposed to most of its tenets. She told Carmella, Your American doesn't go to church. She has strange men in her house (she was talking about Sam and the men from the American base that was being constructed at Moron, whom I had come to know). Your American smokes. She wears unsuitable clothes. She walks around in her bare feet.

Carmella didn't know what to do. You had to pay attention to what people said; otherwise, your reputation was ruined, which was the worst thing that could happen to a woman in Spain. She had a hard time explaining her concerns to me tactfully. Her Spanish—Andalusian Spanish, which included a large measure of gypsy slang—was difficult for me to decipher. Learning Spanish in Andalusia was like learning English in Mississippi. You had a distinctly slurred accent. Often what she seemed to be saying had no relation to the words I was memorizing from *Spanish for Dummies.*

Finally I said, Are you trying to say that if you work for me you will lose your reputation? She hung her head. Do you want to quit? She shook her head. Could you just wear shoes when you go out to get the mail? she asked in slow Spanish so that I could understand. I thought of going barefoot as my signature fashion statement, and besides, the liver-colored Spanish tiles felt so cool on my bare feet that they woke up my brain. I had grown up with the dictum that leaving your shoes off was good for your feet and, for the record, a lot of people had commented on what nice feet I had. They were long and slender like a thoroughbred; I used to think of them as Lady Brett feet.

Okay, I'll put on shoes to go down and get the mail if that makes you feel you can walk down the street with your head held high. Leave a pair of sandals by the door, I said, and I'll put them on when I go someplace where people might see me and mark me down as an immoral woman. Well, I didn't exactly make that kind of complicated statement in Spanish, but I more or less gave her the idea she didn't have to worry. I would only go barefoot inside my rooms.

Actually, Carmella and I got along fine. She kept the place reasonably if not obsessively clean. At my request, she didn't go into my study and move papers around. She cooked small amounts of food at American times and went home to her aged mother at night. What did I need her for at night? I was just daydreaming looking out the window over the Alcázar Gardens at the pointed end of stars or going out most of the time with Sobersides Sam, as I had come to think of him.

Those first days in Seville, I was trying to screw up the courage to call Luis, but I was a coward. I was *always* a coward, I thought, no matter how hard I tried to not to be. I told myself I was really being courageous *not* to call Luis. I had no idea who would even know I was in Seville (except Sam, who was always on my track) when one day the señora appeared, all flustered, and said I had a visitor. The señora knew Sam. When Sam came, she always said, *That man is here to see you again.* In Spanish, of course.

*Un hombre muy importante,,* she said, which roughly translated would be "a man with lots of clout."

*Y me siento mareada.* I felt dizzy, as *Spanish for Dummies* would have put it, and I am not in any way—take my word for it—the fainting kind. I was like a sleepwalker running on the fuel of hope as I went down the stairs to the courtyard where the señora made people wait.

Luis stood tall and formal, his *Cordobes* hat in hand. "I wanted to see you before this, but I had to go to London."

*London?* He must have some special dispensation. It was my impression the Pyrenees locked in all Spaniards unless Franco nodded his head, Okay, this one can go away for a while. We can count on his coming back. This was not something I wanted to think, that Luis could be trusted by the fascists.

"I heard you left Barcelona, and someone told me you went to Madrid." Good, he had been checking me out. "Then I asked a friend at the police station to let me know if you came to Seville. Come on, I'll give you a ride around parts of the city most people never see."

He had an old Land Rover, cranky and uncomfortable. I sat next to him and tried to calm my heart, which beat so fast that I thought it might need medical attention. I looked at his earth hands on the steering wheel and repeated to myself, It's an infatuation, it will wear off. No, it won't, I thought, sitting there waiting for my heart to make up its mind whether or not it was going to need hospitalization.

He was saying something about my maid—"Carmella," I said. I hated it when people referred to her as "my maid." Was it her fault that her fiancé had been blown to bits in the Civil War and she never had a chance to be a wife and have a home and children of her own? Was it her fault that her father had been killed in that same war and she had been left with an old and infirm mother? "What about Carmella?" I said edgily, sick to death of trying to justify slipping her extra money and not making her get down on her hands and knees every day to wash floors nobody had walked on in over a week.

He had heard I was making all the other Americans—a great number of whom were working on the base outside of Seville near his *ganadería* and had brought their families over—upset because their help didn't want to work any longer for the wages they were being paid. To shut the ruckus up, the Americans had had to raise salaries, and they weren't happy about it, not one bit.

I sat fuming, trying to think of some suitable answer where I could stay in the Land Rover beside him and yet not compromise that damned *pundonor* the Spaniards set such store by.

"If we had more people who paid the people who work for them what they're really worth, we'd have a different country."

I couldn't believe my ears. No Spaniard I knew would ever have made a remark like that. The ones I had encountered were inside a society so closed off from the world that they seemed to belong to some long-ago feudal past when a very few owned all the wealth and all the land and everyone else served them. My ex-ballerina friend always said, "It's like the Middle Ages. That's what I love about it."

I had often watched the police cordon off both ends of a street so that there was no avenue of escape and beat people just for the pleasure of hurting them and often arrest them because they didn't like their looks or their clothes or just something about them. These were "incidents," though they were never reported in the United States. Spain was a country of little concern to the American government, which was always guided by economic interests, and Spain had nothing we wanted. Correction: except that base. Count on the military to up their numbers. Otherwise, Spain was just a dried-up, out-of-step spot on the planet with the last of the fascist dictators still in power. It could go its own poverty-stricken way without infringing on vital American economic interests.

It had started to rain. The windshield wipers couldn't keep up with how hard the rain was coming down. Luis pulled the Land Rover over and stopped. He turned and looked at me. I can see that look even now.

"I've been thinking about you ever since Barcelona. I couldn't get you out of mind. That was crazy, because women—" He was probably going to say women are just women—but he plunged on. "Even after I got back here, I kept thinking about you all the time. Did you ever think about me?"

"Yes, I thought about you a lot."

"You did think about me," he said in a voice of wonder. "I thought you were with that American from the consulate—"

"Sam's a friend." I could see from his face there were friends, and then there were *friends.*

He took one of his earth hands off the steering wheel and put it on my thigh. I could feel the pulse of his heart beating through that hand; the pulse of my heart lurched for a moment, and then we were one pulse beating together in slow, regular rhythms. If he kept his hand there, we would be connected for the rest of our lives. If he took it away, our lives would be severed. I put my hand over his to stop him from severing those two tied-together hearts.

I have a Spanish peseta in a round silver ring that I wear around my neck, and sometimes when I touch it, I can feel a pulse there, as if Luis's heart were beating inside that coin the way it had beat inside his hand that day. Sometimes there is nothing but flat, dead metal. At first I didn't know which it would be, but now I am almost always certain when the pulse will be there and beat against my hand. For a moment, I am back beside Luis in the Land Rover, with the rain beating against the windshield, and he has stopped the Land Rover and turned to look at me, and I see that look on his face. It's what I have that will never go away.

Spring comes early to Andalusia. I filled the house with violets and jonquils, two pots of hyacinths. I threw the French doors thrown open to the Alcàzar gardens budding across the high wall that ran all around the palace, birds singing (where I first heard the nightingale); the sun steamed in, the house was aglow with the fresh smell of earth-opening air.

I was so dizzy with spring and love that often, instead of working, I wandered the streets of Seville, happy to come upon scenes I would never have encountered back in the States and knowing that I was going to see Luis, but just not quite sure when. He worried all the time about our being properly chaperoned. I wasn't in the least worried. Why should he be?

I saw two storks nesting on top of St. Lawrence's, where I had gone to see the Jesus de Gran Poder, whose feet, or rather whose right foot, was outstretched as he bent forward under the weight of the cross. That was the foot the devout kissed. There was a young man there, twentyish, very handsome, praying fervently. He bent, put out his hand, and gently wiped the foot with his handkerchief before he kissed it, a strange juxtaposition of intense faith and a fear of germs.

I was holed up in my three cheap rooms in Seville where I sat at my typewriter—so you have some idea of how long ago this was—and worked every morning on a book that was going to be The Great American Novel. It rained every day, not just on the plains, but all over Spain, and when I wasn't working, I spent a lot of time at the window contemplating the fact that I had done the Spanish unthinkable. I had left my husband.

Some afternoons, I took lessons on the castanets from Maestro Realito, trying to learn how to click and clack the right rhythms so that I would be able to do flamenco dances when the rains finally stopped and life in Spain began again. Some afternoons, I met with Porter Tuck and his girlfriend Maria and we drank cheap wine in the gypsy section of Seville. Porter wanted to be a killer of bulls and had assigned himself the name *El Rubio de Boston,* "The Blond from Boston." He was gorgeous to look at and had a slender, willowy body; he was tall for a bullfighter, but blonds are what the Spaniards went wild over.

Porter had had a few scrimmages in small arenas at those villages where carts were pulled together to form a circle so that amateur would-be bullfighters could take on a scruffy animal that came from god knew where and try to display their expertise in the hope that a bullfighting talent scout would just happen to be there and take notice. All Porter talked about was getting a fight in a real ring where real money exchanged hands. In those local makeshift affairs, Porter got no money; he lived mostly by cadging what he could from the few American and British *aficionados* there were in Seville; Maria I suspected worked the streets when things got desperate.

Porter and Maria were the kind of people who inhabited that gray area between what was legal and what was outside the law, what I thought of as "on the edge." After Porter and Maria came to visit me, the mean señora who owned the place told me they were *gente baja,* low people, and she did not want them in her house ever again.

I tried to defend them, but I didn't really have a position that she would understand. I liked them because they took me to places where real flamenco was played, the costumes the dancers wore all ravaged and smudged with sweat. They knew women who threw the cards and told your fortune and looked you in the eye as if measuring you for a robbery and knife thrust later. They ate food as they walked down the street, swallowing bread ravenously and spitting the seeds and pits out of fruit as they walked along. Mainly the attraction was that the three of us were joined by the fact we survived on dreams. My name was going to be mentioned alongside Hemingway's. Porter was going to be as famous a matador as Manolete, and Maria was going to live in a big house in Madrid and invite all the movies stars she admired to drink and dance the night away in a special room she would have set up like a *taverna.*

Every day was an exhaustive effort to believe in these inconceivables, but we were young and in love with life. Then suddenly one day Porter came roaring into my room, the señora shrieking behind him. Porter grabbed hold of me, twirled me around, and sang out that he had got a date for a fight in Valencia. Ships from the American fleet moored just outside of Valencia, and the maestro was sure that thousands of sailors would pay good money to see a real American, a *blond* American, fight bulls in his ring, even if the bulls were the young ones that *noverillos,* bullfight apprentices, fought. What did the Americans know? Bulls were bulls. Porter would be dressed in a suit of lights.

I had to come. I brought them luck, Porter said. The real truth was I was the only one of the three of us who could scrape together the bus fare to get us to Valencia.

We went on a series of buses borrowed from a Keystone comedy. We had to make endless changes, and the buses kept breaking down. Maria had brought a watermelon, and we dripped juice all over clothes that had been decent enough when we started out, but we arrived looking like derelicts. Porter had no money for renting a *traje de luces,* the suit of lights he would need to appear in the ring. It was expensive, I remember that, though not exactly how much I "lent" him.

We stayed in a down-and-out pension, a place filled with filth, fear, and a kind of frantic festiveness. The night before his fight, Porter got drunk, and it occurred to me he was like people who wanted to be have written The Great American novel but didn't want to do the actual work of writing it, something my husband, in his anger, had accused me of.

The day of Porter's debut, Maria and I sat in *sol y sombra,* the medium-priced seats. In those seats, the sun *(sol)* fried you the first half of the fight, and then the shade (*sombra*) sent you into chills the second half. But we never got to the second half. Porter was gored on his first bull. The wound was so immense that the impresario was convinced Porter was going to die and didn't want him to die in Valencia. It would be bad for the reputation of his ring. So he stuck Porter in an ambulance and sent him off to Madrid where the specialists in the Sanatorio de Toreros could deal with him. Probably he would die on the road, and no one would pay much attention. He hadn't made more than two or three passes before the bull hooked him, so nobody knew whether he was really any good or not. Maria went with him, and I took a bus trailing after them.

The ambulance was old and decrepit and broke down four times on the way; the whole journey took nine hours. Porter was more dead than alive when he arrived. The doctors said he had the worst horn wound they had ever seen a man survive.

When I went to see him after an all-night operation, he lay on the bed looking wasted. The only thing he said to me was that he was out of cigarettes. Maria said they had no money, and she didn't know anyone in Madrid. She looked at me with large pleading eyes, and I handed over what I could.

Since Porter was still alive, the maestro in Valencia was interested in him again. He would be a big drawing card: *El Rubio de Boston,* who had survived the worst goring a man could get and still live, would appear in a grand corrida in Valencia as soon as he was out of the Sanatorio de Toreros. I'm finally getting my big chance, Porter told us from his bed in the infirmary. Maria and I looked at each other. He was way too weak to go back into the ring, but he was afraid if he didn't fight right away, the crowds would forget him and the maestro wouldn't book him again.

In his triumphal return, as Porter referred to it, Porter was third on the cartel because he had fought fewer fights than the other two *noverillos*. The most senior of the bullfighters got the first and fourth bulls, the second most senior the second and fifth bulls, and Porter would get the third and sixth. There was a great deal of fanfare, and then the fighters and their *cuadrillas* marched across the ring to martial music. Everything seemed festive and gay. There were hundreds of American Navy men in the stands shouting and pumping the air with their clenched fists. The first bull came out and gored its bullfighter, so the second bullfighter went in and tried to dispatch the animal, but he was gored, too. That meant that Porter had to kill this bull, and then deal with the five that came after, six bulls altogether.

He was, as the Spanish put it, *sin vergüenza*, without shame. He let the men the maestro had hired to be his *cuadrilla* flap their capes as long as they could or would, the audience screaming and shouting and starting to throw things. Then he went in and made no attempt to make any passes. He just wanted to kill the bull in front of him and get on to the next one. Later he told me that his legs were shaking so badly that he was afraid they would catapult him right onto the bull's horns. What he did to avoid the moment of truth was avoid that danger—the one that had killed the great Manolete— by running around the side of the bull and stabbing at him. He kept stabbing and stabbing, until the bull finally fell down. He was booed all the way through the last five bulls, but he escaped alive. He was through with bullfighting, whether he wanted to be or not. No one would ever hire him again. I think dealing with six bulls after being gored so badly had cured him of any romantic notions he might have had about being a bullfighter. He packed up his things and left for the States, leaving Maria to make of her life what she could.

Later, much later, when I was back in the States, I heard he had become involved in some kind of dope deal and had been put in prison for two years. The first day he got out, he took a bus to New York City and ran around Central Park telephoning from one public pay phone after another. "They're after me," he kept saying. "Come get me and help me get away." He was found in a telephone booth with his throat slit. Some accounts say he was shot, but a man I know and trust on this kind of thing said, His throat was slit.

After Porter left, I saw Maria occasionally. She never out and out asked for money, but she looked terrible (who would pick her up looking like that?). Someone—a trick, I suppose—had beaten her. She had lost two of her front teeth. I gave her money from time to time, a "loan," because she might be living on the streets, but she still had that touchy Spanish *pundonor*. The one thing you could never wound in a Spaniard was his pride without making a mortal enemy for life—if you escaped with your life. Salvador de Madariaga, the great Spanish historian, says the English want fair play, the French law, and the Spanish honor.

Anyway, I liked her. She had *corazón*—heart, which was another Spanish way of defining courage. I knew that in her circumstances I would never have been able to exhibit anything even halfway as valiant as the smile she put on her face showing a black hole in the middle of her teeth. I might not have much money (an understatement), but I wasn't poor the way Maria was poor. I never would be. I had been born in a place where there was a little bit of room for women who wanted to define their own lives to wiggle their way at least halfway toward independence—if they were willing to put their pride in their pocket and *smile* when they were put down or passed over for promotion—and learn shorthand and typing before they started out looking for a career.

Porter never wrote Maria after he went back to the States. This was an aspect of love I had not contemplated before, that it was possible that the person who said he loved you could leave you and you would never hear from him again. Maria never mentioned this betrayal. When we got together, it was as if Porter had never existed. She would never tell me where she lived—"I'll drop by and see you," she'd say in her heavily accented English—and she did every other week or so, unintimidated by the shrieking señora trailing behind her, screaming for her to get out.

I hadn't seen her in quite a while when one day I thought, It's been at least two months since I've seen Maria. It came to me that something bad must have happened to her. I went over the bridge to the other side of the Guadalquivir to the Macarena, with its crowded stoops and streets that often erupted in violent confusion, the cacophony of its alleys like an explosion of Rimsky-Korsakov music. I tried to track Maria down. It wasn't hard for me to translate into Spanish "the woman who was with *El Rubio de Boston*." Yes, people remembered El Rubio and they had seen Maria around, but he wasn't with her anymore. He had gone back to America, she was all alone now—some shook their heads—no one had seen her for a while. She seemed to have disappeared somewhere, but then people had been disappearing "somewhere" for years in Franco's fascist Spain. What was one more?

One more: that's one of the things that I brought back from Spain, that we are all just one more. We come into existence and live for a time with our dreams and delusions, and then we disappear and people forget we have ever even been around. For instance, how many people remember El Rubio de Boston? Or have ever read a book of mine?

I didn't get back to Seville until almost a week after Porter had been gored, and then it was late in the afternoon and I was a physical and emotional wreck. When I climbed the stairs to my three rooms on the second floor and put my key in the lock and opened the door, I found Carmella in hysterics. Her nephew had been picked up on suspicion of something or another. When the Spanish police picked someone up, if you didn't find out what jail the person was in during the next twenty-four hours, he would be whisked away to some secret concrete cellblock where he might languish for years, or he could easily be summarily shot. Imprisoned or shot: it depended on the mood of the men on duty. In the case of prison, it might be months or even years before you found out which jail he was in and, even when you found out, there was really nothing you could do. The whole country was under the iron grip of those small, fat hands of Franco.

I remember Carmella and I running frantically from one police station to another. The police treated Carmella with contempt, and they weren't much more civil to me, with my terrible faltering Spanish and my ridiculous American indignation.

Carmella and I stood out in the street—it was nearly midnight— Carmella crying and I in such a rage that my whole body was shaking. Come on, I said, running down the street to a friend's apartment with one of the few phones in Seville. It must have been nearly one in the morning by that time. Someone I couldn't identify opened the door, let us in, and finally led me to a phone. Just getting the phone to work was a task at that time of night. I couldn't call Sam; this was not the sort of thing the American consulate wanted to be involved in. I decided to call the only other person I knew who had power over people like these police, Luis at his *finca* twenty-five kilometers away.

He owned a vast amount of property and had a title, the kind of man the police would listen to. That wasn't the only reason I called him. I called him because if someone asked me, today, so many decades later,

Who was the love of your life? I would say Luis. Luis was the love of my life.

By the time I got through all the problems with trying to make a long-distance call and babbled to someone who answered the phone and couldn't make out what I wanted—I kept shouting *Le Conde, por favor*—it was at least two o'clock in the morning. I kept right on babbling when Luis finally got on the phone. Stay where you are. Where are you? What's the address? I'll drive in and—

But it might be too late by then—

Just stay put. Put your maid on and let her give me the name of the street where you are. I want to be sure I've got right place. Carmella was sobbing and shouting—after all, to her way of thinking, the person on the other end of the phone was an immense distance away. She kept repeating her nephew's name. There would be a pause, and then she would give the street and number where we were. Then she would start sobbing and talking about her nephew, and then she just stood there holding the receiver. Luis had rung off.

Luis got Carmella's nephew out. I never knew quite how. All he ever said was that he went to a police station and gave the name and they told him where to go and he went and someone at that prison said, You'll vouch for him, and Luis must have said yes, because how else would Carmella's nephew have been released? Luis didn't know Carmella's nephew, and he only knew Carmella—she was probably still "the maid" to him—because I had called him and asked him to do something that would give him trouble and it was for my maid, my maid, for chrissakes, and he had done it.

We were watching Carmella and her nephew go down the street into a cream-colored dawn. I was so tired from going to Valencia and the goring and getting Porter and Maria in the ambulance and then going to the Sanatorio de Toreros and then back by bus to Seville and then trying to deal with Carmella's problems that I thought I was going to fall down. My body was so belligerent for all I had put it through that I was sure it would refuse to get up again. "Carmella's nephew was just walking down the street, and these thugs picked him up, and he was beaten—you could see that, his face was all bruised—I'll be so glad to get out of this city—"

"You're going home?" Luis sounded genuinely alarmed. For the first time, I thought I'd have been better off if I'd never laid eyes on him or anyone else in Spain.

"I rented a place in Alcalá de Guadaira last week. It's a lot cheaper, and quieter, and a better place to write." Alcalá was a small walled Moorish village maybe five miles outside of Seville where I meant to finish my novel. Carmella, exhibiting a courage I found admirable, had told the señora that she was coming with me. She knew I would eventually be leaving and that she would have a hard time getting another job, no doubt about that after sticking with me, because the señora would bad mouth her. I told her I'd give her a rave reference in English (big gain) so that she could look for work for the American wives of the engineers working at Rota. They would pay her better and treat her better than women like the señora. She was taking a chance—maybe those Americans wouldn't hire her and the señora would see to it that any other Spanish woman didn't—but Carmella was beginning to look at the world differently. It had finally come to her that getting down on your hands and knees and scrubbing tiles no one had walked over was a matter that could be interpreted in different ways.

I had written to Roy to ask if he would send me some of my things. I needed clothes desperately, I said, and I had to have some books. I couldn't write all day; it was too exhausting. I needed something to read. I gave him a list of books I needed. I'll pay you back, I promise. I knew Roy would get me the books and send me the clothes because he knew what it was like to want to write—and because he was a friend. In the long run, friends seemed to me more reliable than lovers. I don't even enter husbands into the equation.

*Write?* At this moment I felt as if I might never lift a pen again.

A light went on at the end of the street. "Ah, coffee," Luis said. "You'll feel better after you have some coffee."

Spanish coffee is as dark and strong as the rough Spanish tobacco. When I picked up the cup and took a sip, I involuntarily made a face. Luis laughed. He reached across the table and took a cube of sugar from the bowl, then pulled a small silver flask from his pocket—never go anywhere without brandy, he said as if that were one of the commandments—and casually poured some of the brandy over the sugar until it turned a pale ochre. Open your mouth, he said. Hold this between your teeth and sip your coffee through it.

He had made me a *canard*. Instantly, my mind flew back through the dark corridors of memory. It was a word carried over from the days of the *Blotto.*

I don't remember getting back to where I lived, but the Land Rover pulled up and I opened my eyes and saw what might be called "home." I said, "Do you want to come in?" That was the polite thing to do, especially after someone went to a jail and bailed someone out for you.

"You're dead tired. You need to go to bed."

He was being proper. If he came in with me and there was no one else there to chaperone—not even Carmella because Carmella was only a maid and wouldn't have counted much even if she had been there—people would talk.

He didn't want people talking.

The ex-ballerina would have found that hysterical. All Spanish men care about, she always said, was getting you horizontal. They don't see women as people; they're just toys to play with and then throw away. Or they're like brood cows to give them sons, the more the better. It shows how *macho* they are.

"It was a bad night," he said, and he took me into his arms and held me against him. He had on the rough clothes of the country and smelled of that harsh *campo* tobacco he smoked, of arid land and lathered horses. His head lay against mine. I didn't want him to kiss me. I didn't want him to talk. I didn't want to do anything but stay like that for the rest of my life.

"I'll come back tomorrow," he said. "I want to take you out to see *Los Vientos.* I need to run some errands here in Seville, but I'll be through by noon. Go get some sleep, and I'll see you tomorrow." He sounded as if he were talking to a troublesome child; if he had said, Blow your nose and dry your eyes, I would have done it. If he had said, Go in the house and get some things together and come away with me, I would have done it, whether I was a going to be a toy and get thrown away or a cherished keepsake that would stay with him the rest of his life or even a baby-making machine popping out one son after another. He could keep all the bad things in the world away. Hadn't he just proven that?

I would see him in less than twenty-four hours. Anyone can get through twenty-four hours when the world is going to give you what you want.

I tried to sleep. If I didn't sleep, I would have dark circles under my eyes. I needed to look so fabulous that Luis would never forget the face he saw that morning. Carmella kept looking out the window. She was as excited about his coming as I was because, she said, she hadn't thanked him properly for what he'd done the night before. "He's here! He's here, señora!" I don't know which of us yanked open the door and ran down the hall to the ground floor first. We pulled open the heavy wooden door that kept the señora's house safe, or so she thought. She didn't know there were unseen things everywhere that could sneak in like smoke through a keyhole and seize you forever, things far more dangerous than thieves or murderers.

The door of the Land Rover still hung open. Luis hadn't bothered to bang it shut when he started to run up to the house. I was filled with an extraordinary feeling of elation, as if I were on a serotonin high and would never come down.

Carmella was being effusive, and Luis was telling her it was nothing, he was glad to have been of service. I could understand every word of their Spanish as if I had been given an instant injection of *Spanish for Dummies*.

Luis grabbed hold of my arm and swung me down the steps and into the Land Rover and rammed the door shut. He turned the key and cranked the ignition and threaded the Land Rover through the filament streets until we were out of Seville and bumping along rutted roads past the small walled Moorish town of Alcalá de Guadaira, where I would be living the following week.

We made a right turn off the paved road onto a dusty track and slowed down so that I could take my time and see the whole gaunt countryside—long avenues of tall, thin trees and stretching out from them a vast canvas of land, scrubby and filled with brush that looked half dead but had a sweet, seductive scent that hung heavily in the air and in front of me a filmy emptiness as far as the eye could see. There was a hot, dry wind that never stopped, but it was soft against my skin. The road ran on for miles and miles and nothing changed, and yet every view was slightly different, as if someone were practicing to design the perfect place and could not get it quite right. Everywhere was blessedly hard, dry earth, not one drop of water, and I was in ecstasy. I'd had enough water to last me the rest of my life.

Suddenly Luis stopped the Land Rover and put a hand to my face and touched my cheek. I could feel the trembling in that hand. Then he took his other hand and put it on my other cheek. He was cradling my face in his hands when out of the hot, dry landscape came a clattering herd of goats, the bells around their necks ringing noisily, followed shortly by a young boy who immediately came to a stop and lifted his cap and bowed his head.

Luis hastily put his hands on the wheel of the Land Rover. I recognized the salutation but nothing else in the whirl of Andalusian Spanish which came out of their mouths. So much for *Spanish for Dummies*.

The tone of the boy's voice was filled with deference and the boy's face was anxious, as if he had interrupted something he shouldn't and would be punished for it, though he'd had no idea what he had done wrong. He had just been herding his goats along, minding his own business, when suddenly he'd come on the Land Rover. Luis said something very rapidly.

A huge smile split the boy's face. He was obsequious in the profusion of his gratitude. His cap was still in his hand. It was obviously going to stay there until Luis started off.

Reality will always lay its cruel hand on your happiness. What I thought at that moment, and god knows where it came from, was a line from Dostoevsky: *No man is good enough to be another man's master.*

Luis, of course, had no idea I was using literature to destroy our happiness. He was preoccupied with getting the Land Rover going. The motor ground once or twice before catching, the man and boy shouted something to one another, and then we were flying through beige, then ochre, then mauve stretches of land with bluish-green clumps of leaves against the sky, then gold across a whole plain with a small pueblo here and there, another herd of goats—

"Luis, what's the word for goat herder? I know that's not going to be in my abbreviated English-Spanish dictionary."

*"El hombre de cabreros."*

I threw Dostoevsky and the land of literature aside and allowed myself to plunge back into the world of nature.

We passed cork trees, their trunks like naked, bloody bodies, a lone man in ragged clothes leading a burro, endless orchards of olives. If we passed anyone on the road, it was usually a weather-beaten man who took off his hat and bowed as if he were acknowledging his lord and liege. The ochre earth, the wizened trees, the potholed dirt road, all belonged to Spanish gods whose demands were unfamiliar to me. But I knew the wind god well. To hell with the *Blotto*, to hell with the Pope, to hell with Dostoevsky.

This land might look desolate, Luis was saying, but it was good for breeding bulls. The big ranches—Domecq, Villamarta, Carlos Nuñez, Pedro Romero—were not too far off the main highway to the east.

We turned into a long avenue of eucalyptus, and I saw two vast pillars with life-size black metal bulls on top of each and an arch that spanned the two. *Los Vientos*—The Winds—it said in thick black letters, with the family crest underneath. I smelled the air around me, I smelled the earth, the flowering shrubs; I had come home.

Luis eased the Land Rover up the long, tree-shaded drive, and then I saw a great house with large, black double doors and enormous windows that must have been eight feet tall and almost as wide. "I thought this was like a farm," I said, stupefied.

"Well, it used to be a hunting lodge, but I am trying to see if I can't make it self supporting. It's hard going. People don't want to change the kind of lives their fathers and grandfathers and great-grandfathers before them had when the place was just used once or twice a year. My family thinks I'm crazy, especially when I start arguing about how our people could—"

*Our people.* He meant the people who lived in those small pueblos we had passed, the men on the road who had bent their heads in oblation. *Our people* was the way they had always been spoken of and always would be, because those words had been hardwired into the family's brains from birth.

*Los Vientos*, he said, had never been used for anything more than a hunting lodge, and usually only one month a year during the hunting season. "—they could be doing a lot more with the land than was ever done in the past instead of only using it during the fall or spring to hunt—"

I thought I must have heard him wrong. "You mean they only used this place to *hunt*? How big is this place anyway?"

"Twelve thousand hectares." Whatever that was. Twelve thousand anything seemed to me a lot in a country the size of Spain, something like maybe Indiana and Iowa combined. "My great-grandfather got the land from the king for some favor or other he did, and it wasn't considered good for anything but hunting. He built this place, and the court would come down and hunt—"

The court? Did he mean like the king and—"The court came to *this* house?"

"Well, it has forty bedrooms—"

Fitzgerald was right when he said the rich were very different from you and me, and Hemingway was wrong when he said, Yes, they have more money. It's more than the money. It's the power that comes with it that makes the difference. I couldn't imagine what it would be like to have been brought up in a house with forty bedrooms. Or why anyone should have a place like that just to go once a year to *hunt*.

I was filled with the kind of anger that can't quite be identified. It has something to do with injustice, but you can't pinpoint what injustice you want to specify. I said the first thing that came to mind. "I never thought you had someplace with forty bedrooms. Look at your hands. You have earth hands."

"If I have what you call earth hands, it's because I'm trying to make this place something besides a hunting lodge that's only used once a year. Do you think I would be driving around in an old wreck like this Land Rover if I was the kind who thought I deserved to be born into a family that had a hunting lodge that was only used once or twice a year and had forty bedrooms?"

How would I know the answer to that? If the hunting lodge had forty rooms, what did his Madrid house have?

"I can ride over this place for miles and miles and see and feel things I would never see or feel any place else. I wanted you to see it because I felt that you—"

I waited for him to finish the sentence, but he got out of the car and came around and opened the Land Rover door, which stuck. He gave it a slam with his fist and then opened it and waited for me to get out. He wasn't going to help me out. He wasn't going to touch me. He wasn't going to finish the sentence I didn't understand or he didn't know how to explain or there was no explanation at all for all this unearned entitlement we had been passing through and I was now about to see in all the splendor of its forty bedrooms.

The initial thing I remember about the house at *Los Vientos* is coming through enormous wooden portals—they couldn't be called doors—into a huge tiled hall. The first thing I saw were red stains on the tiled hall floor. Someone had just come in from shooting and left rabbits in a pile, and the maid hadn't had time to clean up. The air still preserved the acrid odor of smoking cartridges. Blood on the sand in the bullring, blood on tiled floor, blood on the body on the crucifix—everywhere I looked in Spain there was blood. No wonder I now shy away from anything red.

Sun was pouring through the enormous windows, and I was blinded for a moment. I stood in the tiled hall, my eyes blank with light. I closed them and waited and, when I opened them again, I saw a dark masculine house devoid of the softening touch of female hands. There were no bowls of flowers, no soft cushions, no fashionable magazines, no bright-jacketed books. The halls were racked with guns, and there were two living rooms, one on each side of the large entrance hall that was longer and wider than most people's living rooms. Each of the rooms off the hall had an enormous fireplace; the one on the left had a pool table. The one on the right, which we entered, had the heads of bulls on the wall and antlers from the herd of deer the old count had had imported from England, or so Luis said. Why wouldn't I believe him; who could challenge anything he said with all this corroborating evidence in plain sight?

I had thought I would hate the dead heads, but they seemed right at home here. It was as if the heads said, I came from here, I went to do my duty in the ring, and now I have come home where I belong.

Rare old bullfighting posters decorated two walls and snapshots of the family in silver frames were spread out on tables and the top of a piano, its cover closed; there were a lot of pictures of people on horseback, some of them of people playing polo, and a large, yellowing photo of what must have been Luis's grandfather with someone who could only be a king. The king looked young and boyish, and Luis's father looked hard and shrewd and robber-baronish. Looking at that picture, you knew that Luis's father would be here after the king had gone into exile, that he would keep his land and his silver mines in Mexico for his son, and for his wife and three pretty daughters there would be jewels and fine furs, that he and his kind were stronger than the passing whim of a Republic. He would have rushed to help Franco, I thought, when Franco flew out of exile in the Canary Islands to Morocco and led an insurrection against the legitimately elected government of Spain. I am a woman who believes in equality, and here I stood enthralled with a man who, as Miguel de Unamundo would have said, had the "the mystery of faith sanchopachesque, which, without believing, believes."

On one wall, there was a bookcase of Spanish classics bound in Moroccan leather, a few French paperbacks, yellow with age, some American and English novels, which I immediately coveted I was so starved for something to read, even if they were all outdated. The only reading material on the big wagon-wheel table in front of a leather couch was agricultural journals and a recent copy of the *New York Sunday Times* business section.

Everything was very, very quiet, just the two of us standing in the middle of that room whose photographs tracked a family I couldn't even begin to imagine. Luis put his hand on my shoulder, and the house came suddenly alive inside my head, people opening doors, talking, laughing, bickering, peeling a piece of fruit, examining guns to choose the one they would want for the day, talking about pheasant and ducks and the *ave frio*, the crazy bird, that Luis told me the peasants ate, and saying what a nuisance the rabbits had been that year, though they made good stews, nobody but Luis caring that they got into his private garden and ate all the lettuce and destroyed the shoots of the young vegetables he was trying to raise. I looked around and tried to imagine what it would be like to live in a house like this.

It would be like some children's book where the children find a secret place and never came back out, I thought. Luis stood beside me, his head tilted, his arm on my shoulder, waiting for me to say something. "It's like being in Eden, a different kind of Eden, one without plants and flowers. This is like an Eden where you just see the earth."

"How would that be Eden, then?"

"Because the skin of the earth is more important than the plants and flowers. With water, you go down and down, but with the earth, it's hard and it holds you up. You don't have to be afraid you're going to fall through and never see air again." He didn't have a clue what I was trying to say, and I thought, There is no way in the world I can explain. Then I thought, with a sinking heart, We're so different. Probably we will never understand what we say to each other. We will never know the right answers to give.

He took his hand off my shoulder and put my hand in his—perhaps I *had* said the right thing—and we walked and walked through that enormous house, through the dining room with its table long enough to seat far more than forty people and past the dark portraits on the walls. We went through a study with trophies and plaques and cases of ribbons of triumphs from so long ago that the ribbons were falling away from the pins that held them up in their cases; we plowed through bedroom after bedroom, the mattresses turned up; we walked out into a small courtyard and then into a separate building, a small chapel as elaborately furnished as a miniature cathedral. The clothes on the Madonna sent spangles of color that danced through flecks of light and sent their colored raindrops on the patterned tiles of the floor. There were rows of wooden pews and a small confessional made of some dark wood that gleamed in the light and stations of the cross along the walls. Christ hung in agony over the altar. It was as Spanish and as Catholic as you could get. "I'm going to get married here," Luis said.

Then we went back outside and stood in the courtyard and a man, hat in hand, came up and said something to Luis, and Luis told me he had to leave me for a moment. Why didn't I wait back in the chapel, the one room in that great place that had no place for me, a woman who needed a divorce, a woman who lived alone and let men come visit her without having a chaperone present, a woman who smoked and wore two-piece bathing suits that showed her *bare* midriff, a woman who hated Franco and his feudal fascists and yet had at first sight, as I came through the big pillars and up the eucalyptus lane, fallen in love with this house and would never have changed one thing about it because at last I had found the place where I belonged. Well, maybe I would have gotten rid of that hideous wagon-wheel table.

A few hours' drive from the hunting lodge, Federico García Lorca, the most famous Spanish poet of the twentieth century, had been arrested by Franco's forces for his political views (and because he was a homosexual), then taken into the hills outside of Granada in the early morning dawn and shot. Being shot is a nice way of saying murdered. He was thirty-eight years old. After he was dead, one of his executioners said he had "fired two bullets into his ass for being a queer."

*A las cinco de la tarde* ... at five in the afternoon ... the poem Garcia Lorca wrote on the death of Manolete had probably the most famous line ever written about bullfighting. Even bullfighters who hardly knew more letters than those they could print to sign their names could recite at least part of that poem.

| | |
|---|---|
| *A las cinco de la tarde* | *At five in the afternoon* |
| *Eran las cinco en punto de la tarde* | It was exactly five in the afternoon |
| *Un niño trajo la blanca sábana* | A boy brought the white sheet |
| *A las cinco de la tarde* | *at five in the afternoon.* |
| *Una espuera de cal ya prevenida* | A basket of lime already prepared |
| *A las cinco de la tarde* | *at five in the afternoon.* |
| *Lo démas era muerte y solo muerte* | The rest was death and death alone |
| *A las cinco de la tarde* | *at five in the afternoon.* |

In 1929, in the last part of June or the early part of July, García Lorca chose as his first foreign land to visit not France, where all the famous writers and artists were living, but the United States, in particular New York City—an odd place to go, since he spoke no English and the country was reeling from the worst economic depression it had ever experienced. He was going to study English at Columbia, but after only one week, he came to the conclusion that, like me, he had no aptitude for languages.

He kept his dormitory room at Columbia and devised his own course curriculum: prowling Manhattan and Brooklyn incessantly, day and night, except for a few short weeks in the summer when he went to the Catskills and after that visited a Spanish professor in Newburgh (hardly the place you would think of as a destination for a poet). What he seems to have gotten out of his experiences in America was a sense of the disruptive forces of the modern world and the discovery of his own sense of isolation.

García Lorca left the United States to give a lecture in Cuba in the spring of 1930, and then returned to Spain. So far as I had been able to make out, he never learned more than a couple of phrases of English; all his friends in the States were Spanish or Spanish-speaking. He had almost no money most of the time. He lived on handouts and often was penniless, but he was obsessive about combing streets everywhere from uptown in Harlem, not exactly a safe place late at night, to the Battery and the Bowery downtown and across the river into the bowels of Brooklyn, trying to absorb what the United States was really like.

I imagine him along the waterfront amidst all the enormous transport ships, walking the filthy piers past drunken men who staggered about or slid down some gum-tarred building and lay senseless in the darkness, the exact opposite of Andalusia and its burnt landscapes and tiny church-topped towns. Perhaps that was why he had gone to New York. He wanted to be with water.

The men who plotted his death might have met in this very house. They might have knelt in one of the pews of the small chapel at *Los Vientos*, praying for the success of Franco. Luis, if he had been older, might have gone into battle on the side of the Fascist forces. Even in New York, when Lorca looked up and saw the moon, he thought of it as *la luna gitana*, the gypsy moon—the Spanish moon of pride, passion, and death. He had never dreamed he would be taken out and shot because he was a poet and he was gay. He was thirty-eight years old, and no one knows where his bones are buried, though in 2003, the *New Yorker* ran an article, "Looking for Lorca," that discussed the possible places near Granada where Lorca might have been buried.

> According to some rumors, the Nationalist authorities, alarmed by the attention the poet's death was receiving, exhumed his body not long after it had been buried and moved it. ... Lorca was actually interred in a mass grave known as *el barranco*, the ravine, which is believed to hold several hundred bodies.

When Luis came back, he could tell right away something was the matter. "What is it? He said.

"I was thinking of García Lorca," I said.

"He was killed outside of Granada. That's not near here."

That won't work, I thought. It's your kind of people who murdered him. It's your people who supported Franco. Killed, assassinated, murdered, shot—take your pick, Lorca was as dead as they could make him.

Luis put one of his large, earth-stained hands on mine. "I have so wanted to bring you here to see Las Vientos. Even when you're not here, you're with me. I am wondering if you are thinking—if you were wishing that we would come here and live together and never be apart again."

I looked at him. Surely he could see the answer in my eyes. But in back of that answer, dark figures prowled inside my head—Generalissimo Franco, the Flangists suppressing the rightful government the people had voted in, dead members of the Lincoln Brigade, Carmella's father and fiancé, and of course George Orwell and García Lorca.

We went back into the house. In the dining room there were two places set, his at the head of the table and mine at his right. The china was as thin and transparent as tissue paper, with a thick gold line around the rim and the family crest in the middle. The wine glasses were cut crystal and would probably play a tune if I touched them gently with a fork. I sat bolt upright and looked at portraits as Luis pointed to each one and explained who that person had been in the family line. I couldn't tell one from the other; all the men looked haughty (Fascists! Fascists!) and the women full of repentance. For being born women, no doubt.

I don't remember eating, but I know I drank a lot of wine. I know I smoked. *A woman smoking at the table!* I was *mareada* with despair and wine when we got back in the Land Rover, and I kept talking and talking. I wanted to lock my mouth shut, but I couldn't. It talked on and on. I was under the impression that Luis could follow my mind, which was running a mile a minute—or I probably only liked to think he could. After all, these tirades were spewing forth in English. In a foreign language, where I would have had to slow down, it might have been easier to follow, but people with minds like mine left their sentences always half finished as they plunged from one thought to the next. I doubt Luis had any idea of the confused jumble of contradictory things I was trying to explain to him, though I remember quite clearly repeating over and over that everything depended on how you tried to connect things you had learned from the past to what might happen in the future, that you couldn't decide before hand on how something would turn out if you had never had any experience in the past to make it fit in.

Finally I stopped. I thought I was going to be sick. You're ruining everything, I thought. *You've ruined everything.*

I got out of the Land Rover when we got back to the señora's house and said, "Thank you very much for everything you did for Carmella's nephew and for taking me out to show me *Los Vientos*. I'm sorry I couldn't stop talking. I don't know what was the matter with me." But I did. It was the grapes in the glass that couldn't stop me speaking.

I ran up the walk before he could answer. After I got the door open, I ran to my three rooms upstairs. I slumped down on the floor and held my head in my hands. "You've ruined it all!" I hollered at the top of my voice. "You've ruined everything."

Carmella came running. She thought I had been badly hurt.

I had been. She just couldn't see the wound. The worst wounds you never see. Where had I been all these twenty-six years of my life that I hadn't learned that lesson?


My bad Spanish made Luis happy. He could anticipate my making at least one faux pas that would reduce him to speechless laughter. After I had constructed what I thought a simple straight-forward sentence, I knew from the faces around us frozen in disbelief that I had wandered into some verboten lingual territory. Sometimes he would explain, and sometimes he would shake his head and say, Just don't say that again.

Why?

It's not the kind of thing women say.

But men say it?

Not in mixed company.

If you can say what I said to other men, I don't see why you can't say it to me. Why should you have the privilege of knowing something *I* said and I can never know what it was? Sometimes he would give me a patronizing look and laugh. My reaction was either to refuse to talk, barricading myself in silence, or to lose my temper and say things I regretted later. Either way, he would look at me and shake his head, which would exasperate me further—why didn't he get mad back?

When I had calmed down, he would smile and say, *Mi norteamericana,* and then *No te preocupes, mi compañera.* Don't upset yourself. It was his *compañera* that was so important to me. It meant equal, that we were the same, but the fact was, he had more power than I did because he was a man. Here in Spain. Be honest—anywhere. So he was patronizing me.

Apparently I hadn't disgraced myself after my first day at *Los Vientos* because he came back two days later and said, "I've got a present for you." He held out a small bamboo cage, maybe six inches long and six inches wide, with very thin slats at the sides and on the top, which was made to move back. I peered through the bars and saw a black beetle busily eating something.

"It's a cricket," he said, full of himself.

*"It looks as it's eating itself."*

"When the warm weather comes, its sheds its—what is the English word—"

"Carapace? What am I supposed to do with it? What am I supposed to feed it?"

"A leaf of lettuce, a small slice of apple every day, and some water in one of those caps that come off aspirin bottles" Aspirin bottle caps seemed to crop up in my life over and over. Was there some significance in this? "You can put something in a corner so that it can hide."

"But what is it *for?*"

"It sings. It will keep you company when I'm not around."

I didn't believe this black thing in the box was going to make music. As if to confirm my convictions, the cricket didn't make a peep the first days I had it nestled in its bamboo cage next to my typewriter. Then one day, I heard this odd kind of chirping, and the next day a little singing, and then the damn thing sang so loud sometimes that Carmella and I had to shout to each other to make ourselves heard.

I named the cricket Luis so that I could have the pleasure of saying Luis's name when I talked to it, which was often. I didn't have a radio or phonograph, but I had music, the bright notes of an insect's song, as if Luis had taken a part of *Los Vientos* and brought it to me as an offering, as if he were giving me part of his world, where he seemed to think that I belonged. Geologically, the earth is still a work in progress. So are we all, the cricket sang.

The cricket came just before *Semana Santa* and *feria*. During Holy Week, the last week of Lent, statues of the Virgin and Christ were honored at night by *paseos*, when men from rival *cofradías* (brotherhoods—all male of course) carried the Virgin from their church through the streets of Seville to the cathedral and then through the cathedral, passing before the resplendent statue of the Virgin Mary there; presumably, she blessed it.

There were fifty-some *cofradías* competing to see who had the most elaborate jewels and the most money pinned to their Virgin's gowns and which was the most lavish float that paraded through the streets of Seville to the central altar of the cathedral. The great wooden platforms that held the statues and the decorations around its Virgin and the huge silver candelabras might weigh as much as half a ton, and the procession from the church to the cathedral lasted up to twelve hours. The men who carried the platform with the statue—who numbered about sixty—packed sacks of sand on their head and shoulders to protect them from the full force of the enormous weight they would have to carry. You could just see their feet, because the folds from the black drapery over the platforms under the Virgins only covered their bodies. I thought the floats looked like something out of a circus parade.

A procession started anytime between noon to midnight. The most famous were from the two gypsy quarters, the Triana and the Macarena. People—usually women, oftener than not a gypsy or a Moroccan woman positioned in the window of a dwelling next to the church—sang Moorish *saetas*, songs of lamentation for Christ's pain and the sinful nature of the human race, as a statue left its church. As soon as the *saeta* started, the procession stopped until the singing was finished.

The men of the *cofradías* who were not carrying the Virgin trailed behind the float. They wore hoods like members of the Ku Klux Klan, and many of them beat themselves with chains and whips (think Lawrence of Arabia). Some drove nails into the palms of their hands, and some wore crowns of thorns on their heads (think Jesus). At the end of the procession, there was always at least one man, but usually two or three, carrying crosses so heavy that they could hardly drag them along, barefooted and penitent for the sins they had committed that year. The idea was that the bigger sinner, the worse the punishment.

One of those black-hooded figures had paused beside me and put out a hand to feel my breasts. "*Que guapa,*" he said. How pretty.

He thinks he can get away with this because I'm a foreigner, I thought. He wouldn't do that to a Spanish girl. But of course no Spanish girl would be alone on the street at one o'clock in the morning watching the statues of the Virgins go by. So the blame was on me.

*I wouldn't want to be a Spanish girl for anything in the world, I thought. This is a country for men, not women.* With that in mind, I gave him a good fist in the balls. *That's one for our team.*

When I told Luis about this man touching my breasts, he said, Well, there's always a rotten apple in every bucket.

Barrel, I said. I could tell he wasn't too surprised or outraged.

Each of the *cofradías* wanted its float to be the most memorable and their *penitentes* the most conspicuous. I was told that once, going across the bridge over the Guadalquivir, the top of the Virgin of the Macarena's crown hit the overhead trolley wire. The whole float (as I thought of these elaborate exhibits) toppled over, and all the jewels and coins and offerings pinned to the Virgin scattered every which way. They were worth a **fortune**, everyone who told the story always said. And then, smiling, they would say, Everything, every single thing, was back by the next morning. I was told that story time and again, and though I never contested the veracity of the claim, I would think, Uh-huh, sure. No one took so much as a gem the size of a grain of sand. The truth is, I wanted to believe everything had been returned, just the way I wanted to believe there had been a girl who had raised a pet bull and, after it had performed brilliantly, had gone down into the bullring and called its name, and it had come to her, and they had both walked quietly through the Gates of Fear.

Semana Santa was about a country deeply rooted in religion. *Feria,* which marked the end of Lent and the resurrection and the light of the world coming back on Easter Sunday, went from reverence to debauchery. Nobody prayed, everybody played. From black to bright, I used to think of that last week in April when the bullfighting season officially opened.

At midday, there were parades through the center of town with fine horses and women in fancy, flounced flamenco costumes; there was a bullfight each day at five o'clock in the afternoon (*a la cinco de la tarde …*), and in the evening, hundreds of tiny little private canvas tents sprang up around the perimeters of Seville, creating a city of revelry where people stopped for food and drink and music. You were supposed to have an invitation to visit them, which *of course* only the rich could afford to erect. Not open to the rabble.

But then, very few things were open to the public in Franco's Spain. Except prisons. Every book, all the public oratory, all the church sermons, every article every day in every newspaper, proclaimed how Franco had saved Spain from the Reds and would keep it safe from Communist infidels. Every street, every household was kept under constant surveillance for some state or religious infraction.

If you had fought or sympathized with the Republican government, you could never be free of the notion that at any minute there might be a knock at the door and a pair of Guardia Civil would take you away or demand some kind of payment for leaving you alone or cart you off to prison. The Guardia Civil always traveled in pairs to protect themselves, but in one town in northern Spain, not even traveling in pairs had helped them. They had been lynched. The village thought to be responsible was cordoned off, and all the people in it machine-gunned.

Lucia Graves, the daughter of the English poet Robert Graves, who had spent most of his life on the Spanish island of Majorca, remembers reading as a child a story that ended:

> Marxism, like the ivy that chokes its prey, had tried to spread all over Europe, beginning with our beloved Spain, but like Islam, like Protestantism, it founds its grave in our country! All the people came out of the churches rejoicing, raising their

voices in gratitude to Heaven and chanting Halleluiah!
Lucia Graves, *A Woman Unknown,*
Berkeley, CA, *Counterpoint,* 2010, 65.

Semana Santa was like an official seal of approval of the oppression of the Catholic Church. Feria let off the steam that simmered and boiled under the repressive regime's iron hold. Every noon, there were beautiful carriages pulled by matched pairs of blooded horses and men riding magnificent stallions on special saddles so that a woman dressed in a traditional Andalusian costume could ride behind the man on a small part of the seat with a strap for her to hang onto with one hand; the other went around the rider's waist.

Ava Gardner, the beautiful Hollywood actress who seemed as close to Lady Brett as a real woman could get, had been booed out of the *paseo* one year because she'd been having an affair with Luis Miguel Dominguín. Dominguín was considered by many to be the successor to Manolete as Spain's top matador—in 1959 there would be a famous *mano a mano* between Dominguín and Antonio Ordoñez to determine who was the premiere bullfighter in all of Spain. Shortly before his death, Hemingway covered that competition for *Life* magazine, which ended with Dominguín getting a goring that nearly killed him.

Dominguín was married to a woman everyone respected; she was Spanish, she came from a good family, and she was being humiliated by the press's coverage of her husband's flagrantly open affair with Ava Gardner. There were pictures of Dominguín and Ava in *El Ruedo* and *Digma* all the time; Ava would be sitting at the *barrerra,* the first row of the expensive seats for spectators, with a black lace mantilla draped over her head, and Dominguín would always dedicate a bull to her. He looked like a god when he raised his hat in front of her to indicate that the next bull he fought would be in her honor, then turned and tossed the hat over his shoulder. She caught it, put it on the ledge in front of her, and waited to see if Dominguín was rewarded with an ear, or both ears, and sometimes, for an extraordinary performance, both ears and the tail.

A man never dedicated a bull to a woman unless he was pretty sure he was going to put on an extraordinary performance. It was a great honor to have a hat in front of you, but I wouldn't have wanted Porter

Tuck's hat in front of me the afternoon of his comeback when people were throwing anything they could lay their hands on at him.

The public displays of affection between Gardner and Domínguín had been going on for some time, and the Spanish had had enough of Ava—an American woman coming to Spain and taking someone's husband with not an ounce of remorse in her. When she rode during feria behind a handsome man (not Domínguín; that would have been too much for even a woman like Gardiner), people had jeered and booed. They had even thrown things until she had burst into tears and was taken away, weeping. She could have gotten away with the affair if the two of them had carried on quietly, but it was bad taste to let the press take pictures of them dining and dancing and walking together hand in hand. So far as I know, no one ever chastised Domínguín. Boys will be boys, you know.

During feria, Luis rode a big black stallion in the parade at noon. One of his sisters (I hoped) sat in back of him, the same one who sat in the front row of *sombra* at the bullfights and twice had bulls from *Los Vientos*, when they were on the cartel, dedicated to her. Luis sat in the *toril* making notes on his bulls, and I sat with Sam some rows over. I saw Luis catch sight of me, then look away and pretend he hadn't seen me. That went on the first two days of the bullfights, and I was furious with him.

Then I disgraced myself with the balloons. One night, when we were out at the place where people went to drink and dance, I said to Sam, Let's buy up all the balloons there are. This was a considerable feat, since the small little open canvas "houses" sprawled over miles of the flat dry earth. Sam, who should have known better, said, You want balloons? I'll get you balloons. He started buying up all the balloons he could get his hands on. I couldn't hold them all. Some got away. Some I gave to crying kids. Sam kept on buying. Balloon men were running around trying to sell us more balloons. Children were screaming because there weren't any balloons to buy and they couldn't get near me because I had a huge crowd of kids around me demanding balloons. Drunkards were popping balloons; irate fathers were snatching balloons out of my hands, women were shrieking in my face words I knew were not meant for nice women.

We had been drinking a lot of wine, we were smothered in balloons, and every "house" wanted us to come in, so we kept going from one to the next, drinking more wine, balloons jammed all around us, balloon vendors waiting at the entrances to sell us more balloons.

We came out of one "house," and I saw a carriage. I said, Let's rent that and carry the balloons all around and throw them to all the children we see. I started jamming balloons into the carriage. The man who had been sitting atop the seat waiting to drive the horses began to holler at me, but I just waved my hand toward Sam. Sam would pay him.

There were balloons everywhere. They were hanging out the windows. They were tied to the sides of the carriage. The horses were high-stepping it along when out of nowhere Luis appeared at the window between a battalion of balloons. Hello, Luis, I said brightly, do you want a balloon?

What are you doing? he demanded. You've taken the Duke of Something or Other's carriage. I can't remember the duke's name. After Luis said duke, I knew I was in Bad Trouble, plenty bad.

I thought it was for rent, I said lamely.

Oh, my god, Sam said, the only time I ever heard him take the lord's name in vain. He was wringing his hands and trying to apologize. I thought, Wait until the American Embassy hears about this. Definitely not the kind of thing in your file to put you on the executive track.

We took the carriage back, and the Duke of Something or Other thought my believing his coach had been for rent was hilarious. He was pounding Sam on the back and laughing while Luis looked at me as if he had seen for the first time what I was really like, and it wasn't small and porcelain and pliant. It was *a handful*.

Sam was with me the entire feria after the balloons, and he was happy. I could see how happy he was, and I wanted to say, You've moved along in the alphabet almost to L, Sam. How does it feel?

I had made a spectacle of myself. Not as bad as Ava Gardner, but bad enough.

After all, Ava Gardner was *booed*—Luis might even have been the one she had ridden behind in that little leather saddle that was only used on special occasions—Ava Gardner, with not an ounce of remorse in her, far braver than I could ever be went right on parading around with Dominguín. Still, even being brave didn't have her fare well. The last pictures of Ava Gardner, taken in London where she was living in retreat, showed an old, haggard woman. She had had a stroke, and part of her face was paralyzed. Feckless during her youth, she threw away her beauty, her money, her luck. Frank Sinatra—who had left his wife to marry her before she left him and turned up in Spain to become the love of Dominguín's life and then left him—Frank Sinatra in those last years sent money to pay her hospital bills. He never got over her. Probably Dominguín never got over her, either. But of course he went back home. And of course his wife took him back. Every hour of every day, he must have thought, *Where is she? What is she doing? What is she thinking about? Does she ever think of me?*

The balloon episode, however, was not over. The next afternoon, Luis did not have any bulls from *Los Vientos* on the cartel, so he was not at the *toril*. I looked toward the area in *sombra* where what I hoped was the sister had been sitting, but he wasn't there, either. I was sitting with Sam, waiting for the opening music that signaled the march of the matadors into the ring, where they would salute the judge and then take off their fancy capes, and if they were really smitten with some woman, walk over in front of where she was sitting (women who have besotted bullfighters are always given seats in the first row) and make some flowery speech, then hand his cape up to her. She would spread it out before her and wait for the bullfighter to dedicate a bull to her and throw his hat over his shoulder in tribute to her. She would take the hat and put it on the heavily embroidered cape.

Sam was handing me a Snickers bar, which he had got in the commissary, when Luis pushed his way down to where we were sitting and said, "Can I talk to you a minute?" Pause. "If you don't mind," he said to Sam in a terrible voice.

I got up and said, I'll be right back. Sam smiled at us both, though it was lunatic to think there was going to be any polite exchange of social pleasantries between any of the three of us.

165

I followed Luis up the ramp that led out to the corridor where people pushed and shoved when everyone was let in and nearly trampled you to death when it was time to get out, a dark and gloomy place with a strange smell that I thought must have come from the dried blood of past dead and human animals.

Luis was furious. I don't mean mad—I mean on a real tear. "Just tell me," he began in a voice boiling over with rage, "how you can go all over Seville with that man. How can you do that? Can't you see how it looks?"

"How what looks? He has a name—you know perfectly well that's Sam from the consulate, the United States Consulate, Luis. What are you getting so upset about?"

"In this country, men and women don't go out together all the time unless they are going to get married."

"I go out with Sam because he's a friend. What is the matter with you? You know Sam is just a friend—"

"He—doesn't—seem—like—*just*—a—friend."

The scar on his dark, sunburned cheek was a brilliant white, his eyes flashing with such black rage that I instinctively took a step back. I don't know what I thought he might do—deconstruct right before my eyes? He grabbed hold of me and pulled me against him. I could feel his heart, pumped full of blood, thumping so hard that if I had looked down I was sure I would see it breaking through the traditional bright white starched *paseo* shirt and short black jacket Luis was wearing. It appeared determined to break free—to do what? Change Spain? That's what it would take.

"Oh, god, you don't know how it is to see you with *that* man, the way you look at him—"

"I don't look at him in any way different than I look at any of my friends—"

"*Yes, you do!*" Then he stopped speaking English; what I heard was a long flow of scorching Spanish fueled by uncontrollable rage. I had never seen anyone so distraught in my life, not even my father when he went into one of his monumental fits that meant his fists were itching to get at the strap.

Luis shook me. My head was bobbing back and forth, and I was desperate for air. It was like being under water. I flailed with my arms as if I were trying to swim away from him. Then he pinned my head against him, blazing words pouring out of him. For a moment I thought he was going to take his fists and beat them against my back. This man that I thought I knew from some mysterious connection that had bound us together from the first moment we met had turned into a stranger capable of great violence. His English had deserted him, and I couldn't understand any of his Spanish. There was no scene in *Spanish for Dummies* that even began to cover an encounter like this.

For a moment, both of us strained against one another as if we were enemies engaged in mortal combat. Then the Spanish stopped, he took a deep breath, and he laid his head against mine. "Oh, my god," he said in English. "I have never felt like this about anybody in my life, and I'm so afraid I'm going to lose you. Don't you understand that?"

At that moment I thought, This is not some kind of made-up story. This is real. We need to separate illusion from reality, and our only weapon is the belief that an act of will can overcome anything. Luis had to move on from old beliefs. And me? What was the answer to that?

I was a woman who went out on the streets unchaperoned. Who had *men* who came to visit me with no witchy chaperone to make sure men curbed their lustful natures. Besides Sam and Luis (during the daytime and leaving the door to my house conspicuously open), there were the men from the base at Rota that I went out with, and Sidney Franklin, the American bullfighter Hemingway had been so impressed with. Franklin had written a book, *Bullfighter from Brooklyn*, which made him seem one destined for lasting glory, but I looked on him as lonely, aged, overweight, and in no way a sexual menace. I felt sorry for him. Who in Brooklyn cared about a bullfighter in Spain, and who in Spain was interested in a has-been who had never shown himself especially proficient in the ring? I thought he was probably pretty poor, too, because he eagerly drank and ate whatever I put in front of him, and he often arrived on my doorstep around dinnertime and lingered until he was invited to stay for supper. Carmella thought he was a sponger. I tried to explain that there was an element of tragedy about him, but she countered by reminding me there were never any cigarettes left after he'd been in the house.

I should have said the magic words then: Luis, I love *you*, but I thought women should never be the first to say those words to the man they cared about. They might spook him. "Oh, Luis," I cried, "How can you act like this?"

"Because I can't help myself," he said.

Sidney Franklin was sitting on my couch in Alcalá de Guadaira drinking a glass of wine when he looked out the window and gave a sudden exclamation. A Land Rover was parked in front of my house, and a man in peasant clothes was walking toward the house carefully carrying an envelope as if it were valuable crystal stemware, and if he dropped it, it would shatter. "I know that Land Rover," Sidney said. I knew it, too, but I wasn't going to tell Sidney I did. The less Sidney knew, the better. The less anyone knew, the better.

I went to the door and took the envelope, which was cream-colored, thick, and very expensive looking and, when I opened it, had the same crest that had been on the entrance to *Los Vientos* and on the plates at the table from which Luis and I had eaten.

> *I'm having a tienta a week from Sunday and wondered if you could come. I can send someone to pick you up and take you back. I'd come myself, but there is going to be a lot of company I need to look after. Please give your answer to Pedro, and he'll tell me whether you can make it or not. I hope you can.*

It was signed in an indecipherable scribble.

Sidney had come up behind me, full of curiosity. I couldn't decide whether it would be worse to tell him I was going some place he hadn't been invited or just to pretend it was none of his business. I knew Sidney pretty well by that time. He might turn up and get into the Land Rover with me. I needed haven't worried. He had read the note at the same time I was reading it. He went into a flap, dancing around in dismay and making sucking sounds of distress. "I'm sorry, Sidney," I said, "But the note didn't say anything about bringing anyone with me." I looked at the man who had delivered the invitation, nodded my head, and said, "Sí," while Sidney made a major production of storming out of the house, leaving half a glass of wine so that I knew he was in a serious snit. If he never came back, I thought I could live without fretting too much.

I had a week to wait. I knew I wouldn't see Luis during that time because there would be so much to do to get ready for the *tienta*. When all you are doing is waiting, time seems stopped for hours. When you look at the clock, perhaps three minutes have gone by. At night, I lay in bed and tried to imagine a plotline for the characters in a book I cared nothing about. They were fake people living made-up lives. The chapel was real, sitting in the dining room had been real. The drive home when I couldn't stop talking was certainly real—and terrible to remember.

During the day, I moped about the house. Mostly I sat and stared into space, but I also went back to struggling to learn Spanish. It was my concession to hope—as was the singing cricket who had taken to doing runs up and down the scale that were heartbreaking.

Sunday seemed as if it was never going to come, and by Saturday that seemed fine with me. If Sunday never came, I would have it to look forward to for the rest of my life. If it came, it would flash by in seconds, in another cruel trick time could play. Time has no real tape measure by which it can be counted. It takes us all and lays us down into dust, and all those minutes and hours that tormented us or gave us hope and joy, all those sweet moments that transfixed our lives and made them seem to stand still, are gone and there is no one left, certainly not us, to remember them.

But one thing you know: Sundays will always come, and they will always go.

The drive to Luis's *finca* was about an hour, but seemed to go on forever when there was only the driver and me bumping along the dirt road. Suddenly I saw the two immense pillars with the bulls on top and the iron gate. A gatekeeper gave a grave bow to us as he let us in. When I got out of the Land Rover, I stood staring at a crowd of people staring back at me—friends, politicians, old family retainers, bull breeders, visiting beauties and their chaperons, people I couldn't identify. Then I heard hoof beats, and Luis galloped up and jumped down from his horse, hanging onto the reins with one hand and taking my hand with the other. "I'm so glad you could come." He was breathless. "I was afraid you might not come—I mean, after the last time I saw you, I thought you might be angry with me. I'm *so* glad you came."

Before I could answer, someone took the horse, and Luis started introducing me to people whose names I would never remember. The women all looked dainty and decorative and were dressed for a fiesta; they were the kind who got big photos in the newspaper when they announced their engagements. The men all wore long, tight, charcoal-gray pants with black bolero jackets, flat-topped *Cordobes* sombreros, and very stylish boots with an inch or an inch-and a-half heel. This, I would later learn, was the *traje de campo,* the traditional dress of rich men for a country outing. I stood in my blue jeans, totally out of place. I wished I had never come, and I never wished it more than at the large luncheon where I was the only American. The only thing I could follow even halfway was when the conversation turned to talking about the bulls.

I had been fairly inconspicuous during the morning when the heifers were being tested. These were worked with a cape or a *muleta,* but the bulls destined for the ring were never allowed to see a man on foot until they come into the ring. They did get a sort of testing out in the field when men on horseback came riding up and flipped them over with long poles. If they got up and charged, they were fine, but if they ran away, they were sent, like the cowardly heifers, to the butcher.

Luis had been carefully watching everything each cow did and meticulously making notes in a big book, which I later learned had all the information about every bull and heifer that had been raised on the *finca:* the animal's birth date, name, number, parents, and the performance during the testing when a man, usually shouting and waving a cape or a *muleta,* would try to entice the cow to charge.

I will a pay a lot for a bull, Luis said, but I will pay even more for a good cow. Good cows are what will make *Los Vientos*'s name in the end, because they are the ones who send the bulls out for glory. So, I thought with satisfaction, even cows—the *women* of the breed—have a place of honor.

There were several bullfighters making fancy passes and grinning every once in a while at the crowd, which was noisily enthusiastic. Not Chamaco or Litri, though Huelva was not that far away. Chamaco and

Litri were still in the north and couldn't take time out to come to a ranch whose bulls were in—say—the B category. Or maybe they would have realized that Luis would tower over them and make them seem pale and listless next to him. Wouldn't have been able to spit, I thought, when they were with him.

How would I have explained if Chamaco had come up to me and begun chatting in such a familiar way that everyone would have been able to see we were what Luis's guests would have immediately called *good friends?*

Why shouldn't I have Spanish friends? Because these people would know how to differentiate between A friends, B friends, and C friends. I could see them labeling me, in the style of a trashy romantic novel, as "a spirited girl." Spirited girls in those books didn't do any of the things I could imagine them accusing me of doing in their minds. She's a married woman who doesn't have her husband with her and she has *men friends.*

Probably having Sam as a friend was all right. He was an American, and he worked for the United States government, and who cared about what Americans did amongst themselves? I tried not to mention Sam when Luis was around after our scene except to think, Ah, he was jealous! Good! For the most part I tried to hide any time I was spending with Sam, which wasn't actually much these days.

Would *men friends* include Sidney Franklin? No. He wasn't even in the C category. People like Luis and his friends were all As. A-pluses.

Twice, Luis himself got down in the ring. I held my breath, because though the cows were only two years old, they were still dangerous. It occurred to me that he could be hurt again—it was a cow who had caused the scar on his cheek and had torn his arm to pieces. Or he could be mortally wounded like Manolete at Linares. *I can't feel anything in my right leg. I can't feel anything in my left leg. I can't see.* I put my head down. I couldn't look. I think I, who didn't believe in god, was doing something like praying. My mouth was so dry that the top felt as if it were stuck against the bottom. If I had had to speak, the words wouldn't have been able to get through my teeth.

I remembered Porter Tuck with the horn driven ten inches into his chest. I thought of Chamaco lying in the Sanatorio de Toreros, and his eyes said it all, I have to go back, I have to go back. A man next to me tapped me on the arm and said what I took to be, It's all right, you can look now. You know how it is: Luis likes it to live a little dangerously. You know he likes to fight for the fun of it.

For the fun of it?

Maybe that explained me.


The morning went on and on. Spanish lunches are usually served at two. I was tired and hungry and cranky with all these chattering people I didn't understand. A man I didn't remember and whose name I never learned took me up to the house when it was time for drinks. Waiters in livery, or what I thought of as livery, were passing glasses of sherry. Mirth, merrymaking, laughter, dazzling smiles, exuberant conversation. I would not have been surprised if a troupe of beaming shepherds pranced forth and sang pastoral Iberian ballads accompanied by rebecks.

So far as Luis was concerned, I might just as well have not been there. Nothing is more damaging to one's ego than being ignored. I went over to the wall of books and looked blankly at Spanish titles. I even took out a book and leafed through it as if I were fascinated by the contents. Why had this man invited me to something that would make me feel so out of place and ignore me as if I did not exist? I was thinking about going up to him when we were all summoned into lunch and saying, Thank you very much for inviting me, but I have to go home now. Could you get someone to drive me?

Why was it such a painful thing to love? Why do facts have to get in the way of how you feel? I thought of my family (hardly a sacrifice if I stayed in Spain), my friends (they could come visit), the language and culture (no way to rationalize the difficulties there), leaving my own country for what amounted to forever (could I do that?). Exasperated as I often became with it—and had the *right* to feel cheated of the false expectations it made for women—I was an American, and nothing I ever learned, not even its language, would make me Spanish. It is one thing to be Spanish, and another to be American. It's no coincidence, I was thinking, that an ocean separated the two countries. Between the two there be dragons and evil enchanters.

Forty people might have been put up for the hunts during Luis's grandfather's time, but there were a lot more than forty people at this lunch, and there was still plenty of room at the table. To my astonishment, I found that I was seated two places down from Luis. There were men on either side of him, and then myself and a pale slip of a girl across from me, and then men on either side of us. I suddenly realized how few women there were. The men mostly talked to each other. Every once in a while, one of the men on either side of me would ask me something in Spanish. I told them I could talk about bullfighting, but not much else, and they seemed to think this was very engaging. Eventually I had something of an exchange that seemed to go all right. I stayed away from politics and tried not to make any reference to Franco, though I heard his name on all sides of me; occasionally Luis would look up and stare at me for a moment, and I would stare back, and that was pretty much lunch. A lot of food I didn't eat, a lot of wine I did drink, and both of us (I thought) suffocating with desire in the midst of all these people, for I could see that Luis was only toying with the food on his plate; he had hardly eaten a thing. Everyone else ate as if this were the last meal the gods were ever going to grant them. Drank a lot of wine, too. Well, I was no slouch in that department myself. By the time we were ready to get up from the table, I was thinking I could go back and tell Sidney Franklin he hadn't really missed anything.

Then Luis casually reached across the table and picked up a square of sugar and laid it on his plate. He took the brandy decanter and let it drip over the sugar. When the color satisfied him, he picked it up and leaned across the table, right past the man sitting on my left, and said, "Here," holding out the cube between his thumb and forefinger. I took a teaspoon—at least I had enough sense not to grab it with my hand—and held it out. Then, when he put the sugar in the teaspoon, I transferred the sugar to my mouth and drank my coffee sip by sip through the brandied sugar cube the way Luis had taught me.

In all those back-street, run-down cafés where there were real flamenco guitar players, singers, dancers that we went to see, he would always order two coffees and two brandies. He would automatically make a brandied sugar for me, I would open my mouth, and he would put the cube between my teeth. His hand always lingered for a moment on my lips as I took the sugar. We passed into our own world in that moment, and no one around us existed except the two of us.

When Luis passed me the cube of sugar at the table, it was as if he was making a public announcement, as if all these people he had assembled were props so that he would have an audience to witness this intimate act between the two of us, as intimate as if we had got up before them and started to undress one another. Everyone at the table suddenly stopped talking and stared at us. We're shades of a Chinese circus, I thought, putting on an indecent show for them.

There are plainly black and white lines here that cannot be crossed, I thought, and Luis has just crossed one of those. It was not about money, and it was not really about class, though something of class was certainly involved; it was about turning his back on what was expected and doing something he knew was out bounds.

These people would never starve or be homeless or worry about money. There would always be a place for them, and knowing that, they were free to live as they wanted while others toiled to make them happy. To them, there were two classes of people in the world: those who were meant to be served, and those who did the serving. I was someone who could not be put in either category. They didn't know where to put me, or what I was doing here, or why Luis was treating me as someone he considered special. I wasn't rich, I didn't have a title, I came from a country most of them considered uncivilized; surely I wasn't someone he was thinking of marrying. But he had just done something that said I was special to him, more than anyone else. But the truth, to them, was that I didn't belong.

Nonetheless, after lunch they went to great pains to be pleasant to me. In their own way. But I did not believe one person should own villages of people and direct their lives; on the other hand, in so-called free societies, there were millions of people starving and leading barren lives. Was it Luis's fault he was born lucky? Would I rather have seen him walking down the road in threadbare clothes behind a donkey?

I had driven myself into a corner.

I looked across at Luis, who saw himself—or I saw him—as a bridge. *Bridge* was not the right word. I wasn't sure there was one. All

I knew was that he thought we could combine two worlds that were essentially at odds. Somehow, it occurred to me at that moment, he saw me as part of that link. There was the hunting lodge that was no longer going to be just a place of pleasure. Now there was going to be the kind of woman he wanted to go with it.

He's got this vision in his head, I thought, and it might just work, but again, it might not. The point was that he was trying. In all my life, I had never known, I realized, anyone like him or this place, this country, these people. Looking at me, they must also have thought, What a strange species our friend has found and brought for us to view. What's he going to do with this oddity?

The women stood up abruptly, filed out into hall, and across to the living room with the bullfighting posters and the horns. They were busy looking for things, which turned out to be materials to sew on. They had linen tablecloths (some of them so intricate I didn't see how they would ever finish), some small towels that I identified as possibly guest towels on which they were carefully embroidering their initials; they had nightgowns and slips and god knows what else. They immediately sat down, put on thin gloves (gloves? Oh, okay, not to soil what they were working on), and industriously began to push their needles and thread through the hoops and frames in front of them. Then they began to talk. Mostly about servants. Clothes got some concern. Now and again, some piece of gossip about someone I had never heard of slipped into the conversation, and they would giggle conspiratorially together. They were the kind who had *very* small purses.

I sat dying for a cigarette and resenting every last one of them. I even resented myself. Most of the time they spoke Spanish, but once in a while, being polite, they addressed some innocuous remark in English to me. They had upper-crust British accents. They could have been hired out as food and fashion consultants. They often said *My husband* before they went on with the sentence. It was worse than Indianapolis. At least my relatives fought and screamed and slammed doors; these pretty women were so passive that they could have been crushed down to lie in a pile with their linens and never complained.

The pale slip of a girl who had been across from me at the table I learned was called Maria Concepción, a woman who I thought (but wasn't sure) probably was one of Luis's sisters. At least I always think of her as Maria Concepción, because I saw her as conceived and being a part of *Los Vientos*. Who knows what her real name was? Maybe it really was Maria Concepción. One ting I knew: She belonged here and I didn't.

Maria Concepción went off and came back with a large velvet box and a key in her hand, so I presumed she had unlocked a safe to get it. In the box was an incredible array of glittering jewels, rings with gems as big as grapes, necklaces and pins studded with valuable diamonds, rubies, sapphires, emeralds, opals, you name it. If it was expensive and could be locked into silver or gold, there was a representative of it in that velvet box. All over Spain, people were starving or lay wasting in prisons, and these girls were squealing over a lot of expensive rocks. When she held up a three-strand pearl necklace, I wanted to say, Pearls melt in vinegar, as if that would absolve me.

"Try this one on," the one I thought was the sister said.

"This one" was an emerald as big as those round erasers I used to remove something I had typed by mistake. It seemed to me obvious that my fingers were too large for the ring to fit.

"I have big hands," I said. Big *American* hands, I felt like saying into that sweet face. "I don't think it will fit."

"Why don't you put it on and see how far it goes?"

Why on earth should I try on a ring that obviously wouldn't fit? All the women around me were so small and delicate that at five-eight, I towered over them, even sitting down. They were passing pieces of jewelry around and talking about embroidering tablecloths while the men were in the poolroom across the hall laughing their heads off. A man just wants to sleep with you; he does not invite you to his house in front of his friends and let his sister pass you an emerald that would cover half your finger if you could get it on.

Luis's sister put the emerald back and began taking other rings out of the velvet box, trying to push them over my large American knuckles. She seemed determined to find one that would fit. We went through an assortment of emeralds, rubies, diamonds, sapphires, and some stones I couldn't identify, Class B stones probably, but she insisted on my grappling with these as well. At last she gave up, pressed the jewels back into the velvet box, and disappeared. The other girls stood up, shook themselves down to get their clothes in line, and then went off. Everyone seemed to have somewhere to go but me.

An afternoon wine headache was taking hold. I began to think this was going to size up as one of the bleakest days of my life when Luis came bounding into the room and said he was going to take the Land Rover out to the outer bounds of the *cortijo* in order to see the corrida bulls. There were no roads, he would cut overland, it would be a rough trip, but it wouldn't be dangerous, just bumpy and disagreeable. Whoever wanted to go was welcome. The women weren't keen on going, but I was; I didn't care about being bounced around. Anytime I could be near Luis, I was ready to endure pain and/or punishment.

We went out on the porch, and some men said they might like to go. Then they would look at Luis. After a moment, they would say something in their rapid Spanish that I took to mean, I don't think I'll go after all. Then they would give Luis one of those smiles you'd like to wipe off their faces with a baseball bat.

Only the two of us got into the Land Rover. At each jolt and every rut, I was conscious of the big warm body next to me, the large, square, tanned earth hands so close, gripping the wheel. The yellow light was on; the terrain was very rough; Luis was concentrating.

We paused briefly so that I could watch a field of thoroughbreds running back and forth in excitement down a long, sloping field, like a set from some movie. Then we moved on, and when the Land Rover reached the edge of the range where the bulls were grazing, the look and smell of the land made me understand why Hemingway had chosen Spain as his other country.

My husband had said Forster's "Only connect" was the answer to everything, and maybe he was right. For the first time in my life, I felt a connection that I believed could last forever. I had regained the ability to see the world as a place of possibilities for joy and happiness, a belief I had lost in Boulogne when I'd looked at the map and realized my husband had been lying to me about how far we would have to go on open water.

Luis stopped the Land Rover and turned and smiled. "If you've got one to spare, I'll take one of your American cigarettes."

A couple of the bulls had looked up, but when they didn't see anything that looked as if it might be a threat, they went back to placidly grazing.

"Maria Concepción told me you girls—"

Girls!

"—were looking at the family jewels."

"She kept trying to make one of those rings fit. None of them fit. Maybe I'm not the big-ring type."

Luis looked puzzled. Doesn't understand American slang, I thought. He went to school in *England*. British monarchy and the crown jewels, all that. "I'm more into trying to learn Spanish and being able to hit a bird without endangering the spectators than I am into diamonds are a girl's best friend."

"You didn't like any of those rings?" He sounded enormously disappointed. I couldn't figure it out. I could not imagine why he would care if those rings fit or not.

"It was just that—well, I don't always understand what they're saying most of the time because my Spanish is so bad—"

"It wasn't just that you couldn't follow all the conversation, it was the people too. I know that you haven't got much in common with them, but they mean well—"

"That man next to me said he didn't see how anyone could think you could trust goat herders—at least I knew the words for that because you told me—that you couldn't trust people like that with any responsibilities because they didn't know anything but how to herd goats and you couldn't blame them because that's all they'd ever known all their lives, all their fathers and grandfathers had known. If they tried to do something else, they wouldn't be any good at it, and then they'd lose their *pundonor*. He said that as if goat herders couldn't possibly have the same kind of honor as he did. He said that some people are born to herd goats, and some people are born to do bigger things—I believe he said something about noblesse oblige, but I'm not sure because by that time I was so—let's just say you're lucky my Spanish is so limited, but I understood what he meant. He didn't know, that man, that you came and helped get Carmella's nephew out of jail, did he?"

"I hope not. It would not do me any good. Those people were born into families who have always had money and prestige and power.

They've never known anything else. Why should they want to give up what they have?"

Who can deny that? I held my breath before I let it out to say, "Do you know how many people are in all those jails?"

"That's something people don't talk about. No one wants to be talk about the war. It brings back all the terrible things that happened, on both sides."

I wanted to say, Your father supported Franco, didn't he? But I really didn't need to ask. *I knew.* I felt a chill pass over me. I must have shivered, because Luis took my hand and put it to his lips. "They're up at the house. We're here. I don't want to talk about them. I don't even want to think about them right now. I know I should be worried if they're having a good time, but I don't care. You don't know what these last days have been like. I keep thinking you're with that man from the consulate and—Oh, god, you don't know what it's like to think of you with someone else and imagine—"

I put my arms around his neck—I had to twist and turn to get across that damn clutch to do it, but I would have walked over an army of machines to get to his mouth. I was suddenly filled with courage. At the gate to the *toril,* I would have had no trouble at all when I went to spit.

For a brief moment I was part of the orchards, the hills, the land, and above all, Luis.

"Oh, god," he said at last. "What are we going to do?"

How would I know? We sat there like statues who between them didn't even have one good eye.

"We should go back," he said. "People will start talking if we don't go back."

Didn't he know they were already talking?

I was not in charge of myself. I was getting ready to do some stupid thing, the way my husband had made that scene in the Barcelona consulate. Sam was right. People in love lose control of themselves. You cannot reason with them. They lose their lifelines.

I've got no lifeline, I thought. I can't even remember where I put my purse. *Where did I put my purse?*

"Do you remember where I put my purse?" I asked in a panic.

After that, I became a regular at *Los Vientos*. Luis never had me come when no one was around. There were always people to chaperone us, as I guess he thought of it. He had a shotgun made for me with a silver barrel decorated with intricate designs. It was light enough for me to lift easily and didn't have a kick that would knock me over when I was brave enough to fire it.

It was late spring, and there were hunting parties once or twice a week. We went out into the campo, Luis and I usually alone in the Land Rover, the others following in jeeps, and the servants in mule-drawn carts carrying the food and wine and the men and women who were going to prepare it. We sat in blinds, and beaters drove birds and animals toward us. I was always afraid I would bring down a beater instead of a bird, but Luis was patient with me. I became a good shot. (*You went to bullfights and you shot birds!* my veterinarian daughter says to me now, shocked. I am somewhat shocked myself, but that was in another country at another time, and besides, that wench is dead.)

We went early in the morning, sometimes before light, and by lunch I was famished. There were long rows of boards set up on big empty wine barrels covered with long slats with linen tablecloths over them and beautiful silverware, big crockery soup bowls, and thick utilitarian wine glasses. We stood around drinking sherry from Jerez and eating *tapas*. The bread was never ready. It was set into big iron ovens to cook over an open fire, and it took a long time to bake. We usually had gazpacho, not like the kind you get here, but real thick, garlicky soup with coarsely cut-up vegetables that made it a meal. I ate so much gazpacho in those days that I can't even look at it now. Then came an enormous meal. If there had been a deer killed early in the morning, it would be skinned and put on the spit, but mostly it was young goat roasted over live coals. Cheese, fruit, big pitchers of sangria, that wine that is flavored with fruit and a dash of brandy and a spritz of soda, constantly replenished. I napped in the afternoon on rugs spread out under the olive trees while the men went back to the blinds.

Spain might be black funeral robes on more than half the women, who, with their husbands or fiancés dead, were left with only the consolation of the Church and the shrill, nagging, cloistered lives that were presumed to promote virtue, but—if you believed that virtue needed to be active, as I did—I could see no hope for the future. I'd never really had to undergo the daily struggle for bread that people like Carmella had, I'd never really had to fight for everything, *everything,* not just some things, and I was like Luis and his friends in that, as much as I didn't want to admit it. I held the privilege that an American passport gave me, and that people all over the world wanted. I had been singled out in some way for that luck, maybe not as much luck as Luis and his friends, but by billions of other people's standards, I was rich, and what was I doing about it? I wasn't out on the street distributing the little I had to the poor and needy. I hadn't pledged myself to Mother Theresa (I guess not—she didn't believe in birth control or abortion). I hadn't joined the Salvation Army to stand on street corners ringing a bell and soliciting funds. I was not one of the *penitentes* during Holy Week, or like Luis lamenting the new tractor that had been ruined by a man who didn't understand it. I would never, because I had never heard them, regret the absence of peasants singing on a summer evening as they wended their way home from the fields of *Los Vientos* where they had been working all day.

Spain was Franco and prisons and people who were afraid to speak out for fear someone would turn them in; Spain was the iron hand of the repressive religion of the Catholic Church, which imprisoned women with rules that made them nothing but servants of the men around them, things I hated, but what was I doing about that? I was out in the campo swilling sangria and filling myself with fine food. I never thought of anything but joy on those mornings Luis and I went into the olive groves and passed the horses and bulls. I didn't want, on those days, to know why other people's lives didn't work. I didn't even want to admit there *were* other people. It was just Luis and me and the earth all around us shining in the sun and the wind blowing across the dry plains and making our faces warm with its memories of the Sahara.

I wrote and wrote. A novel was coming to life under the keys I punched every morning until I was so empty that I couldn't think of one more word. I lay down and listened to the cricket's song of *Los Vientos,* and then I arose, took up my Spanish grammar, and tried to learn some new words. I was going to learn Spanish. I was going to—the gods themselves know what. I knew what I thought—that I could have *everything.*

I remember the first time I danced with him. We were in the living room sitting around the big wagon-wheel table (that I thought was so ugly) with maybe half a dozen Americans from the base having drinks. Sometimes a wife or two came, but often I was the only woman. I think of this as Luis in his American period. He was a great hit with the commander at the base who brought over big-shot guests to introduce to "his friend the count."

We had just come back from looking at the bulls from the Land Rover. Luis put on a record, old, out of date and scratchy, like everything else in Spain. He said, Would you like to dance? I got up, feeling very conspicuous, and went to Luis. We stood there awkwardly. Our hands had touched, but never our bodies. We moved slowly toward each other. Luis put out his arms, and I moved cautiously into them. The others were watching us. They'll know, I thought. One of those men wanted to marry me. I had been dating him on and off for months and didn't know really how I felt about him. But as soon as my body touched Luis's, I was sure it was like holding up a large sign with big, thick, black capital letters: THEY WANT EACH OTHER.

I was sitting at the typewriter one morning in my faded culottes and an old ripped tee shirt stained brown from the French canal waters, trying to rewrite a scene that had come out all wrong. I had my bare feet hooked around the runners of the chair, although I loved the cool feeling of the tiles on my feet. Carmella didn't complain if I went barefoot in the house. She had a pair of sandals by the door of my study, and she had come to believe my theory that bare feet kept the tile floors cleaner than shoes.

Luis was always dropping in unexpectedly. He would stay for lunch, which was apparently permissible, but never dinner. Carmella could serve as a sort of chaperone during daylight, but she went home at nightfall. As soon as it started to get dark, he would immediately be on his way.

We never knew when he was coming, so we always had to be prepared. There was always food leftover, because Luis was always bringing me things from the *finca* and buying exotic foods in town. Keeping food was a problem—no one had a refrigerator. Even Luis didn't have one out at the *ganadería*. I had Carmella take the leftovers home. I liked to think of Carmella's mother eating those exotic, expensive things she had never tasted before in her life.

When Luis came, my days were radiant; when he left or didn't come, I was plunged into despair. Without him, my life seemed to have no purpose. I would try to conquer the feelings of being bereft by working all day and into the night, and still I felt the sick sensation that I was nothing without him. I remembered his saying, I can't lose you, and I would think, I can't lose you either, but I don't know what we're supposed to do to get past all the differences.

I was sitting at the typewriter in my ratty old clothes, my working clothes. I didn't think Luis would come. I had seen him the day before, so I really didn't expect him to turn up for lunch. My face and fingers were smudged from the new typewriter ribbon I had been trying to insert, and I was not in a good humor when Carmella (in shoes) came in and said, *Una señora. Muy elegante. Aqui. Para usted.*

Carmella gave me one of her looks. I put out my cigarette and dutifully donned my sandals and pattered down the hall where a woman stood who, had I been back in Indianapolis, would have been making an unannounced visit to check to see if I were a fit candidate for proposing membership in the Junior League.

"I'm Luis's mother," she said in English.

She had on elegant shoes, which I thought must be Italian. The Italians make the most supple, beautiful shoes in the world. I had always wanted an Italian shoemaker to take my thin foot in his hand and marvel at its shape. Oh, he would say, I can make you the most perfect shoes in the world.

There was Luis's mother, in her perfect shoes, and there I stood in my cheap sandals. It seemed like a parable, but I am capable of finding parables and symbols anywhere I look. It is the curse of the writer.

It wasn't as if I weren't expecting something like this, just not today, when nothing was going right, and I looked like the rag picker's daughter, and my novel was lying on my desk DOA with no hope of resuscitation.

"Can I have Carmella get you some coffee or tea?" When all else fails, be polite. Polite people have the advantage—and those who speak first always lose. So in the cosmic scheme of things, I was fifty/fifty.

Luis's mother sat down. "I expect you're wondering what I'm doing here." Unlike Carmella, she paid no attention to my ill-shod feet and faded culottes, an outfit "a proper young lady" should not have been wearing anywhere at any time of the day, especially in Spain.

I thought she had come to tell me how inappropriate it was that I had been seeing her son. I had no idea what I was going to say to her. It was obvious that someone as elegant as she looked hardly deserved "It's none of your damn business."

"The truth is—" She paused, obviously as uncomfortable as I was. "The truth is Luis has talked about you—"

And you've come to see for myself.

"Let me ask you if Luis has talked to you about his sister, Maria Concepción."

"I just know he has a sister named that. I think I saw her once at the bullfights in Seville, but I don't think he's ever really talked about her, not really about either of them." The other one had me try on those rings, I thought. Then it struck me: he had wanted a ring to give to me. Like an engagement ring. And none of them had fit. How apt.

"Maria Concepción has had a very bad time. She married a man we all thought was going to be just right for her, and it turns out he has a very bad temper. He beats her—"

I sat up with a start. I was remembering my father, the man who beat his wife and children and made everyone around him constantly fearful waiting for his next outburst. People who looked like this woman didn't have people like that in their families.

"There's not much we can do about it. Luis has told him if he does it again, he will—well, he will take measures. But I don't really think there's much he could do, short of killing him, and of course he can't do that, much as he might want to. She has three children, and she can't leave him."

I wanted to say to her, Where is your imagination? Why don't you plan a little hunting "accident"? People are always out at *Los Vientos* shooting. It's what the goddamn place was given to you for. Surely some kind of plausible shot through the head could be arranged.

She was saying, "If she left him, he would keep the children. Yes, he could, and there wouldn't be anything she—or anyone else—could do about it. She has no rights. Women in Spain don't have any real rights at all."

Not keep her children? Of course she would leave with her children. She was their mother. Then I remembered the story about the girl who had raised the bull and pleaded with her father not to send it to the ring, and he had sent it anyway.

Luis wasn't like that. He would never have sent the bull.

How do you know that? You don't know that. You just want to think that.

"I know from what Luis tells me that you have a mind of your own. I think that's what he likes about you. I know when you got married you weren't married in the Catholic Church, that you aren't Catholic."

Here we went with The Church again. "I was born Catholic, or at least brought up Catholic, but I haven't been to church in years—"

"What I meant—" a long breath—"since you weren't married in the Catholic Church, you weren't really married in the eyes of the Church. You could be married in the Church now, and it would be like you had never been married."

"I'm not a Catholic, and I'll never go back to being one. I've seen enough of what goes on in the Church."

"That's not the real problem. One way or another, that could be dealt with. If you have money and friends in the right places, you can make problems like that go away." How could Luis's mother cast out the Catholic Church so glibly when for centuries it had been the bedrock of Spanish life? It occurred to me you had to be really rich to be able to do that. I wanted to say, If you can fix the church, can't you manage to make it look like an accident when someone shoots the man who beats your daughter?

"The real problem is that you'd have to become Spanish if you stayed here." It was obvious I didn't get it. "Become a Spanish citizen. And you'd have to live like a Spanish girl." I stared at her in complete disbelief. "All foreign women who marry Spaniards have to take out Spanish citizenship."

*Become a part of Fascist murderers?*

"But it wouldn't only be that. You'd have to *live* in a different way. You'd be Luis's wife. I sympathize with you," she said earnestly. "You don't know how many times in my life I've wanted to speak up, to talk back, not to be just a wife. I went to school in England; it's why I made sure all my children went to school there. But they came home, their lives are here, they are Spanish, not English. I tried to do what I thought was best for them. I wanted them to know something besides how things are here. Maybe it was a mistake."

I had pictured a woman full of fire to protect her son from a *married* American woman who was going to ruin his life. What I saw in front of me was a woman who wanted to save me from living a life that she thought would ruin both his and mine.

She would be right. If I stayed, I would be aligned with the kind of people who murdered Garcia Lorca and at least a hundred thousand others who wanted the legitimately elected government to remain in power. I would be a writer who lived amongst people who hated poets like Garcia Lorca because they told the truth.

"He loves you," she said in a helpless way. "I can tell from the way he says '*Mi norteamericana*,' and sometimes it's as if he isn't even listening when I talk to him—even though he's standing right in front of me. He doesn't see me because he's so caught up with what's inside his head." She paused and then went reluctantly on. "I suppose you're with him, even though you're not there. He's so jittery all the time, as if he can't stay still a single minute. Sometimes when I look at him, it's almost as if I don't know him, he's changed so much. Men and women can't live at that kind of fever pitch."

They have a name for people like me in India. It's Mahamaya, the Weaver of Illusions, the woman who trapped men with passion, which was like, the Indians said, the trap of death. I know that because years later I went to India (several times) trying to track down my karma. It's still there so far as I know, because I never found it. Well, there were men who were traps of death, too. Why wasn't there a name for them?

"They have to go back to the ordinary world, and then they look at each other, and what do they see?"

She waited for me to answer. I thought of the bullfighters who showed their bravery at the Gates of Fear by spitting contemptuously before the other dry-mouthed fighters to demonstrate their courage. This woman across from me would have had no trouble at all spitting at the Gates of Fear. She loved her son with the kind of love I had longed for from my mother all my life. If I had cut my throat to show my mother how much I cared for her, she would have complained I was getting blood on the rug.

This woman loved her son—of course she loved her son—but she could see that if her son got the woman he thought he loved, that woman would soon be so constrained by the society around her that she would turn into somebody else, somebody her son wouldn't love. When we sat at that huge table in the dining room and had guests and they talked about Franco, he would see the hate in my eyes. Perhaps I would even look at him one day with hate.

In Greek myths, when the gods give you something, they can never take it back, but if they become unhappy with what they have given they can make the gift one that poisons your whole life. Homer tells us that Apollo loved Cassandra and gave her the gift of prophesy if she would love him. She took the gift and then turned her back on him, so Apollo made it so that when she prophesized, no one believed her. Cassandra would have saved Troy if the Trojans had believed her. They would not have taken the wooden horse into the city. But they didn't believe her. And so, rejoicing at their having driven the Achaeans away, they dragged the wooden horse into Troy, drank themselves senseless, and lay besotted when the wily Odysseus and his band of warriors came out of the wooden horse, opened the gates for the rest of their army, butchered all the men in Troy, and made the women their captives.

Cassandra saw her own future. She would be taken as a slave back to Agamemnon's palace and murdered by his conniving wife and her lover. She saw Agamemnon caught in a net as he washed the war off of his skin and was slaughtered before he could do more than cry out. Cassandra had warned him, but of course he didn't believe her.

This woman was warning me. She had displeased no god who would make what she said not be believed. I saw into the future she was painting, and the image was so bleak that there wasn't one bit of brave hope left in my heart. The only consoling thing I could think was that it would be all right to stop trying to learn Spanish.

"We have always thought—we've always thought there was a girl he would marry, a girl he's known all his life, and we all thought he cared for her." Luis's mother was pointing out to me what I already knew: in Spain the family is the center of everything, binding generations together, insuring continuity and place of position. Luis was the only son. They were all depending on him—and the woman he would marry. What did I have to recommend me? I couldn't even speak the language, and language is the glue that holds people together, that permits them to take their proper (so far as Luis's mother was concerned anyway) place in their rightful world. When you can't understand what is being said around you, you are cut off from that world.

I had thought Luis and I might be a bridge to a new way of getting out of what I considered a constricted feudal world. What I saw in his mother's eyes was that love wasn't sufficient for the task. It couldn't keep up the strength needed to succeed. I didn't want to be a *Spanish* wife—meek, subservient, the doting mother of as many children as Luis put in me because there was no birth control in Spain. I remembered almost being arrested for indecency because I was wearing a bathing suit, even if in my eyes it was modest enough. It had had a little skirt, for crissake! That bare skin at the waist had been a means for Satan to use his black power to provoke the evil passions of innocent men: the Virgin Mother or the temptress Ava Gardner, one or the other. A woman couldn't be both. Luis's mother was looking at me and seeing temptation, ruin, and damnation. I was looking at me and seeing an imprisonment that I would never be able to escape. I had got away from my other jailers, my father and my boat-husband and Indianapolis, but if I married Luis, I would be in a country that put me behind bars forever and only let me be a baby machine and a husband's toy when he fancied one, less even than a second-class citizen.

Luis couldn't bring into his world a woman who looked in contempt at all the Falangist men that surrounded her. Such a woman would be a threat to the whole family, not just Luis. "I'm sure he cares for this girl, but he—but he doesn't love her, not the way he cares about you. In the beginning it would be all right, but then the passion would die down—passion always does, my dear, whatever you think—"

I had come to the time when I realized you could come to curse the gods for the good things they gave you.

"—and then everything would start to go wrong. Men here think they have the right to have any women they want—yes, they do, they *all* do—and they hit their wives—yes, they do, all of them."I pictured Luis's father hitting this beautiful, elegant woman, and I felt so sick that I couldn't speak.

"Even if you wanted to leave and somehow got out, you would have to leave your children behind. You might not be able to leave at all."

She seemed so sure of what she was saying that I imagined things I wouldn't even have been able to imagine five minutes before. I thought of that day in the corridor of the bullfight ring when Luis had my head pinned against him and the words kept pouring of him, when for a moment I thought he was going to take his fists and beat against my back, how I had panicked, as if this man I thought I knew might be capable of a violence I couldn't even imagine.

"I can tell from the look on your face that you understand what I'm saying, and that you must love my son, too, or you wouldn't have that look. Being in love is one thing, marrying another. Believe me, my dear, marriage brings out the worse in people. And believe me when I say that you would come to hate it here."

*"Oh, my god," he had said in English, "I have never felt like this about anybody in my life, and I'm so afraid I'm going to lose you. Don't you understand I can't lose you?"*

Everything had been built on illusion. Luis's mother was trying to make me see that. He would never be mine. He had never been mine.

I pictured Luis standing before the altar at the chapel at *Los Vientos* with its crucified Christ waiting for a woman who had no face as she came down the aisle in a froth of white; she who would change everything about the house, she who was Spanish and would have Luis and the gods that inhabited *Los Vientos* and everything that for a moment I had thought I might one day claim as mine.

"I wanted to see you and tell you not to do anything you would regret, that would ruin both your lives. I wanted to ask you to do what has to be done, and to ask you not to tell Luis that I came. Will you be kind enough to do that?"

I couldn't talk. I just sat and looked at her. Spanish men put such emphasis on bravery, but it was the women who were the ones that truly had *corazón*.

When a bullfighter retires, he cuts the *coleta,* that knot of hair that he wears in a small bun tied up in a ribbon under the back of his hat when he goes into the ring. Some of the men let their own hair grow long and then, when they are never going to fight again, they take that hair in their hands and cut through it. Some of them have a little artificial knob of hair that they attach, and when they retire, they take that *coleta* and burn it. You never throw a *coleta* away. Sometimes you even see one on a private altar of a bullfighter who has left the profession. Cutting the *coleta* for a bullfighter meant everything that mattered to him was at an end.

I am going to cut my *coleta,* I thought.

"Will you promise me you won't tell Luis I came here to see you?"

"I won't tell him."

She was at the door before I had even gotten out of my chair. I ran to the window and watched her walk down the path to a long, gleaming black car. A man with a peaked cap got out and opened the door for her. She turned and looked up at the house and nodded once. I nodded back, a kind of pledge of honor, and then she got in the car. The chauffeur closed the door, and I could no longer see her behind the tinted glass. It occurred to me there must be some symbolism between the Land Rover and the Bentley, but I was in distress. I couldn't connect anything, least of all the symbols or signs the gods were giving me.

Nothing seemed to be what I had thought it was. Luis's own mother could picture him as unfaithful, brutal, a bully to his wife. I wasn't who I wanted to think I was—someone resolute and strong, committed to a future that would put meaning to my life. Luis's mother had painted me into a corner, and the only way I could get out was to walk over wet paint.

I knew that if I said I was leaving he would try to make me stay, just for a little while, he would say; if I stayed, the longer I stayed, the harder it would be to leave. I might never leave.

I was afraid even to see him. I knew that if I saw him, I would at some point or other agree to stay to think it all over. I would even tell him his mother had been to see me. I wouldn't be able to stop myself, and I could think of nothing worse for him. His honor would be offended, *his mother* interfering as if he were a child, *his mother* bringing shame on him. He would never forgive either of us. But if I left without out a word, I would shame him, too. He had laid his kingdom and all its jewels before me, and I had turned my back on those offerings. He would have felt his *pundonor* had been tarnished forever.

I closed my eyes and tried to remember the smell of *Los Vientos*, the *Los Vientos* that could have been the winds of change; I thought of that crooked look Luis had; I was even haunted by that goddamn Land Rover. At that moment, I would have given half my life to sit in it again and look out at the road as we started out toward the meadow where the horses and the bulls were placidly grazing under Luis's Spanish sky. I thought of his earth hands on my shoulders pulling me around to face him. I thought of him saying, I thought about you all the time. I couldn't get you out of my mind.

I knew I would never get him out of my mind, no matter how far I went or how long I lived. I had to leave right away, or I would never go; there was no way I could see him and keep my resolution. I sent him a note. *I don't think this is going to work.* What else was there to say? That the great Spanish knight errant Don Quixote tilted at windmills? Sorry, no happy ending. Cervantes didn't have such a hot life, either. Maybe nobody does.

I left so fast that I gave most of my clothes to Carmella. I like to think of her in a Peck & Peck suit going out to market through the narrow, crowded streets of the Macarena. I like to think some man will see her in her splendid suit and think, I want to know that woman. A woman like that would make a fine wife.

If there were cosmic symbolism, I would have found the cricket dead the morning I left. It hadn't died, but it wasn't singing. I took the small bamboo cage to Carmella and said, Will you take my cricket?

My mother would love that noise it makes, Carmella said. It will keep her company while I am away.

I can't believe that I broke down, that I was weeping over an insect.

I went by ship over all that water; there was nothing but water everywhere I looked, like a punishment. The trip took nearly a week. Then I was back home. Well, I was in America.

He never came to get me. *That* was my moment of truth, and it was as if all the waters of the world closed over me.


"Remember," says that encyclopedia of last resort for those who want to learn Spanish, *Spanish for Dummies, as* I thought of it, "that Spanish is a very precise language. In Spanish, you have two forms of 'to be,' each with a different meaning, to supply more precision to your statements. Unlike in English, when you talk about *being* in Spanish, the verb you use removes any guess work about what your meaning is.

When you speak of permanence in Spanish, you use the verb *ser,* but when you want to indicate something that is a temporary state (being ill, for instance, or just passing through), you use the verb *estar.* So in Spanish, it isn't "to be or not to be," but to be (forever (*ser*) or not forever *(estar).*"

*Estar* is where I am.

Cretan vaulters somersaulting over the horns of the bull

A *rejoneador,* on one of his special horses

The first Chamaco

Tip of bull's horn sawed off before a fight

Porter Tuck in his suit of lights

Luis branding a calf at *Los Vientos*

# FIRE

There is something rather
noble about junk—selected
junk—junk which has
in one era performed
nobly in function for
common man—has by
function been formed by
the smithys hand alone and without
bearings roll or ball has
fulfilled its function, stayed
behind, is not yet relic
or antique, or precious
which has been seen
by the eyes of all men and
and left for me—tobe found
as the cracks in sidewalks
as the grain in wood
as the drop in grass
out of a snow hummock
as the dent in mud from
a bucket of poured tones
as the clouds float and
as the beauties come
tobe used, for an order
tobe arranged—tobe
now perceived
by new ownership

**David Smith**

The first thing you are probably thinking is, Why didn't she (meaning me) clean that poem up and get rid of the mistakes—change *tobe* into two words and put an apostrophe in *smithys*. When I asked Susan Cooke, who overlooks the David Smith estate, that question, she gave me an insightful answer. What Susan Cook said was "some may just be careless mistakes, or errors, committed while writing hastily. Others, such as his habit of writing 'to be' as 'tobe' doesn't seem to me to be an error, but instead he seems deliberately to be conflating the two parts of the infinitive for 'identity' in the same way the he conjoins distinct physical elements to make a sculpture ... the poem is transcribed directly from Smith's sketchbook."

I picture David stopping work for a moment, frowning as he digs around in a pocket for his notebook and scrawls out his thoughts. To hell with punctuation or apostrophes, but *tobe* he deliberately makes one word. He can do that if he wants, can't he? He's David Smith, and what he does is break rules. He does it with huge pieces of metal; certainly he can do it with something as small as a pencil. He means the world to see it as he sees it. That's his mission in life.

In 1969 the *New York Times Magazine* declared that David Smith was "America's Greatest artist." Well, the *Times* hedged a bit. They quoted a critic, Clement Greenberg, who had always championed David's work.

**The Late David Smith—"America's greatest artist" at work—** that was Greenberg's appraisal, not the *New York Times*.

I recognized the bulky figure whose back and bellicose headgear filled the front-page magazine picture, except that I couldn't see his hands, which were occupied with shaping metal in a workshop. I had been in that garage-like building many times. The picture was right for David, though: An enormous piece of metal is dangling from a thick chain in front of him. Sparks spangle the air around him. Smoke hangs over everything. ***The world conceived in his fire.***

Huge piles of scrap metal, broken appliances, strange discarded tools, indefinable iron objects would be haphazardly stacked in corners of a workshop that looked like the devil's inferno: David Smith, the American Hephaestus. What he molds into his metal sculptures is like nothing that has ever come before, though there will be countless imitators that come after.

I would have reprinted that cover here, but the *New York Times* informed me it would cost me *$1,125* to do that. After a moment's consideration, I decided that readers who wanted to see the cover could look it up on the *Times*, which I was assured by the woman at the *Times* was free if readers would sign up:

> Please be advised that linking to an article on the *New York Times* website is free of charge and does not require permission. You do, however have to use the publisher's URL, which will take your readers back to the *New York Times* website, in which they have to be member, or become a member.
>
> Membership is free of charge and only takes a minute to complete. For further information on linking, please see the URL:
>
> http://www.nytimes.com/membercenter/faq/linking.html
>
> If you wish to use any other copyright content (i.e. logo), then permission is needed and copyright fees will apply. Thank you for your consideration.

Actually, if it hadn't been for Greenberg, David might never have received the universal (well, at least in the Western world) recognition he deserved. Greenberg immediately saw that David was someone with an American passion for individualism that, combined with his indigenous stubbornness, would lead him to create a form of distinctly American sculpture.

David would have been happy the *Times* put him on the cover of their Sunday magazine section and not at all happy that no one could tell what he looked like because the picture on the cover was of his *back*.

*David who?* a friend of mine that I used to believe had a large IQ asked. What kind of person can't remember the name Smith?

David Smith, the person who has changed the way people look at sculpture, I said dogmatically.

I don't think I've ever seen any of his things.

Where were you not looking? At the Met, at the Tate, at any

prestigious museum where there is at least one Smith piece? I didn't say this. I've given up thinking most people care anything about art, have ever bothered to learn the basic Greek myths that have shaped Western culture, have read *any* part of the Bible, have any knowledge of the great epics of ancient times from *Gilgamesh* to the *Ramayana,* know anything about the history that has given them their present civilization. TV is their educator. They get their world view from something that looks like a large, living postcard.

Inside, in the article, the *New York Times*'s caption underneath the picture of David's back reads, "David Smith working on a sculpture with an acetylene torch in his studio." It was not gas acetylene at all, but electrical arc welding that David was using in that photo. Can't the United States' greatest newspaper even get that right? Then again, who cares what he was welding with? Well, David would have.

David would have banged on his huge work table in frustration. I loved that large length of wood that for some reason I believed monks had once supped upon. It had cost a pretty penny—he would never tell me how much—and it was lovely, a refectory piece (I think) from the seventeenth or eighteenth century worth a fortune. I could not believe that on that priceless piece of furniture he was constantly drawing with pen, crayons, watercolor, charcoal, pots of enamel, paint sprays, anything that came to hand when he was in the middle of scrawling as fast as he could something he saw inside of his head—human figures, animals, birds, insects, landscapes, mythical creatures, symbolic arrangements, abstractions and nudes nudes nudes, all of it giving (at least to me) an impression of an interior raging fire trying to be transferred outside onto paper. It took too long to make one of his gigantic sculptures without an initial plan to guide him. But mostly I was worried about the table.

"You shouldn't use an expensive table like that," I said primly. I was living on so little that seeing something so expensive being mistreated shocked me. We all set our idea of what a price should be in our adolescence. In mine, it was the five-and-dime; now it's the dollar store, and I understand they're going to change that to the dollar ninety-nine.

"It's *my* table," he said testily. Then I noticed that he was always careful to cover the table with paper from an enormous roll he kept stashed in the corner before he began to draw. He no doubt knew the value of that table down to the last penny, and he belonged to the five-and-dime generation. In time, I came to see he was exceedingly careful about his investments (and that included past wives) but not so stringent about his own expenditures. Frugal is the New England word I believe would cover it, though in point of fact he had been born in Indiana in one of those places that think art is Elvis on velvet.

At least you have a decent name, I remember saying to him. *Smith?* he hollered at me. You think *Smith* is a decent name? There are millions of *Smiths* in the world, probably millions of David *Smiths.*

Well, at least people can spell Smith, I said. Nobody spells my last name right.

I too came from Indiana, I had a last name nobody could spell, and my first name had an ugly sound about it. Having a name you despise is a disadvantage from the day of your birth; it's as if your parents wanted to give you that ill-favored name the first time they looked at your small, red, wrinkled face so that you got payback because they wanted a boy and got a girl. Jean. Jean Marie. This is hardly a good start for someone who wants to be a writer who will be remembered far after her body has fed the worms.

David also hated the name Jean because it had belonged to his second wife, from whom he had not parted amicably. He avoided using the name I preferred for myself—Rik—by referring to me as "Girl," a generic term I imagine made it possible for him not to bother learning the names of any of the various women in his life. I think he also said "Kiddo." He belonged to the generation that called women girls and used outdated terms like kiddo without realizing it classified him as Over the Hill. He didn't seem a lot older to me, though in point of fact he was more than twenty-five years my senior, because he had so much energy and such enthusiasm for life.

Years before I went on my excursion on the *Blotto,* Roy Bongartz had taken me up to Bolton Landing to meet David. Very few people knew who David Smith was then, but Roy was always ten years ahead of everyone else in discovering up-and-coming artists, the way he always knew good restaurants before they became popular or could tell a film of resonance from one that had popular appeal.

Roy drove the two of us up to Bolton Landing in one of those clunker cars he was always nursing along. When David came out to meet us, I looked in disbelief at this man who seemed all bulk. He didn't even look American. He didn't look like any nationality, unless it was something odd like Latvian or Estonian, one of those offbeat countries I'd heard about but could not have located on a map. He had enormous hands and feet. His chest was so broad that even in a triple-X shirt, he would have strained the seams. His voice boomed out of his body like some great gong you might find in a Tibetan monastery.

Roy was leaning out the car window explaining who I was. I'm not even sure David remembered Roy, but he roared we were welcome, come on in, come on in and have a drink, it must be cocktail hour time somewhere.

David shepherded Roy and me into a house made of cement blocks, pulled out a bottle of something, and led us through the kitchen into a smallish living room with a large picture window that looked out on an endless parade of enormous pieces of sculpture.

The house seemed cramped for so large a man, who at that moment sat in a worn, overstuffed leather chair talking his head off. I could see behind him into the kitchen where this pretty woman was at the sink violently scrubbing something (baby bottles?), two toddlers hanging off her. She never came into the living room; I don't remember David even introducing her. It seemed to me she was at the sink the whole time I was there. I had the impression she was tiny and frail, but Michael Brenson, who is doing the definitive biography on David, told me she was tall. About my height, he thought. I think I thought she was small because she had no role that day except as a drudge.

Why doesn't she speak up? I thought. Why is she letting this man get away with behaving as if she didn't even exist?

Maybe they'd had a quarrel before we came and weren't speaking. Even so, he should at least have introduced her. That was just common courtesy. Perhaps he thought he was punishing her by ignoring her existence.

At that first meeting, I thought, There is something the matter here. I don't know what it is. Maybe it's just the usual fight for power between a man and a woman who have had the misfortune to marry one another.

Don't let him get away with this, I wanted to shout at her. Start a new life. Get a pail and scrub brush and wash away the print marks from where you walked out of the house. Throw away the shoes you walked out in. Go buy a great new purse and begin a new life. Be somebody besides a bottle washer—advice she must have eventually given herself, because the second time I saw David she was long since gone.

He arrived at ten thirty at night (odd-hour encounters were, I was to learn, characteristic) with a *Life* photographer in tow. I had just moved into the Bolton Landing cottage overlooking Lake George a couple of months or so before, and I had dropped David a note asking him if he still had that small piece of sculpture *The Puritan* that I had admired years before when Roy Bongartz had brought me up, before Roy had met Cee.

Probably David didn't even remember Roy Bongartz or me. Why should he? Who were we but a couple of drop-ins without any interesting credentials?

Two, maybe three months went by. I had forgotten the note when one night, the house began to rattle and shake. My daughter was asleep, and I was afraid that gigantic rumbling would awake her, and I ran to the door and opened it to find David and an exceedingly tall, thin man identified as the photographer from *Life*. David had a quart of whiskey in one hand. He uncorked it between his teeth, spit the top out, and clumped into the cottage. It took several episodes of cork disposals for me to realize that he meant I'm not taking any home. We're supposed to drink the whole damn thing.

Fifteen minutes and two drinks later, he disappeared. He was on his way, he informed the *Life* man and me, to get some lobster. An hour passed, then maybe thirty minutes more. My god, I thought, he's probably gone all the way to Albany to get the lobster.

We had just had a blizzard. The *Life* photographer and I gazed out on a world of endless chalky drifts. We had run out of small talk, and god alone knew what had happened to David. The *Life* man began to prowl about restlessly. There wasn't much room to prowl. Finally, anchored at a window bleakly looking out at all that white, he said, "Got any candles?"

I handed over my supply. He bundled himself up, went out into that winter wasteland, and ran from drift to drift, scooping out altars in the snow then setting lighted candles in the niches. Presently a world of flickering snow altars lay outside my kitchen window. Inside, the prodigal returned. David was at a skillet doing something ambrosial with lobster, wine, shallots, and rice. Nothing, but nothing, has ever tasted as good as that dish which David tried unsuccessfully time and again to duplicate. At David's funeral, I ran into the *Life* man again. I thought he had no recollection of that night; too many other, more interesting evenings had intervened. That turned out not to be true. He remembered very well. He had even taken pictures of my daughter amongst the sculpture, though I had cut her hair so short that he kept referring to her as "your son."

Years later, I tried to trace those pictures. I thought my daughter would like copies of that special time in her life, something she would treasure, but by then Dan Budnik had become of a something of a recluse and never answered my letters. I thought I understood; at that time, I was also hiding out from the world. I didn't want to go back in time to those memories. So many of them were too painful to resurrect.

I must back up. What am I doing in Bolton Landing with a small daughter with hair cropped so close to her scalp that she has been mistaken for a boy?

After I got off the ship in the United States in 1959, I came back to a country I didn't know what to do with. I had no idea at all what had been going on in the United States. In Spain, few American magazines or newspapers had been available, and the ones that were on newsstands had been so heavily censored that sometimes the articles made no sense.

While Luis was in Spain riding one of his blooded stallions through heat and scrub and a vast vista of bony landscape, I was in the land of the free and the home of the brave trying to make some sense of what I had done. I told myself, Two headstrong people can't live in the same house. They run up against each other's oddities and eccentricities, and they feel crowded and trapped. But a voice inside answered back, *Los Vientos* was a *very* big house. The two of you might not have been so crowded that you came to wonder what had ever brought you together in the first place, an idea that might be described as a martini of the mind.

The risks are always great when any momentous change is to take place. Luis had had the courage to try. I had not. At the moment when I most needed courage, I had failed. That indictment shadowed me endlessly, refusing to go away.

Besides my political innocence about the United States, I knew nothing about the latest fads in food and clothes, had never heard of the plays on Broadway and Off Broadway; didn't recognize any of the titles of the new films in the movie houses; couldn't fathom the music that was being played on the radio, loud and raucous and full of allusions I didn't understand.

The college friend I was staying with and with whom I had shared my most intimate secrets a few years before now seemed like a visitor from another planet. Yet I was one of the people who could only be called American. It said so on my birth certificate, on my passport, but I didn't feel as if I were the same nationality or had been raised in the same country or even came from the same human species. *Death in the Afternoon* was no longer of any use to me; I bought the bibles of the new America, *Howl* and *On the Road,* and went to poetry/jazz readings of Allen Ginsberg and his busy Beat friends in Greenwich Village but more often around St. Mark's Place. The Village had become too expensive for artists, who had begun to migrate toward the east side of town, around Second Avenue and St. Mark's Place, where I hung out trying to learn the argot of the Beats.

Try to imagine a time before computers, cell phones, Blackberries, credit cards, e-mail, fax, the Net; CNN, CSpan, *Entertainment Tonight*; a time before globalization, with its rapacious robber barons whose special interest groups controlled the government; before agribusiness, green house contaminants; when the Cold War was in full throttle and no one had heard of AIDS; a far-distant time when American citizens were enamored of Naugahyde, rumpus rooms, Tupperware, polyester, split-level track houses that ran for hundreds of miles where once there had been leafy trees and quiet creeks and green groves that shadowed the nests of breeding birds.

When I landed in New York City, I was overwhelmed by spires of metal, plastic and tinted glass, by millions of manically energized people racing from one place to another who gave off a kinetic energy like that of high-wire circus performers. My lungs took in soot and smoke until my heart slowed so that I felt as if it were ticking to a stop. At last I understood the phrase "stranger in a strange land."

The women on the TV in front of me wore fancy color-coordinated clothes to show they were safe in the suburbs, these perfectly dressed and coiffured wives performing menial tasks who never sweated, never wept, had never thrown a dish against a wall, had never been on a small boat in perilous seas, or had never known what it was like to stand in wide open spaces gazing out at running bulls. They were appliances, these women, like their new magic dishwashers and washing machines. In some ways, Carmella was better off than they were. These women were domestic servants who didn't get paid a wage. Carmella could at least go home at night and get out of her uniform—but don't forget the old, ailing mother, I thought, and the room with a single overhead bulb burning a hole in the dark, windowless room. The only real light to that room came from the door that opened onto the covered veranda that ran all the way around the building and looked out over the yard where the washing and water drawing were done. I saw Carmella walking down the street in one of my outfits and Luis running up behind her and grabbing hold of her and pulling her around and—

And what?

And he cries out in dismay. I want him to suffer, the way I was grieving, thinking I never should have left, and there was no going back, even if I wanted to. I didn't have two hundred dollars in my bank account to buy a boat ticket back. I owed my boat-husband a thousand dollars. I didn't even have a completed book. What I had were fear and trepidation and a collection of papers that didn't seem to go together to claim they were a novel.

While you are getting ready, Luis, to go on your honeymoon (and where would that be, if I may be so bold as to ask?) with you and your lovely bride disporting on beds both lengthy and luxurious, I am lying in the dark trying to put the pieces of each time we were together where they belong, but they won't fit, or I have lost or misplaced some of the parts.

You cannot even write me a letter, Luis, and say I had made a mistake—you could never in a million years know where I am. You probably don't even give me a moment's thought. *NO*, I don't believe that. I don't ever want to believe that.

Writers, it has been pointed out again and again, are close friends of despair. And don't forget poverty and alcohol, Henry Miller had added. The people of my unfinished novel moved about in my mind more real than the people around me composed of actual flesh and bone and blood, more real even than you, Luis. And who were you, Luis? The man I brought home with me inside my head, the man I remembered—or the fragments of what I remembered—or someone I had concocted, someone who didn't really exist at all, an illusion, one of those tricks that make you think you have found what you've been searching for, and it's going to last forever, but when real life intrudes, it's gone, and you have to live with disappointment and regret for the rest of your life.

It occurs to me (too often) that I have made up Luis out of what I wanted him to be, that I in no way know who Luis really was. So I have lost him twice—once when I left him, and now as I tell myself that he was only the illusions I had brought back with me from Spain.

I am back in a country I don't know or care to know, with its raucous, crazy, cacophonous pace, while you are back home, Luis, tumbling around on the sheets with your new wife, or shortly will be.

His mother got into that big black car. She had my word.

So at least I left the arena with *pundunor*.

**What if his mother had been lying?**

No, she would never do that.

How do you know that? What if she *had* been lying?

I should have said to the mother, I can't make you any promises.

But I have a genius for making mistakes.

Each time I have loved, says Susan Sherman in *The Color of the Heart*,

> I have left part of myself behind
> until now I am mostly memory
> mostly dream

I myself feel stripped to the essentials, like plain little Emily Dickinson, though I am probably a whole head taller than the Maid of Amherst, who with her prim, spinster ways secreted herself away, writing poisoned poems that would screw themselves into your brain until you couldn't get them out. They would hunt you down no matter how far you tried to run from them. Did Emily Dickinson really know what a demon she was, sitting there in her starched white dress putting the pen between her lips to think,

> For each ecstatic instant
> We must an anguish pay
> In keen and quivering ratio
> To the ecstasy.

I'm getting close to the time, thirty, when you're not forgiven mistakes: you have to have justification for your behavior. I don't have much time left. While you are back there getting ready, Luis, to walk down the aisle (or have already taken those steps), I'm here in the United States, and I need a new me, Luis. What I tell myself is, A hardened heart is a powerful tool.

I don't care if women writers aren't taken seriously. I don't care that I am relegated to the category of "woman writer," which means that the books I turned out are supposed to be books that only *women* buy. I am going to write the books I want to write. I am not an auth*oress*.

It is not only Spain, I see, that puts its limitations on women. It is the fact that I am **a handful**. I have always had the instantaneous suspicions of the outsider, always been restless and questioning, and I'm not going to change. That much I know; I don't care what the cost.

People do change the conditions of their lives—but, and this was a big *but*—in the midst of inventing a new life they always have, alas, their same old selves.

This is not a comforting conclusion.

I believed, like Roy Bongartz, that shallowness was a sin, but despair might be the most serious sin of all, worse even than murder, because it meant giving up on life. Churchill used to call that cornered feeling The Coming of the Black Dog. Vachel Lindsay drank Lysol to get away from it. Chatterton hanged himself. He was only seventeen, a beautiful boy who wrote wondrous poems, but even at seventeen he didn't want to deal with the black dog. I had learned a lot of references to things that went wrong in people's lives from my boat-husband on that long ride on the water, the waters of life you might say, and then from the parched lands of *Los Vientos* where my heart lay, not even decently buried, waiting for Luis's wife to walk over it in beautiful high-heeled Italian shoes and grind it into the ground.

What I needed was luck, but the gods are not in the luck business. They've got other priorities.

Anyway, religion is the opium of the people.

*Opiate!*

Whatever.

He had been ready to take a chance, and I had not.

I had choices, however. I could be like Roy Bongartz, who had unaccountably arrived at our place in England with a woman, a very beautiful woman—Cee her name was, and she was a vegetarian, at which time my husband and I looked at each other wondering how in the world we were going to feed her for the three days they were scheduled to stay. It was very odd to think of Roy attached to someone. He had always seemed to me a solitary savant. His ambivalent attitude to an extended romance demonstrated itself the next day, when he went out into the middle of that deserted dirt road in England where we lived, my boat-husband and I, in an authentic Tudor house that sounds romantic but had no plumbing, electricity, or heat, and only one tap of cold water with no way to bathe except by bowl.

Roy carried a suitcase out to the road that ran by that thatched- roof cottage and sat down on it in the middle of the road and just sat there hour after hour. Finally, Cee went out and said to him, What the hell are you doing? Roy said, I am giving up.

If I were to choose a metaphor that would have been more *accurate* to describe how I felt on my return to America, I would say that I felt like one of those Aztec sacrificial unfortunates, the beating heart torn out of me, blood running down the ridges of my body, my arms and legs amputated to be sold later as meat in the people's market.

If someone else had showed such self-pity, I would have been filled with contempt. Nothing *really* bad had happened to me. I wasn't driven out of my house, whipped into a cattle car, and carried away to a concentration camp. I wasn't being systematically tortured (I was doing that to myself). I wasn't dragged into the weeds and gang-raped until my insides gave up so much blood that I died. I wasn't led out to stand in front of a ditch and gunned down so that my body conveniently fell over into the ditch where dirt could be thrown over me and I didn't take up any more time in being dispatched than was absolutely necessary. I just hadn't got what I wanted.

But every day that Luis didn't come to get me—I still clung to the hope he would—made the hole in my heart larger.

So I had a hole in my heart. Probably everyone over ten had holes in their hearts. Why should I be any different from the rest of the world? Because that had always been my goal. How egocentric can you get?

Some days, I was so overcome with pain that I was ready to go out into the road the way Roy Bongartz had and give up. Don't you *dare* think like that, I would tell myself. You rode all over *Los Vientos* on horseback. You bumped over all that rough ground in the Land Rover and never once complained. You even wanted to help brand the calves. You were indefatigable. Luis would put his arm around your shoulder and turn you toward him. His eyes were shining. His mouth was twisted into a smile. *Muy fuerte, mi northeamericana,* he would say proudly.

What did he mean, **my** *northamericana*? I'm nobody's anything. But at the time, I loved him saying that. It sounded as if he would keep me with him the rest of my life. I won't forget you, I promised the empty air all around. Please don't forget me.

You know I will never forget you, he tells me inside my head.

I had $179.32 in my bank account and a book that still needed to be finished. Not that I knew what to do with it if I ever got it done.

My husband called me and asked me to lunch. We were to meet in the lobby of one of those new modern buildings that look like a stack of large, discarded kitchen appliances. I stood by the information desk watching identical-looking men in gray flannel suits striding purposefully by. They had no distinguishing characteristic to tell one from the other. I did not recognize my husband when he came up and stood beside me. He might have been any one of those hundreds of automatons scrambling out into Manhattan madness. He had to tap me on the arm to get my attention.

"You're wearing a hat." It sounded like an indictment, though the gray little hat with its understated row of small brass buttons in a circle all around the brim was, I thought, just the sort of thing Lady Brett would have worn to undermine an opponent. I will **never** tell anyone how much I paid for that hat and for the expensive gray matching gloves. I had on one of the great dresses of my life, red wool with a high, rounded collar and very subtle crisscrossing diagonals of gray that the hat and gloves reflected. I had donned my *traje de luces* and was going in the ring to face my Miura bull.

I still mourn the loss of that dress, the way I mourn that dress I spilled wine on the first time I met Luis. The moths ate holes in it that couldn't be camouflaged. It became a dress to let in oxygen. Everything needs air, even apparel.

I didn't want my husband back. Why then had I squandered money to make him sorry he'd ever lost me? We had lived together for nearly eight years. Surely when he looked at me, he could see the damage reflected in my face, which should have been a source of satisfaction to him. He could file it with all those other horrible accounts he collected: wives who were stoned to death or buried alive; traitors whose death came by small, slow slicing; Mogul rulers who had the teeth of their enemies brought to them in soft suede bags; prisoners left chained while the tide was out so that they would drown slowly as it came in; an antagonist's heart cut out and put through a meat grinder to make succulent patties to serve to the enemy.

We went out a revolving door, my boat-husband and I, into a street frothing with lost souls. The restaurant had faux Rococo fittings and was so expensive that the prices weren't printed on the menu. My husband was spending big bucks to impress on me what an idiot I had been to leave him.

My husband began talking about his teeth. His dentist was charging him an arm and a leg to fill all the cavities he had developed overseas. He said *overseas* the way someone says Auschwitz. He said his bills were going to be over a thousand dollars, and he needed the thousand dollars I owed him. He leaned forward and said, "Right away," about two inches from my face.

We were not married. We were not divorced. We were not anything except a lender and a debtor.

He could give me the name of his dentist. My teeth must be a wreck too, but don't expect him to help pay, even if we were still legally married. He didn't have any obligations to me. Actually, he could sue me for desertion if he wanted to. I waited for him to say the magic word **adultery**, but he didn't seem interested in any sexual misconduct I might have been committing while he was starting to climb the corporate ladder. Correction: that I wish I had been committing.

Where was this big book I had spent all that time on in Spain? If it was going to be such a sure-fire success, I'd have plenty of money to pay him back. I could get an advance. It was perfectly obvious from the sneer on his face that he knew I hadn't finished the book. Okay, fair enough. I had just come from a fascist country, I had loved a man who consorted with friends of Franco's. My husband had points on his side. Just don't be so despicable about your advantages, I thought.

How had I come to marry someone who seemed worse than a fascist? He was handsome. He came from an Ivy League school. He had a Norman Rockwell family that I thought could replace my own dysfunctional one (did the words dysfunctional family even exist then?). Above all, I had wanted out of Indianapolis, and this man now sitting across from me flashing his repaired incisors had seemed to provide the perfect avenue of escape.

I thought about the call I made to my mother the first night I was back in the United States. The first thing she wanted to know was if I had gone back to my husband. I said, No, I'm going to try to make it on my own, though it doesn't look as if that's going to be easy.

I know you must be hard up for money, she said. I would like to help. I don't know about your father, you know how he is, and anyway I don't know where he is. As I wrote you, I've left him. Your brother would know, he's still in contact with him. He's doing so well, your brother. I'm short in through here because I've just given him some money for a down payment on this great house he's going to buy. It has five fireplaces. He and Jan can't live in that apartment anymore. She's going to have another baby. Maybe I could let you have a hundred or two. After all, I want to be fair.

*Fair?* I can't even rent an apartment because I didn't have a down payment, and she's helping pay for a house she tells me has five fireplaces. I decided that I'd commit hara-kari before I'd take a cent from her. The logic of her reasoning was not lost on me, though: the man establishes the house, and the woman lives in it to polish it and provide him with all the comforts he desires. I believe the saying then was, It's a man's world.

I looked at my husband. He *was* handsome, but not the way Luis was, burnt black by the Andalusian sun with fierce, villainous eyes that made him look like a Barbary pirate. He had an almost menacing mouth (yes, I remember that mouth, Luis, I remember it very well). I thought of the muscular fluidity of Luis's beautiful body. The man sitting across from me was not really handsome; he was only a good-looking boy with professionally repaired teeth. Then again, the devil often hath a pleasing countenance.

My husband was holding the menu casually, as if he were used to eating in expensive restaurants and not having to check out prices to see if he could afford all the shrimp in Barcelona. All I had was my hat, my gloves, and my great dress. I didn't think those were good enough to do battle.

"You want a drink?"

I rose, picked up my gloves, and said, "It would be a waste of money to spend anything on me except your share of a divorce, which I think will easily add up to a thousand dollars. I'll let you know if you owe me anything more."

That's my girl, Luis said inside my head.

I was supposed to be meeting Sobersides Sam the Peanut Butter Man from Seville at the Met after I lunched with my husband. What is Sam doing in the United States and how did he find me? I am living in a small back bedroom in the downtown apartment of an old college roommate. Sam should be in Spain doing his consulate thing. He doesn't belong in New York City telling me on the telephone that he wants to see me.

"How did you find me? No one knows where I am."

"This time it was a little harder." After a moment, he made a funny noise in his throat. "There are always ways in the service to find someone if you want to hard enough. I'm going to be transferred to Hong Kong. That's why I'm back in the States. I have a couple of weeks to get my affairs in order."

When he said "get my affairs in order," a message appeared in my mind in neon lights. He was going to ask me to marry him, and I had to keep him from doing that at all costs. He was a nice man, one of those brave men whose courage had cost him all he had to give. One who had always been good to me, who I could see thought I might give him back the sense of joy that waited inside each of us to flower, the roots of which he had lost in Korea.

I knew just what he would say after I said No, I can't marry you. He would say, Well, I can always hope, can't I? And I would say, Sometimes hope is not an option, and then Sam would say, It's better than nothing. I don't love you the way you deserve, I would say. You deserve someone better.

Surely a man like Sam *did* deserve a wife who loved and honored him. Maybe I could just say, Think of all the trouble I had trying to learn Spanish. I could never in a million years manage to learn any of those dialects in Chinese. On the other hand, considering the circumstances, Sam might not find that funny.

Sam is better to me than in any way I deserve. Why can't I love him the way I should?

The obvious answer is that I have a severe barometric deficiency in measuring men.

I was so nervous when I came up to Sam on the steps of the Met that I began to speak so rapidly that he wouldn't have time to get any words out first. "I wore your shawl the other night. Everyone thought it was so beautiful. I said it came from Seville. I miss Seville so much. Tell me all about what's going on in Seville."

Sam was not dumb. He could see I was trying to steer him away from what he had come to say. "I guess you heard your friend—the count—is getting married. I suppose you know that already."

*We have always thought there was a girl he would marry, a girl he's known all his life, and we all thought he cared for her. I'm sure he cares for her, but he—but he doesn't love her, not the way—*

My face felt as if it had been sitting in a freezer for a month. I had just realized that for the rest of my life, one way or another, I would be encased in that moment when Luis's mother had said, Men here have the right to hit any women they want—yes, they do, they **all** do—yes, they do, **all** of them—and I had pictured Luis's father hitting that beautiful, elegant woman and had seen her heart turning glacial. Every day the ice expanded, until one day it had completely enveloped her. I thought of Luis in that dark passageway of the bullring holding me, so out of control that I was sure he was going to start pounding on my back because in the state he was in, anything was possible.

The cortex of my brain shut down, but my heart beat on, repeating over and over, *I hate you, Sam. I hate you. Don't you know that in Greek plays The Messenger is always put to death? Hasn't anyone ever told you it is not good to be The Conveyer of Bad News?*

The next thing I knew, I was lying flat on the concrete steps outside the Metropolitan Museum of Art. A crowd had gathered round me. Are you all right? Sam, who was kneeling beside me, kept saying over and over. Why the hell would I be all right if I were lying on the steps of the Met? I couldn't speak. It was an effort even to open my eyes. Why should I open them, anyway? What was there I wanted to see?

Years later, I read that Frida Kahlo was convinced that the trite expression "broken heart" had a basis in real physical sensation—a sense of fracture in the chest, the sensation that a sword was turning and twisting in an ever-expanding wound. By this I assume she meant the knowledge that came from that moment that made her understand that all the hopes her heart had held were shattered, and nothing or no one could ever mend that pitiful organ again.

Sam finally helped me to my feet. We stood on the Met steps and looked at American traffic, which was the exact opposite of what we would have seen on the streets of Seville, with its ragtag carriages and battered cabs. Sometimes all life can often be reduced to comparison and contrast. I don't mean the real difference is between illusion and reality; I only want to suggest that comparison and contrast are often the keys that lead to understanding the difference between illusion and reality.

Sometimes it's better to be a friend than a lover, I should have said to Sam. Friends last longer. Shallow, Roy Bongartz would have said—and he'd have been right. I had taken Sam's shawl and let him squire me to places in Spain I wouldn't have been able to go on my own; I had let him wine and dine me, I had *used* him, which was one of the worst sins someone could commit. I could make a list, I thought, of the hundreds of crimes I had committed against Sam because he was a nice man.

Goodbye, Sam, I said. Thanks for everything you've done for me. I wanted to say, I'm sorry, I really am, but I didn't have the emotional energy.

I kissed him on the cheek and ran down the steps of the Met. I never saw him again, but we wrote once in a while. Two or three years later, he sent me a wedding announcement. When I think of him, I think of a man of great *pundonor*.

I had mismanaged my life to such an extent that I was wondering if it was so smashed up that it couldn't be fixed, that all the good pieces had been lost or misplaced and may have disappeared forever.

Memory has become my lover, but if I am the keeper of those moments of love left behind, I am a poor protector. I will never be able to retrieve everything, no matter how hard I try. It is possible that at some time in the future, Luis won't recall me at all. Someone will say something about "that American girl," and he will have no idea who that is. You know, the one that bought up all the balloons at *feria* and took the duke's carriage. Perhaps he will have a flicker of recollection, but it is also possible that I will be completely gone from him. He will be in his other life, the one his mother knew was waiting for him.

I am the woman who has a sick feeling in the pit of her stomach the first moment of waking because all night long she has been the victim of night demons and who during the day hefted such pain that the only way to stop it would be to cut out her heart or drive a nail through her brain. I eat jelly beans, pretzels, and gum drops and smoke cigarettes (well, Virginia Woolf smoked like a fiend) instead of consuming food. I drink too much wine, *Spanish* wine, that I pay outrageous prices for because it has the word *Spain* on its label. I play a record of gypsy music I have brought back from Spain over and over until the needle sticks and all I hear are the raucous sounds of a needle stuck in a track and still I don't shut the record off. I am waiting for the disk to heal itself and give me back music that will transport me back to the sandy soil of southern Spain.

I am the woman who does not understand the country she is in and cannot go back to the one she loves. I am the woman who reads a newspaper that advertises a cat collar for $12,000. It has diamonds studded into the collar, but would the cat know that? I am the woman who stares at a page of the *New York Times* ("All the news that's fit to print") and sees a purse made of crocodile skin that costs $15,000, its clasp in solid twenty-four carat gold. *This* is fit to print? That cat collar, that crocodile purse cost more than the average Spaniard made in a lifetime. There are *shoes* advertised that cost more.

I am the woman who knows that though I will never see Luis again, I must make some accommodation to life or I will not be able to go on. But I can't give Luis up. I don't care if he marries and has children and even finds that he has come to love his wife. All I want to know is that he's occupying the same planet I am. The Earth will be all right so long as Luis is still inhabiting it.

I never take the pesata coin around my neck off, and every once in a while, I put my fingers on it to feel the burning fire of its heart. I hadn't lost Luis; he was just in another place. Every day I would remember less and less, but there will never come a time when I wouldn't be prowling the corridors of my mind searching for misplaced and lost pieces.

The peseta represents a world where people go on picnics and drink a lot and don't get a hangover, eat whatever they want and never gain weight, are always slim and trim and twenty-five; a world where everyone had the body and face he or she had always wanted, and if you got tired of that, you could turn it in for another and there were no restrictions on how many times you could make changes. A world where the temperature was always seventy-five, the sun always shining but it didn't make you sweat, the food you ate didn't need hours to prepare and more hours to clean up, a world where the dust disappears by blowing on it and the floors shine if you wave your hands over them. Most of all, I am a woman who wants a world where there was an agent who wanted me because he thought I was going to become a great writer. An agent like that is far more important than any other man could be, I tell myself.

The usual way that most people got an agent was to have someone recommend them. I didn't know anyone who had those kinds of connections. I opened the phone book to Agents, Literary, and started going down the list. I began making the rounds, but I never got past the secretaries in the fancy offices—"Leave your name and we'll get back to you." Yeah, sure, when bulls fly and someone gives me a lottery ticket that turns out to be worth twenty million dollars.

When I was well down the list, I climbed the stairs of a not very prepossessing building and found a one-room office, dusty, disorganized, and filled with draughts that lifted and lowered the papers scattered over everything. "A girl," as she was always referred to, sat behind one desk and a spidery little man behind another that dwarfed him. He admitted to being a literary agent, though he looked like one of those B-movie gangsters who get murdered the first half hour of the film. He told me to sit down, and I looked around for a chair that didn't have something on it. Finally I wedged my way in amongst a pile of papers.

He had an odd face, and he began talking a mile a minute in an accent I couldn't identify—I don't think I was able to interject a whole sentence during his half-hour gabfest—and then finally he said, "Bring me a sample of your work."

I came up with two chapters, about fifty pages, that I had taken to carrying around with me in case someone showed even a faint whiff of interest and handed them across the desk. "Call me the day after tomorrow, and I'll let you know," he said in his oddly-accented English.

It turned out he was a Dutch Jew who had escaped the Holocaust by fleeing to England (the rest of his family went up in ashes). There he taught himself English by reading Shakespeare, so his conversation was filled with antiquated expressions like *perchance* (as in, perchance might there be more action in this scene) and *albeit* (as in, albeit when I was passing by the public library I ...). I think he took me because I was tall. Short men often have a thing for tall women. He was very good to me, but he extracted thousands of grams of gratitude.

I wined and dined him for *years*. Some of my friends revolted and said they weren't spending one more evening listening to him talk about himself, but I hung on. He had been there for me through the really bad times—though he didn't like any of the husbands I collected and made no bones about it. (Fie on you that you should have made these miserable choices!) I felt an obligation to him for taking me on when no one else would and for finally getting me into print.

He was going to write a book himself about all the famous people he knew, but he should have concentrated on the bizarre episodes that occurred in his own life. It wasn't just that he had escaped the Nazis; it was also that he had fled with a woman who was genuinely certifiable. She had been a dancer once. When drink inspired her, she would suddenly rise and fling herself about like Isadora Duncan without the scarves, endangering the furniture with an energy that was appalling. It seemed that nothing would ever exhaust it. After a time, her husband would rise and take hold of her and say, Okay, Rudalee, we get the idea, and throw her down on the couch. She would lay back à la Mata Hari and sob, I would give my life for a Turkish cigarette.

If she had no energy for housework, she had an amazing affinity for dalliances, especially with dangerous men. My agent was always being called to the local police station to bail her out because she had been with some ne'er-do-well who had become involved in something criminally unacceptable. I think the cops felt sorry for him. It was obvious that with this woman, he was in way over his head.

Nothing she did deterred him from loving her. Don't ask me why. She was a terrible housekeeper, a terrible cook, a terrible driver, and she cuckolded him every chance she got. But you don't get to pick out the person you love. Love is thrust upon you when you are unaware and unarmed. You can try to run from it, but it's attached, like your shadow is, something you can never get rid of.

Once Rudalee ran off with a carpenter and married him while she was still married to my agent. He went to the police, not because she was a bigamist, but because he wanted her back. The police were all well acquainted with her and might know where she had gone. Rudalee, fearing she would be arrested for bigamy, fled to Mexico, where the carpenter for some reason dropped dead. She was terrified of the Mexican police, as well she might be, so she propped the dead body up on the passenger side, weighted it down with stones so it wouldn't fall over, and drove back over the border, pretending the dead man was just asleep. When she got to Texas, she was afraid of Texans as well as Mexicans, which we have all learned is a wise idea, and drove straight through until she pulled into the driveway of husband Number One with dead husband Number Two, whose torso was somewhat the worse for wear. She broke into tears, and my agent went about seeing there was a decent burial. She was back. That was all he cared about.


I was desperate for money to finish my novel. Besides the fifty pages I had given my agent, I had maybe a hundred more, but I couldn't write a novel when I was spending every waking hour working as a freelance writer for the *Encyclopedia Britannica* and a supermarket encyclopedia for which I carved out articles on the Japanese Beetles, Riddance of: Perennials, Easy Ways to Grow a Permanent Garden; African Violets, Care of and Problems With. My agent tried to peddle the *Gourmet* book, but editors would say to him, We can't use that because it's libelous. Has she got anything else? As if I kept old novels in drawers just waiting for a moment when someone would want them. Come to think of it, I'll bet there are writers out there who have lots of old novels waiting around, like inventory.

A Saxton Fellowship was a very prestigious award during that period. I believe—alas and alack, as my agent would have said—they now no longer exist. My agent took the opening chapters that I had been working on for the novel about my family and gave them to some woman at Harper's and Brothers, which gave me a Saxton Fellowship, which was enough money ($2,500 in those days went a long way) to live on while I finished the book and tried to think of a cheap way to rid myself of my boat-husband. Harper's would have first refusal rights when it was finished.

I worked like a dog. (Where did this expression come from? I don't know any dogs that dust and vacuum, prepare food and clean up the debris, get down on hands and knees to scrub the kitchen floor and the toilet bowl.) I thought I should be writing nine to ten hours a day. I know there are people who *say* they put in a punishing schedule like that, but I don't believe them. How could anyone be full of the fire for eight and nine hours without ending up ashes?

James Joyce's advice for the artist surviving in the modern world was silence, cunning, and exile. I felt as if I were in exile, but a writer cannot be silent. Speaking up is what the craft is about, and I did not know how to be cunning. I didn't fit the definition, but work was what I had to hang onto, the only thing that seemed to make any sense in a world that would think someone like Barry Goldwater could be a savior of the nation.

When I finally finished the book, I had almost a thousand pages, which I dutifully took to my agent, who passed them along to the woman (I wish I could remember her name—on second thought I'm glad I can't) at Harper's. She read the book and *hated* it. I'm not talking about mild dislike here, or maybe there are some weak sections and the end doesn't really work but I think these can be fixed. No, I am talking, *The whole thing is terrible. Get it away from me.*

My agent took it across the street and sold it to Viking. He didn't tell me until later that the woman at Harper's had violently rejected it ("It had vexed her mightily" was how he put it).

To be a recognized writer in those days was to be someone worshiped the way rock stars are today. Anatole Broyard in *Kafka Was the Rage: A Greenwich Village Memoir* has said of those times, "We didn't simply read books; we became them ... Books were to us what drugs were to young men in the sixties." People like Norman Mailer and J. D. Salinger belonged alongside Ulysses and Agamemnon in the pantheon of the gods.

At that time, publishing houses were not owned by huge conglomerates. At Viking, the owner, Harold Guinzburg, had started the company himself and was interested in seeing that the literature he published had value. Viking was the imprint for people like John Steinbeck, Saul Bellow, Malcolm Cowley (who was also an editor), and now me.

The first time I went up to the offices, I felt the same excitement I had that day Luis drove me out to *Los Vientos* and the men along the way took off their caps and bowed their heads as we drove by.

At Viking, writers were treated with reverence. They might not sell huge amounts on their first or second or even third books, but if they had talent, Viking kept on supporting them. Eventually, Harold Guinzburg believed, a great book would come out of that support and garner enormous amounts of readers.

I realize now I had really very little idea then how to write a book; no creative writing courses existed at that time to teach even the basics. Writers were either born to the craft or expected to learn by reading. Apparently I hadn't absorbed all that I ought to while I went feverishly from one Nancy Drew book to next, curled up under the dining room table while my mother and father conducted their war against one another overhead. Nor did I get it by reading recipes at *Gourmet*.

I was assigned an editor, a *real* editor, not some twenty-something who spells **a lot** as one word—or, worse, **allot** as in allot of your ms. is of intrest[sic]—or asks what a chapbook is, as so many editors are wont to do today. Helen Taylor worked with me for over a year to get the massive manuscript into publishable shape. She taught me the rudiments of writing: that you couldn't change points of view in the middle of a paragraph, that description should be suggestive, not overwhelming; that if some image appeared in the beginning of the novel, it ought to have reverberations all the way through to the end of the book, what Helen called a running metaphor (think the use of the circus in this book). A book should be complex, with twisted skeins of meaning that finally emerged as a central theme or themes (think of the loss of love and what the world is really like for women born before the feminist movement of the 1960s). A great book should have a fire all its own (I'm trying to do that with the word *fire* as a recurring image in this section). She would say, If you don't feel the heat as you read back what you've written, something is the matter.

Helen prodded me to cut the book almost in half. In the end, I rewrote it three times. Once a week, I went in with what I had done, and we reviewed material from the week before. Helen pointed out what was making the book stronger and what wasn't working. She never said I *had* to change something; she just showed me where she thought the novel was working and where she felt it wasn't working.

*Weak* was a word she used a lot. It seems to me this scene is weak. You haven't used your central metaphor (and I would think, *What* central metaphor?) to keep the theme going (*What* theme?). You haven't shown any change in this character from what has happened (oh, okay, I see that). Mostly her suggestions boiled down to, It worked or it didn't *seem* to be working. From time to time, Harold Guinzburg would wander back to see how I was getting along.

When the manuscript was finally finished in Helen's eyes—it has fire now, she said—and okayed by Harold Guinzburg, I was consulted on the cover (I *hated* the first cover, so they sent word back to the designer to try something else). We could never find the right name for the book. As a working title, we had used *The Timbles,* the name of the family around which the book revolved, but that sounded too much like thimbles. Though this was suggestive of a thimble of life, I thought that was a pretty corny implication. Right up until the end, I was frantically looking for a title.

At Christmastime, someone sent me one of those horrible mimeographed letters about the family's activities for the year, and it started out Dear Ones All. The people in my book were exactly the opposite of *dear,* and everyone liked the irony of the phrase. We settled on *Dear Ones All* as the title.

It took me a year to realize the initials DOA usually stood for Dead on Arrival, which certainly seemed to suit the mood of the novel. My agent (the carpenter six feet under, Rudalee reinstalled in his house) said that there should be a razor blade in a small pocket at the back of the book so that the reader could slit his/her wrists when he or she finished reading the last page. In other words, this was not a hap-hap-happy book. How could it be? It was about my family.

I was sent to an expensive photographer to have a picture made for the back cover; the publicity staff pretended they loved me; I was made to feel as if I belonged at Viking with people like John Steinbeck and Saul Bellow, who was then—at least according to the pictures on the back of the dust jackets of his books—the handsomest man in America.

Bellow's editor, Denver Lindley, had an office right next door, but Helen went out of her way to make sure I never met Bellow, though she herself eventually married Denver. To this day, I can still reproduce that keen sense of disappointment I would experience when Helen would say, Oh, I'm so sorry, but Saul's just left. Oh, it's too bad, but Saul isn't coming in today. Oh, I think Denver and Saul are working very hard; I wouldn't want to interrupt them. Well I would, but I didn't say so. Dumb me. I had somehow gotten it into my head that Saul Bellow could cure my obsession with Luis. His Jewishness seemed to me to make him like someone from a foreign country, one I could substitute for Spain. As someone who didn't feel she fit in her own country, I was in the market for a substitute culture.

When my book finally came out, I was given a reception, and Harold Guinzburg invited all kinds of famous people, most of whom didn't come—no Saul Bellow—but I had a roomful of friends. I sent Sam in Hong Kong an invitation and half expected him to pop up; instead he sent flowers. I did not send a book to Luis because it was a book about growing up in the Midwest; there was nothing about Spain in it, and even if there had been, I would not have given pain to his new wife. I might hate her, not for what she'd done but for what she'd taken, but if the beginning of the burgeoning women's movement was teaching me anything, it was that one woman shouldn't inflict pain on another. The easiest way to do that was to seize somebody else's husband.

If anything was holding me together, it was my book, which had consumed four years of my life. It was started in England and toyed with occasionally on the boat, but the major part of it had been written in Spain and through the pain of leaving Spain, then continued under conditions of what could only be called penury in the United States. It had been revised and those revisions revised, but finally I had finished it. It was in print.

It was getting good reviews, especially from Orville Prescott, who was considered an A-list critic. A friend had to call me to tell me it was the feature of the day in the *Times*, and it was a rave review. I had to run out and buy a copy; I was too destitute to be able to afford buying the *Times* every day. The book even managed to stagger onto the now-defunct *New York Herald Tribune* best-seller list for one week. One week. Sometimes I kind of think that sums up my life

I decided to get a Mexican divorce. It would be cheaper than going to Reno and having to pay for six weeks' residency. I could live in California with my father, who was working in a job I did not understand for a company whose product made no sense to me. We shared a small San Diego apartment, in a complex grim with the canopy of failed dreams that hung over it. The thing I remember most about California was that the lights never went off; it was the first time I had ever encountered stores that were open twenty-four hours a day. The people in the complex led the kind of dead-end lives that made them do their washing at night—the washers and dryers were in an open space under our little flat—and so besides the nights never getting dark, a constant whirring went on from sunset to dawn. I would go sometimes to the beach and sit, trying to work on my manuscript while the wind blew sand all over me. When twilight fell, I went home and sat and looked at my father, a man whose office always had a sign that said **"Results, Not Excuses,"** who had ended up living in a dreary, furnished, one-bedroom apartment over washers and dryers.

I slept on the couch. We ate the strange, starchy meals of the poor. My father believed I was making a bad mistake getting a divorce. What's the matter with him? he asked me. No matter how many times I explained that I didn't *like* him anymore, he had no idea what I was talking about. My father's face filled with scorn at my innocence when he said, Well, that's not the end of the world.

I never told my father about Luis. I did not tell him about the American field engineer working in Spain who kept telling me, via the snail mail of those days, that he still wanted to marry me. I never really told my father anything of significance. All I remember from those California days is the smell of detergent and the whirl of spinning blades either in the washer or the dryer. California must be one of the worst places on earth to be a failure, but at least my father didn't have to die there. By the time he got sick enough to die, he was working for his brother-in-law in Indianapolis. A Hoosier doctor bungled an operation on my father's prostate (I'm going to learn to sing soprano, he wrote on my birthday card—no check enclosed—just before he went into the hospital). His sister got a lawyer who said, Yes, it was patently a case of malpractice, but there was no point in suing. My father was too old for his life to be worth anything. Even if he won her case, he wouldn't get enough money to cover her lawyer fees.

Meanwhile, my boat-husband was becoming a well-known editor on the New York scene. Much later, when my fourth book was published, he paid me back for ruining his dream of sailing the Adriatic in a small boat by writing a review for that well-known magazine where he worked in which he compared my book to a book the woman he was getting ready to marry had just written. Guess which one was the success and which one was the swill. I pictured him sitting at a desk writing with such relish that every once in a while he would raise his fist over his head and pump the air, hollering, Yes, *yes, **yes!***

My editor at that time, Joyce Engelson at the Dial Press, was enraged. She demanded an equal opportunity to respond. *Esquire* never even bothered to answer. I remember in particular my boat-husband's snide remark (mentioning that he had once had the misfortune to have been married to me) that he could see from the evidence in my novel that **no** man could possibly live up to the standards I felt necessary to make a *real* man.

I had the living proof to refute him at *Los Vientos*, but of course he may have been drawing on all those men in gray-flannel suits he knew, and that was how he came up with such a conclusion. He had long ago swept out of his life old friends from the past like Roy Bongartz. I see now that he wanted to erase that past and substitute his shining step up the literary ladder, where people thought of him as da man.

How does he have so much luck, and you seem to have so many mishaps? my agent asked me.

Which god do you think I should ask?

The one who rules over writers.

He doesn't even know I exist.

I married the engineer from Spain, the one with the buzz haircut who had said he was going to marry me, just wait and see. I tried to look at the move as a positive step forward, but maybe I was engaging in what psychiatrists call counterphobic behavior—substituting a new kind of bad pain in order to overcome an existing one.

It wasn't until after we were married that he let it spill he had once sold asbestos siding for a living. He was also a wife beater and a man of a million schemes in which to lose money. Other people's money. He wiped out what little savings I had in less than a month. But he was chipper, full of false confidence and larky ideas as he went on to devastate his naive brother's bank account and to smash up his sister's car in a DWI so that the insurance company didn't want to fork over any funds, a man who had spent three years in Spain and spoke better Spanish than I did but who had no idea what the word *pundonor* meant.

I asked Roy Bongartz what in the world had made me marry him, and Roy said, *You* told me that once when you were in a car with him in Seville, he found a parking space that was too small to squeeze into, so he hired four Spaniards to lift the car up and put in the space. You said you needed someone who could fix things in your life.

Oh, I said. I guess I didn't look far enough into the matter.

Roy tried to be kind. You weren't really you when you married him. I was always afraid when you tried to smile, your face would crack.

Roy had married Cee by that time. They stayed together until she died, very young, of a brain tumor. They had adopted a half-American Indian little boy, Joe. He's my yiddisher Mohawk, Cee would always say. She had great grace, that woman, because Roy was not always easy to be with, but she loved him to the end. By that time, I hadn't seen them in years. I think they went west and I went to an assortment of places, still looking for my substitute Spain.

My second husband had absolutely nothing to recommend him, if you discounted his ability to move an automobile into an impossible space. Maybe I was trying to get back at Luis, but that seemed too chowder-headed even for me

I had a daughter with Buzz Cut and left that husband. I hid from him in the Adirondacks, where I had found a cheap cottage out in the boondocks. Late at night, I played Spanish music and drank Spanish wine and looked at the telephone and said to myself, No. *No.* **No.**

Sometimes, I think, we do good acts for their own sake. I don't think I do them very often, but I like to think that not picking up the phone and calling Luis was one of the times my better nature shone through. There aren't a lot of those times, so perhaps that is why I celebrate the few there are.

I was beginning to wear out with disappointments, but a first book is like a first love. You never forget the euphoria of seeing your name and your writing *in print*. It's better than sex. You've got something permanent—well, pretty permanent—whereas when the orgasm is gone, it's vanished as if it had hardly taken place. Let's just say that for a writer, having a first printed book in hand is an experience close to Eden without the snake and minus Adam bitching about how he doesn't like apples.

The Adirondacks turned out to be one of the stops on my relentless pursuit of a Spanish substitute. It was there I encountered David Smith.

By the end of the 50s, when I arrived in Bolton Landing, David Smith had begun making money, big money, and that made grandiose gestures like throwing the cork from the top of a bottle of really good whiskey into the bushes as he arrived an easy way to demonstrate his affluence. Having money meant he could buy many of the nice things he had had to do without for much of his life. Lastly, money meant power, and if there was one thing David Smith liked, it was the control power gave.

I think of him out in his shop welding huge, monolithic pieces against a background of fire, an enormous figure looming up through showers of sparks, or up at his house scribbling out sketches, constantly interrupted by the ladies who came on hired buses to gape at his grounds as if his house were a public park. The place did have a kind of Dada Disneyland look, with the lawn filled with enormous abstract pieces so huge they had to be lifted by cranes, pieces of such enormous weight that they could not be displayed in an ordinary gallery because they would buckle the floor and plunge downward through the broken boards. There were over eighty pieces in that field in front of the house. It was like no other place in America. It was like no other place in the world. I had found another country.

My platinum-haired daughter was two years old by the time I arrived in Bolton. I liked to think she was a tradeoff for her father, who was genetically programmed for a slash-and-burn, take-no-prisoners, scorched-earth policy in dealing with the world. Leaving him had been one of the pleasures of my life, getting rid of him a two-year battle that cost everyone but him money. I went to the Adirondacks in the hope that he couldn't find me.

I think David did not want to see my child's mother unhappy, because that would make the daughter worried and unhappy. Children should not have to be around people who are preoccupied a good part of the day and who, by nightfall, become so sad that you do not want to go near them. Scott Fitzgerald was wrong about there being a three o'clock in the morning feeling. You can get that feeling the minute the sun goes down. Or comes up. Actually, at any time of the day or night.

David was crazy about my little girl. Perhaps my child became something of a substitute for David's own two daughters, who lived the major part of the year with their mother, far away in another city. David would toss my daughter high in the air and catch her, shrieking with happiness, as she came down. He would take her into his studio and put her inside one of those gargantuan pieces of sculpture he was working on and hoist her with the winch way up into the air while I stood, terrified, saying over and over, Hang on, hang on, don't let go. Don't you think I'd catch her if she fell? David would demand angrily, which was tantamount to saying, I am the master of my fate, I am the captain of my soul, I am the arbitrator of the universe. I can catch a small child if she falls.

My daughter had no fear, swinging back and forth thirty feet over our heads. She gasped and panted with pleasure. As soon as she saw him, she ran towards him and said, Put me up, put me up. If we were at the cottage, he hoisted her over his head and threw her as far up in the air as he could. For a moment, she was like a rocket going into outer space. If we were in the field in front of his studio, David asked her which piece she liked the best. She always took her time deciding, standing very pensive as she examined one piece after another before she pointed to one of the multitude of choices she had.

David gave her a silver dollar for luck, which she carefully put into my hand. "I lose things," she said solemnly. In every way, she was a solemn child. Often, she seemed older and wiser than the adults around her. I worried because I didn't want her to learn the lesson I had when

I was near her age, that adults are dangerous, that you have to keep on the lookout all the time when you are around them or you would most likely get hurt. Nor did I want her to know at such a young age that love makes you a loser. She had plenty of time to discover that.

I saved the silver dollar for thirty years in my safe-deposit box. I had married again and had given motherhood another try—being so pleased with my daughter that I wanted to hit the jackpot again—and years later I decided my son needed all the help he could get in life. At that moment he was in his sculpture stage, which had followed his deciding to be a master chef and needing four hundred dollars for knives; which came after his foray into mathematics, when he thought he would solve the problem of infinity by doing something with multiple fractions. I remembered the lucky silver dollar David had given my daughter, and I asked her what she thought about giving it to her brother for Christmas. A great idea, she said. We can have the coin pierced so that he can hang it on a silver chain around his neck

My daughter understood the potency of wearing a coin around your neck. She knew I never took off my peseta. Once she wanted to know why I never took it off. I said I wore it around my neck because it meant that I kept in touch with someone I never wanted to lose. How is that? she asked. It's like magic, I said. It can't be explained. So when we gave my son David Smith's silver dollar, it was as if we were giving him some of David's magic.

I don't know if my son even still has it, let alone ever wore it. He took it out of the box and looked at it, puzzled. We explained that David Smith had given it to Allison, and we wanted him to have it because it was a good luck charm. He may have thought that we were trying to pressure him to work hard, the way David did. Certainly he would have remembered how often we talked about David's dedication to his work. Perhaps he took the medal as our way of saying, You don't work hard enough and was affronted.

He had been down so many blind roads. He would decide he wanted to do so-and-so. Then he would change his mind. I don't think I understood that was his way of looking for himself. I had forgotten his telling his kindergarten teacher and me that he was looking out the window to see where things come from. That perhaps is another way of my wanting to know what things mean.

What he has finally settled on is robotics. He wants to make a robot that thinks on its own and doesn't obey instructions when it makes up its mind that the instructions aren't to its liking. A free-thinking robotic, which I find a scary idea but, all things considered, not unlike what had gone on in David Smith's head. We are too much alike, my son and I, and that's a formula for trouble. It's the closest I've come to an explanation of why we always seem at odds.

The cottage my daughter and I and our Siamese cats shared was exceedingly small—the largest room was the kitchen. The whole place was crowded with manuscripts and beer-making apparatus. I was poor and all my friends thirsty; homebrew worked out to about five cents a quart. Even a moderate amount was practically guaranteed to put you over the moon. The children's toys, abandoned shoes, and shirts that go with small children were scattered all over the miniscule living room. I had seedlings, three stone heads I'd picked up after they'd been abandoned in a previous apartment, skis, and so many books the floors groaned when you walked on them, ready to give way from the weight of all that overhead literature. The small living room was almost all bookcases surrounding my desk, with its messy papers scattered about and an old upright typewriter, at least fifteen years old. In a corner was the coach-bed where my young daughter usually slept. There was a tiny bedroom where I lay down at night and stared at the ceiling and wondered how I was going to pay the rent for the coming month. The kitchen had a small bathroom adjacent, and the cottage itself a view twenty miles down Lake George that was stupendous (when the lake wasn't frozen over and looked like normal land covered with snow). People hardly ever used the living room, because it was really my work area. If people weren't in the kitchen, they usually sat on the porch and read, drank, played chess, argued, and chased wasps.

One afternoon, David and I arrived to find the place a complete mess. Since we had left only a little more than an hour before and the cottage had been reasonably tidy, David was aghast, though why he should have taken such a Puritanical attitude was beyond me. His place was *always* a mess.

"My god, people have been here while we went down to town. There are strange people's things all over the place. Books, glasses, tennis rackets, swim suits—"

"It's probably just Tom and Joe—"

The notion that people came, let themselves in (in those days people never locked their doors; I don't think I even had a key), settled down, and then went their way to turn up again at will mystified him. "You mean you *allow* that?"

"But, David, they're my friends."

My friends all seemed to him dangerous interlopers who needed attention that I now realize he regarded as rightfully his own. Once an old friend from my *Quixote* literary quarterly days turned up to spend a few days. I was sure David would like him, and I spent a week of preparation with humorous anecdotes about what a funny fellow Dick was. I got in return the well-documented Smith sulks, a very large man on a very determined pout. About eleven o'clock the first night of Dick's visit, my daughter and I had gone to bed together in the miniscule bedroom. Dick was lying in his pajamas on the couch/bed my daughter usually used.

Suddenly the house began to shake. When David tramped up the steps onto the small porch in those big, ugly shoes on his huge feet, the whole frame of the cottage went into a spasm. Then I heard voices, banging, more talk, the house shuddered some more. The cats were running around like crazy. Dick came to the bedroom door and said, "Rik, the fish man says to tell you he's here."

David just happened, he explained, to be passing by (at eleven o'clock at night, which, after all, for him wasn't unusual), and he just happened to have all these perch, and he just happened to remember I loved fresh fish. Big and belligerent, he stood in the doorway holding an enormous pail. Then his face allowed itself a smile. The sleeping arrangements met his idea of what was proper and what also posed no threat to his feeling that I was, in the end, exclusively put on earth to meet his needs. I didn't take this in any way more than it was meant: he thought that about everybody. That night, he thundered back out to the Mercedes and brought in wine, salamis, bread, jars of preserves, pickles, and olives he just happened to have with him in case we felt like a snack.

He stayed until four o'clock in the morning. We did things like that in those days. It would kill me to stay up until four o'clock in the morning now.

My friend Dick was as puzzled by David as David was by most of my friends. "You mean he does this all the time, just stops in at eleven o'clock at night and expects you to act as if it were an ordinary visit?"

Well, yes, he did.

He was, after all, America's premier sculptor, and geniuses get away with behavior that other people wouldn't get away with for five seconds. Think Jackson Pollock peeing in the fireplace at Peggy Guggenheim's apartment. Think Jack Kerouac drunk in the Viking offices, throwing things out the high-rise window, the staff terrified a pedestrian below might get bonked on the head and they would be sued. Think Van Gogh and the ear, Gauguin and his kinky sex with the South Seas islanders. Think Manet telling everyone he had rheumatism when he had syphilis. Manet's left leg went black from gangrene; the operation was a success, but recovery killed him. Think David Smith in one of his monumental rages as he screams into the phone at his second wife, "I'll hire paid killers and have you bumped off!"

"David!" I hollered at the top of my voice. "You're on a party line, and they all listen in."


I always thought David made nothing but monstrous abstract (perhaps allegorical) figures, but one day he took me down into the cellar of his house, where hundreds of small pieces crowded against one another, some almost recognizable facsimiles of everyday objects—animals, birds, insects, humans—and mythical creatures amidst the symbolic abstractions. He seemed bent on trying to capture the essence of every thing, and each piece (at least to me) gave an impression of violence, a rage of monumental proportions against the world around him, as if he were trying to bring order to chaos and could never quite do it. Now and again, I would see a piece that seemed very still, as if he had caught for a moment the vision inside his head and had frozen that moment forever, immobilized in time. Some pieces were so abstract that you had to look at them for a while before you realized what they actually meant. Sometimes they didn't seem to have a literal meaning at all. David had just named them whatever came to mind. He was not big on helpful titles.

Most of all, he loved his monumental pieces, so abstract and yet so individualized that they conveyed a man who knew exactly what he wanted to say. And what, may you ask, is that? Well, I think it was that he had a fire inside so intense that it needed to explode into individual flames of fire, for, like Hephaestus (minus the lame leg), he was a great artist at the forge.

Outdoors, the ones I liked best had been polished and repolished to reflect the seasons of the year, the multiple twists and turns of their forms mirroring the changing surface of the sky, especially in those sculptures that had vast circles and rectangles. Clouds crowded into those open spaces and seemed to reorganize their forms. Years later, when my daughter and I were in an elevator at the Met going up to the "sculpture garden" on the roof where a special exhibit of David's work was on view, I was happy to think he was past even A-list artists. He had gone into a category all his own. "David would have loved all these people coming to see his work," I said to my daughter. The elevator operator, overhearing me, said, "They don't care about no sculpture, lady. They're just coming up for the view."

Let me be perfectly clear about this: I don't care why the people were on that elevator at the Met. David is now part of the myth of my life, where he is like my boat-husband on his Ulyssean adventure or Luis turning his *finca* from a sandbox for adults who had never outgrown a child's view of life into an adult farm where people harvested the food they ate. We all try to mold our lives into some kind of myth so that they have purpose.

"They don't care about no sculpture, lady. They're just coming up for the view." *Just coming for the view.* Those women scrambling out of the buses had also just been coming for "the view." Those ladies who climbed off the bus at David's house and *picnicked* amongst the great monoliths and threw their wax sandwich wrappers and apple cores under the Cubi masterpieces that were so much a part of his being "America's greatest artist." After all, if you are America's greatest artist, you lose your right to privacy. The trouble was that the *New York Times* article hadn't come out then; those women arrived because they had read in a Bolton Landing brochure that the field of sculpture was worth "a detour," and they needed distractions so that they didn't have to sit home wondering what their lives were all about. Correction: They did know what their lives were about. That was the trouble. It can easily be analyzed as *I know what I have to do today, and I don't want to do any of it.* I can identify with this. I am getting up every day with at least twenty things I *have* to do, and there's not one of them I give a hoot about.

I believe this applies to most people's lives. We could make it a general question about the quality of a life: Do you *want* to do the things you have to do when you get up in the morning? If the answer is no, then you have identified the problem. But identifying a problem does not provide you with a remedy. Remedies are the hardest part of the equation, and some equations have no remedies. The ladies on the bus knew that, perhaps. I was so condescending about them at the time. Now, as I write this, I am filled with compassion. I know I should have tried to explain what was the matter with them to David while he was out erecting wooden barricades and putting up a sign: THIS IS PRIVATE PROPERTY. DO NOT ENTER.

At that time, my contempt for them was bottomless. I believed those women thought themselves entitlement people, the ones who believe the rules the rest of the world had to obey didn't apply to them. They moved the wooden horses, the two-by-fours, the painted sign. It might have been that they even saw David's place as a foreign country, where you took a picture to prove you had been there.

From the cinderblock house that David and his first wife, Dorothy Dehner, had built, I would gaze out at the bus-ladies peeking into the studio and picking flowers out of the gardens. The only deterrent to denuding the masses of blueberries out in back of the house was Jo-Jo, that vile-tempered horse that David had bought for his daughters' upcoming summer visit, who chased anybody away who came near the fence.

The women held up their cameras, laughing fit to be killed in front of those enormous cosmic pieces that would later make such moving problems for the Tate and the Guggenheim. The ladies saw them not as works of art but as backdrops against which they could pose prettily and say, This was taken at that man up in Bolton's place—what's his name? Doris, do you remember what that man's name was?

Some even climbed up on the statues and sat in the open spaces, smiling into the lens, while others ran around screaming, "Look at *this* one, isn't it killing?"

Fighting the refrigerator door (which always stuck), David would be filled with anger and indignation. I always wondered if rage isn't often the result of disappointment. He wanted accolades in the art magazines, his picture on the cover of *Time*, a Nobel prize if they ever gave one for sculpture—or, better, they could make an exception, and he would be the first sculptor *ever* to win a Nobel prize, not caravans of women on an outing trashing up his yard. Once he banged out the door and hollered, "Go home! Get out!" They paid no attention, too busy having their hysterically funny pictures taken.

"Maybe they need visual aids to understand what the word *private* means," I said. "You know, something like those barbarians who used to pile up the gouged-out eyes of their enemies as a warning there was unwelcome territory ahead. They kept human dogs, too, filthy old men who never washed and had long, matted hair and could only gibber and bark. They were chained to stumps to keep intruders out. When people came that they didn't want to come in, the dog-men would run at them and try to bite them."

"Where did you hear of such a thing? A pile of eyes—men chained to posts—"

"I had a husband who collected the macabre. One of his favorite stories was about how Hart Crane threw himself off a boat on his way home from Mexico. Some people think the hand he held up as he went down was a salute of farewell, as if he were saying, You keep on, I can't. My husband thought that Hart Crane had changed his mind, he didn't want to die, and the hand was a helpless attempt to get someone to come rescue him. My husband really took to people who were manic depressives, like Darwin, or paranoid, like Newton, or crazy, like Robert Lowell, who was in and out of mental institutions all his life and spent the time in between terrified of the next episode that would get him locked up again so that he never had a moment's peace. Maybe that was his favorite, Lowell who never had a moment's peace, though he was partial, too, my husband, to Goya, who went deaf and numb with despair at the end of his life; and Beethoven, who also went deaf, which might have been worse, since he was a musician. He liked Milton being blind and Nietzsche raving inside a lunatic asylum that chained its madmen to the wall when they got too vociferous. I think he's probably somewhere right this minute thinking, I hope she never has a moment's peace." I didn't say he'd got his wish, because the look on David's face was so fierce that he was like Charlemagne, who had had 4,500 Anglo-Saxons beheaded at Verde on the River Aller in northern Saxony because they had irritated him in some way or other, maybe because they were pagans and wouldn't kneel down before The True Cross. Who knows with these religious cranks?

David came over and sat on the arm of the chair where I sat slumped with the knowledge I must be one of the few people in the world who quite often saw inside my mind piles of gouged-out eyes.

"Someone ought to find that son of a bitch," he said, "and castrate him."

What a lovely idea.

Without the art critic Clement Greenberg's support, I think it would have been very difficult for David to be accepted as the genius he and (Greenberg) thought he was within David's lifetime. Gertrude Stein told Picasso that all original art was irritating to the public before it became acceptable, and it is certainly true that in the beginning many people considered David's sculptures as nothing but a combination of trash he had haphazardly welded together.

He could be violent about everything—working, eating, drinking, talking, loving, the ways of the world. He would bluster about and pronounce this and that, and there was no disputing his opinion without unpleasant consequences. He would swagger when he had had too much to drink or sit waving his cigar imperiously and reciting some theory he had about another artist, who might be good, but naturally not as good as he was. In those moments, I used to think that the stars grow hotter as they age, getting ready to burn out completely, and perhaps all life is part of some larger myth we do not understand, filled with mortals, gods, demigods, and lessons we seem unable to learn, that time itself has made everything, even death, irrelevant.

I think I had some idea of the angry frustration David so often felt.

He could not transfer the visions on fire inside his head into the metal he was molding in the forge in front of him. He never seemed to learn that it is always this way with artists: none of us ever end up duplicating the initial image inside our heads.

If that initial vision could be reproduced exactly, the work would be easier. It is bad enough that the original image is constantly changing and evolving, but to be interrupted in the midst of trying to capture the essence of that image (think chattering women climbing down off a bus and running around shrieking at one another; think quarrelling children or a bothersome spouse), then there is bound to be an unusually high level of frustration—the angry outburst that seems to come from nowhere, the fist through the wall.

I have a theory that one of the deepest divisions in David's life was his conflict about wanting a wife and not wanting one. For better or for worse, marriage means compromise. All his life, David had fought against constriction and rebelled against authority. I'm not sure he ever understood what the word *compromise* meant. (In Spanish there is *no* word for compromise, think about *that*.) But in marriage, someone who insists on having all the authority is a bully.

The real truth is, I don't think either one of us was very good matrimonial material. We had not had the right experiences with love or—if we had—we had not understood them properly. Luis—or the Luis I had constructed inside my head— had spoiled me for anyone else, and David struck me as someone who didn't really know how to love. He knew how to give—generous to a fault—but giving isn't love. It might be a symptom, but it's not the disease itself.

It was no doubt a romantic illusion for me to believe that at *Los Vientos*, I would have become immersed in Luis—and the children we would have—and that I would have ceased to care about writing. Luis no doubt would have felt all those hours that I shut myself up in a room and put up a sign, DO NOT DISTURB, would have been time taken away from him. Luis would have gone off without a thought to do what he wanted, but he would have felt that I ought to have been at his beck and call when he wanted me, no matter how inconvenient or disruptive that might be. I can picture him shouting or pounding on the door, paying absolutely no attention to the DO NOT DISTURB sign, like the ladies who ran around David's property. We're talking choices here, not ones *you* make, but the ones that someone else makes for you. That's not a choice.

 

I didn't any longer have a clear picture of what Luis looked like, but even so, I couldn't escape my sense of loss. It would often strike me when I least expected it. There were moments when I was nothing but that pain, and I believe it was that pain that defined me. It seemed all in the entire world that I could count on. We should pay attention to what the mind can do to the body—we know perfectly well how the body's malfunctions intrude on the mind—how there is a dual-control knob that turns without our fingers touching the dial.

David seldom asked prying questions about Spain or what I had been doing before I came to Bolton. I would have told him if he had shown any interest. He volunteered almost no information about how he had grown up or what he and his first wife had done together or how he felt about those things in the past that had molded him. It was as if we had no pasts. We were supposed, I guess, to be living in the moment, but we weren't making a very good job of it.

People who don't talk about their childhoods usually have something to hide. I can't ever remember David mentioning his mother and father. Were there any siblings? Did he ever have a dog? He didn't own a dog or cat when I knew him, but I think I would rule out cats. He was more of a dog person. Perhaps he saw himself as someone who had fashioned himself in the image of who he wanted to be, that he was *not* the son of a working-class family who had little interest in art or artists. It's all speculation of course, but I know that by the time I knew him he was consumed with longings for things he didn't even know how to put names to, and those febrile cries of *I want, I want* often come from those who grow up feeling deprived.

I had to look in articles in art encyclopedias and go to the Net to find out his history—a couple of years of mechanical drawings, the only college experience a year at Ohio University in Athens (what an appropriate place for the heir of Hephaestus), where his grades were dismal except for an A in art structure. He got a B minus in drawing. After that, he dropped out of college. That was the encyclopedia information; what it didn't tell was that he was a prolific reader who had educated himself in so many areas that I was always amazed when he came up with some observation that no one but a specialist in the field would have known. Perhaps David's lack of academic credentials contributed to his bluster, but it also came from an outsized personality that matched his bulk. If you say you are a giant, and people look at you and see that in size you are one, does that make you one?

Nobody who had a choice would opt to be born in Decatur, Indiana, like David, or grow up in Indianapolis, like me. I said we both shared the stigma of being Hoosiers. I wanted to blame everything on Indianapolis, which was absurd, but David never said so. What he said was, Put it on paper. Get your anger out there.

I remembered the Hoosier snobbery of my childhood and how names counted. He came from such-and-such a family. Her father was so-and-so. But Smith is a generic name; it is impossible to pin it to an ethnic identity. Lots of people with unpronounceable names who passed through Ellis Island were given an easy-to-spell and easy-to-pronounce American name: Smith, Jones, Roberts, whatever popped into the immigration officer's head. Since David never talked about "his people," as my mother would have called them, I have no idea what his blood lines were. But you don't get a physique like David's unless you have peasant blood in your veins.

Decatur, had had a population of less than ten thousand when David Roland Smith (oh, I love it! Roland, Roland of Roncevaux, I think, where did that come from?) was born there on March 9, 1906. It was impossible to imagine David (Roland) growing up there, standing on the sidewalk watching a Fourth of July parade as he waved a small American flag, impossible to think of him as a member of a high school softball team or taking part in the Decatur vs. Greenbury school track meet. Greenbury had been written up in Ripley's "Believe It or Not" because its courthouse had a tree growing out of the courthouse tower. Who wants to come from a town like that?

Whatever David had been or done in Decatur, he had banished it to some compartment that was tightly bolted, and he would never deliver the key to open it to anyone else. I think the important thing to David was that he got out, for the same reason I did—he felt such an outsider.

I think David believed that life only made sense in its arts. Or perhaps he thought that even if it didn't make sense, people had to pretend that it did. He wanted the world to sort out evil from good and reward the good and punish the evil. History does not bear this out as being true. Still, what was history to him? Hadn't he spent his life proving he could rewrite the history of art? Take out the sculptures of his dreams? Hadn't he constructed his own world at Bolton Landing? Luis got to stay in the backdrop into which he had been born. I got to be the wanderer. David got to be one of the master creators.

I doubt David had had any idea at all when he went to work at the Studebaker plant in South Bend, Indiana, that his job would teach him a lot of the skills he would use later in life to become one day "America's greatest artist." Probably he thought he would be America's greatest something. Some people seem force fields unto themselves.

During World War II, he welded tanks in a defense plant in Schenectady. (I never was given the story of how he got from South Bend, to Schenectady, New York.) After the war, when David finally arrived in New York City, the art world was in turmoil. Painters, writers, sculptors, musicians were all looking for new ways to break through to the next level of their media. They were afire with new ideas, new methods of using old materials, unorthodox ideas that they fell on with the relief of the inventor. David fit right in. Revolt, not Roland, should have been his middle name.

David decided I was living in the Dark Ages of Art, which was probably true, considering I had been inhabiting a country fixated on crucifixion figures, Madonnas decked out in jewels, martyrs and saints who had met dreadful demises. (My favorite picture in the Prado in Madrid was the martyred woman who carried a tray on which lay her hacked-off breasts, the places where they had once resided filled in with painstakingly realistic veins, arteries, bone, and whatever else make up breasts.)

I'll say this for David: He was a good teacher. He saddled me with books. He talked at me until I felt numb from an endless onslaught of words. He insisted on making me tell him what I *thought* I saw when I looked at a picture in one of his art books. He told me his theory that canvas was the base and painting was the sculpture. He said that he wanted his pieces to look like free forms, but also to incorporate the negative empty space around them as part of the overall design, that he was producing "drawings in space."

I would look at one of his huge metal mélanges and think, Well, I guess you're drawing in space as well as incorporating the negative space around the piece to make a statement that is more than just a lot of metal welded together, but I'm having a hard time getting there. If art could answer back, I think it would have said, Of course you are. It's a *new* concept, one nobody else has ever conceived.

He only became himself when he was putting himself into metal. Everything else out was outside and essentially unimportant. He was only himself when he went inside and saw shapes and took up the metal and put it to the fire; then the vision he saw emerging stopped all questions and regrets, the disillusionments and guilt. In his work, he became whole. I understood that. I had begun to have some kind of understanding that the only way I felt whole was when I was writing. In my writing I was defining who I was and why I felt the way I did, which so often seemed to be at odds with everything I had been taught with most of the people I knew. I, too, saw outside. It was then I was happy, the way David was only happy when he was out working in his studio. We were learning the basic principle of creation, that it was the only way of life that made life bearable.

We liked being together because we saw the world in the same way. Besides, I had a good time with him, and I couldn't say that much about the landscape of the Adirondacks where I was living. I belonged to dry, sandy soil and lightly silvered leaves, to a place that sucked your soul into its earth, not to the dour threatening molehills all around me that people who lived in the Adirondacks pretended were mountains. I did not understand these people who lived within this dark, verdant vastness any more than I had understood the Hoosier flatlands back home in Indiana.

Sometimes I felt so estranged that I would sit on the steps of my porch and try to keep from splintering into small pieces that would scatter all over the steps. My daughter would never know *Los Vientos*. It was, I thought, one of the worst things I could possibly have done to her.

These gloomy Adirondack forests had been one of the last parts of New York State to be populated. Their winters were long and the growing seasons short—three months if you were lucky. In the 1900s, there had been one year when there had been no summer at all, and ice had formed on water on the Fourth of July. I could not comprehend how, after a year of enduring such an abusive climate, people would elect to stay on. A lot didn't. Back in the dark, sour forests, I would find the remnants of cleared meadows going back to wild grass and sprouting scrubs. I saw the remnants of abandoned farms, often only stone outlines of a house and the battered boards, caved in, of what had once been a barn, all that was left of owners who had finally admitted defeat and fled.

The fact that David had chosen to live here the major part of his adult life mystified me. I wanted sun and warmth, and if there had to be mountains I wanted real mountains, not green struggling stumps. Perhaps one day, they would really be mountains. David told me that the Adirondacks grew something like half an inch a year.

You mean these are mountains that grow?

You can't see them grow of course, but they do grow. I read it in a book.

The way he said *they do grow* made it obvious that David loved this dark, closed world. He embraced the black shadows and dense forests, the lumps posing as mountains.

Did you ever recognize, David, that since fire was your medium, living in a land of ice maybe wasn't the best idea in the world? I wanted to ask him. It was obvious that nothing gave him as much pleasure as finishing a new piece of work and getting it hoisted onto a flatbed and driven out in the field that sloped down the hill in front of his house as if he were making the statement, Look, I am growing, too.

He always knew where he wanted the piece to go. It would be juggled into position, and he would pull out a big cigar, light it, slump down on the grass and look at it. That look said, I made that piece. I own this land. I built my own house. All this is mine.

He was a dark, dense man and these dark, dense woods had always attracted dark, dense men. First, in the eighteenth century, came trappers, and then, in the nineteenth, big, muscular, hard-drinking loggers. Whether they were trappers or loggers, they were violent. Their cruelty seemed absolutely matter of fact. Boys cornered animals—rats, pet dogs and cats, squirrels, rabbits, deer, feral dogs and cats—solely for the purpose of tormenting them, backing them into corners where they could not escape and shooting them with BB guns, pounding their paws with rocks, throwing kerosene on them and setting them afire, shoving objects up their rectums and down their throats, poking their eyes out with sticks. People criticized bullfighting because it was cruel, but what went on in the bullring paled beside these random acts of cruelty.

When the men got into fights, they used every method possible to kill or maim an opponent. The story I hated most was of a fight that had taken place in a Warrensburg tavern where one of the men pinned down the other, seized a pool stick, and put out his opponent's eyes. This was not a story from the distant past. The blind man could be seen tapping his way down the streets of Warrensburg every morning at eleven when he went—this seemed unbelievable to me—back to the same tavern where his eyes had been put out to have his first drink of the day.

David *looked* like one of those men. No one messed with him, not just because of his size, but also because he had a dangerous predisposition to go out of control at unexpected moments. The man who ran the gas station told me to look out for him. He didn't mean David was predatory in sexual matters; he meant that if I did something to make David mad, he would lose his temper. People got out of his way when he lost his temper.

I didn't say that I had come from much more perilous situations than anything David Smith could cook up. He might lash out with words and sulk in silence, but he lacked the killer instinct. Believe me, I know it when I see it. My father and my daughter's father made sure I had learned that.

"I think maybe I brought a lot of my unhappiness on myself," I said to David one night. I finally began to tell him about Spain, what I had loved about the country and what had puzzled me and what I didn't understand and how I hated fascism and Franco, but I never said to him, I really left most of myself in Spain because of a place and a man I loved and couldn't have. I never once mentioned Luis. David was as close-mouthed about his life outside of Bolton as I was about my life without Luis, if you could call it a life. I don't see how you can do that, now that I look back. Both of us were secret keepers.

When I said, "I think maybe I brought a lot of my unhappiness on myself," he leaned forward, his dark eyes scanning my face. "What do you mean you brought your unhappiness on yourself? What unhappiness? You always seem fine to me."

I didn't say, This dark, cold place is killing me. What I said was, "I expected too much."

"We all do, at the start."

"So then you get to a place where you lower your expectations?"

"Something like that."

"Like *what*?"

David's face had that intense look someone gets when he or she is imparting very private, special information that has never been told to anyone else, not even a priest or a psychiatrist, and I was straining to hear what he was saying, but I was so suffocated with sadness that it was impossible to put his words all together. I heard, Mumble mumble like rocks... mumble mumble ... heart ... won't mumble mumble work mumble mumble you know ... mumble mumble ... what I mean ... mumble mumble.

Was he trying to tell me what it was that had kept him here, what secret he had discovered that had transformed these cold, sullen mountains and dour trees?

David hadn't come alone, and that may have made the difference. He had come with a woman, his first wife, Dorothy Dehner, who was a painter and sculptor herself and who had an inheritance of two thousand dollars a year, which gave them an edge on independence. The pieces she produced, especially in the later part of her life after she left David, seem to me every bit as extraordinary as anything David ever made. But while she was married to David—from 1927 to 1950—she put David's career before her own.

They first met in New York City, where Dorothy Dehner had gone to study at the Art Students League. She was five years older than

David—I find this very significant. After Dorothy, David always picked what you would call young girls, at least twenty or more years younger. He would be the leader, the teacher, the one with power now, because Dorothy had been five years older and already in art school, a mentor I am sure for David, who, the day after he met Dorothy, immediately enrolled in the same school where she was studying. In many other ways, I am sure that Dorothy was the leader (and don't forget she had the two thousand dollars, which went a long way in those days), though David would never in a million years have wanted to explore those paths of speculation. What matters in the end is that during the twenty-some years Dorothy and David were together, they made the main work in their lives making David famous, a goal Dorothy devoted herself to until she left David; then she began to concentrate on her own work. While she was with David, I'm sure he found ways to keep her from working. Men do that when they are in competition with the women in their lives; for a marriage to succeed, there can only be one star.

I never met Dorothy, but I loved a small piece of hers that was in the permanent collection of The Hyde Collection in Glens Falls, where I first saw her work. Later, in 1993, the Hyde had a one-woman show to celebrate her upcoming ninetieth birthday. I was overwhelmed by the depth and breadth of what she had done throughout her long life and how much like David's her work was. Or was it that so much of his work was like hers?

David had been twenty-three and newly married when he and Dorothy visited friends in Bolton Landing. It was the Depression, and land was cheap; by the end of that summer, he and Dorothy had purchased seventy-seven acres on a mountain overlooking Lake George. Beginning in 1940, when David was thirty-four, the Smiths spent every summer in a dilapidated farmhouse that had been built in 1800. It had a leaking roof, cracked chimney, broken plaster, a house Dorothy Dehner said "should never have been built in the first place."

A small, broken-down shed near the house was made into a studio for David. During the bitter Adirondack winters, he and Dorothy went back to their Brooklyn apartment, where the landlord made it clear he did not want David doing any welding.

The Smiths were walkers. They ambled all over New York and Brooklyn, and one wintry day they found "a long rambly junky looking shack called Terminal Iron Works." David returned the next day and said he needed a welding outfit and a place to work. The people at the Terminal Iron Works made him feel at home, and he went there almost every day to work. Later, he would name his Lake George studio the Terminal Iron Works after the factory that had provided him space for his first struggles to break through space, materials, and concepts.

In 1940, David and Dorothy moved permanently to Bolton Landing. Dorothy spent most of her time trying to make the house habitable while David was out constantly scouring the area for discarded machine parts—pipes, scrap iron, any piece of metal that he thought might come in handy one day. I don't think David himself knew what use some of these things would ever be, but they must have evoked strong feelings in him when he came upon them, because he would put them in the back of his truck and haul them home, where they would hang about in his studio until one day he took hold of one and saw he could use it in a piece he was working on.

The Smiths began to construct a house of concrete blocks. David was also outgrowing his small studio. A new one was built out of cinderblocks and sheet steel, large enough for him to construct huge pieces of sculpture and situated near the road so that his work was easier to load and to move.

I've heard some people say David abused Dorothy. I don't know if this is true or not. When I knew David, she was gone, never referred to, just as David never gave any indication he had spent time abroad, but I discovered, in looking through a book my daughter gave me, that in their early years he and Dorothy had traveled to the Virgin Islands, France, Italy, Switzerland, Greece, as well as making a short stay in Russia. In 1962, he was invited to take part in the prestigious Spoleto Festival in Italy where, in a month, he was expected to produce one or two works. He took over an old, abandoned factory and from the junked pieces he found produced twenty-eight pieces, which came to be known as the *Voltri* series. I pictured a scene out of Dante's Inferno, with David standing in the midst of fire like a madman wielding pieces together that took shape while the Italian workmen stood by and stared, awestruck (or, perhaps like the lady picnickers, both amazed and amused).

I would never have guessed he had ever left the United States. Why hadn't he ever said anything about having been abroad? I talked about Europe all the time. He sat mum as marble.

A year after David and Dorothy were divorced, David married twenty-year-old Jean Freas, the girl I had seen at the sink with the two small children clinging to her. Jeannie, as David had called her during the good part of their marriage, had been a Sarah Lawrence student— she was perhaps his trophy wife? She was certainly decades younger, exceptionally pretty, and (I imagine) must have been somewhat in awe of David. They had their two daughters together, and here was this bright (when I later learned she became fluent in Swahili, my admiration jumped twenty points) beautiful young woman with a demanding husband, two small children in diapers, and people wandering in and out of the house all the time, the house looking as if it had been rifled by the police. No doubt she worked hard to try to bring order, which could not have been easy. David was always throwing things around and letting them settle where they fell. But he always knew where they were, so *don't* touch them.

Whenever I think of the 1950s and early '60s, and myself at that time in America, or of David's wives, or of women in general, I think of what third- and fourth-class citizens we were, and not just women but also Jews, blacks, Catholics, anyone handicapped in any way, even with a stutter—and that discrimination was not only perfectly legal but taken for granted. Ads read "male wanted" (and could specify no Jews need apply in code language; no blacks would of course even think of applying); married women weren't hired for good jobs because they would become pregnant and leave or, if they were hired and they did become pregnant, would immediately be fired. Women didn't need careers. They only worked to earn pocket money until they got married. If, unfortunately, that didn't happen, there were few career paths open to women—teaching, being a hairdresser, a librarian or nurse, taking care of the old and infirm at home ("resident homes" didn't really exist). Pay discrimination—men making many more times the salary paid a woman doing the same work or even a higher level of work—was expected; promotions were not. If a man made sexual jokes or advances to a woman, that was her worry, and you never heard a murmur of outrage about it. Though women had shown during World War II that they were as capable as men, even in doing hard lifting and easily carrying out physically demanding jobs, when the war was over, they were expected to put down their hammers and pull on their aprons. *It wasn't until 1964 that the Civil Rights Act was passed.* Ask any black person, any woman, any person with a disability, about how they feel about their civil rights, and the answer you will get is that the Civil Rights Act still hasn't been fully implemented. Women still earn only 79 cents to the dollar a man makes at the same job, and I myself would qualify that as white women. The talking heads are always pondering why Hillary Clinton's supporters were so angry that she didn't get the presidential nomination. The answer is that older women remembered back to the time they trained young men, and the young men got the promotion while they stagnated in the same job for decades and had no recourse to change the status quo.

Young women don't get it. The talking heads don't get it. Most men still don't get it. The crushing fight for equality and recognition is beyond their imaginations because they haven't had to pay the penalties for being female. I'm glad Obama got elected, but you might argue that it is easier for a half-black man to be president than a woman, though I would be the first to admit Hillary ran a disorganized and ineffective campaign. There is one thing *no one* ever pointed out: Hillary would never even been able to run for president if she hadn't been Bill Clinton's wife. She got close to the White House door on Bill's coattails.

I can remember a seminar on Staten Island that James Baldwin and I were part of. He was introduced as representing black writers, and I was introduced as representing women writers.

The white male writers were very condescending to us. We were supposed to ride in the back of the literary bus. They went off together for a drink after the lecture and question-and-answer period, leaving Baldwin and me looking at one another.

It is characteristic of the time period that I had felt honored just to be asked, and I was hurt instead of angry when the white male writers ignored me. Baldwin was livid. We went off together and had a drink, probably several drinks. Baldwin was a happy drinker at night, as if he thought of his black life being best lived out in the black night, and talked about what it was like to be marginalized. "I am a writer," Baldwin said over and over to me, who certainly wasn't going to deny it. "I am not a black writer. Those condescending bastards don't see me as just a writer. They want me to be a black writer so they don't have to be judged with me. I'm better than they are, and they know it."

They also knew that they could get away with treating both of us badly. I was a woman and he was black, and the time had not yet come when whites were conscious of their bad behavior toward minorities.

Baldwin did not even look like someone who was a writer, let alone a major writer. He gave the impression he hadn't been put together right, his head too large for his body and the body itself strangely proportioned, the legs too short and thin to fit the design of his upper torso so that he loped along in a loose kind of shuffle, with his large prominent head thrust forward, accenting the pop eyes and large buck teeth.

It was Baldwin's voice that was the most notable thing about him. Out of this small, black, ugly little man's throat came the sepulchral tones of one of those revivalist voices spun from the depths of doom and death.

Baldwin had been born to acquire a voice like that, his father a Harlem street-front preacher and Jimmy himself a prodigy famous for the mesmerizing sermons he gave before he was fourteen. Even after he lost his calling to save the damned—well, perhaps he never did lose that, he just changed gears on how to address being one of the damned— he went from the Pentecostal lilt and flow of black sermonizing to the raging words of his polemics. The spectral tone remains in all his writing. It cropped up in most conversations you had with him. It became more and more pronounced as he began to supplant Richard Wright as the preeminent black writer of his time. Actually, Jimmy had given Wright the *coup de gras* himself in an article repudiating Wright as the black spokesman of his generation, coupling Wright's work with protest literature like *Uncle Tom's Cabin*, which Baldwin called a bad novel and implied *Native Son* was just as bad.

The two were both living in the Paris at the time and had a bitter confrontation in the Brasserie Lipp, a hangout for American expatriates. Wright accused Baldwin of trying to destroy his reputation. Baldwin tried to defend himself and later wrote an essay—"Many Thousands Gone"—in which he admitted *Native Son* was "the most powerful and celebrated statement we have yet had of what it means to be a Negro in America," but concluded Wright's work belonged to the past and that new black writers were far ahead of him in defining what it meant to be black in America. His polemic essay "Notes of a Native Son" did not help rehabilitate Wright's reputation. His famous inflammatory book *The Fire Next Time* takes its title from a Negro spiritual:

God gave Noah the rainbow sign,
No more water, the fire next time.

That book was on the *New York Times'* best seller list for forty-one weeks. Both Wright's *Native Son* and Baldwin's *The Fire Next Time* were in effect acts that amounted to the son (Baldwin) slaying his spiritual father (Wright) in order to ascend the throne as king of black literature.

People took sides. For a time, it seemed as if Baldwin had won—his portrait even appeared on the cover of *Time*—and then he did a very curious thing. In New Orleans, he had himself photographed by *Life* (ah, the photographers from *Life* seem to be a reoccurring motif, it seems, in my life) amidst the poorest Negro quarters of the city. Baldwin was wearing outlandish outfits with plenty of conspicuous bling in poses that emphasized his homosexuality.

I was so naïve at the time that I didn't understand why I found the photographs so distasteful. Now I think my dismay was a reaction to the rubbish and decay all around him, which was accented by the garish jewelry and emphasis on the white clothing that Jimmy had insisted on wearing. The pictures seemed somehow deliberately meant to be in bad taste. A lot of other people seemed to have had the same strong negative reaction to the incongruity of the man in his exotic clothes and outsized jewelry juxtaposed against the ruins of the lives in the places *Life* photographed him.

What had made him do that? By "that," I mean deliberately affront people's sensibilities. Surely he couldn't have been trying to distance himself from the black poor amongst whom he shone in his white jacket and glittering jewels? Did he think somehow that he was proclaiming himself special, not the usual idea of how black people lived? Hubris has its hidden reasons, often rooted in feelings of inferiority.

One minute Baldwin had been the most important black writer in America, and the next people began to turn against him. His books sold poorly. He was less in demand to take his place as a television pundit. He came back to America, went back to Paris, then went to Switzerland to write more books, each one selling less than the one before, until in the end a review of his latest work would be a small part of a column in the back pages of the *New York Times'* book section. He was no longer in vogue, and the tragedy of his life was that it worked itself out in front of his enormous bulging eyes.

I recall a picture taken late in his life, when he looked fragile and defeated, strikingly black in a room all in white, spooky to look at. It seemed to emphasize how far he had fallen, and the eyes in the picture said he knew every bad thing that was happening to him. The young ones are coming up, Roy Bongartz always said, and you need to cover your back. What Baldwin had done in dismissing Wright's work other new black writers coming up were now doing to him. The fire this time was aimed specifically at him, to extinguish his reputation the way he had ravaged Wright's.

Baldwin was a lovely man when I knew him, young and dynamic and full of a zest for life that always lifted my spirits. He would come to St. Mark's Place when I was living in New York—before St. Mark's became the hub of the East Village. He would sit drinking happily and talking in that Negro preacher's voice. He was a brilliant conversationalist, though I never really got used to the sermon tones in his voice or the fact that he would lean forward, pointing a finger, and say things like, I was imprisoned on a ship and sold into slavery, not literally meaning he himself had had this happen but that he stood for all the injustice and crimes that had been committed against his race. He was making everything more vivid by personalizing it. Such a technique was at first extremely effective, but as he used it over and over, it became a device that seemed overdone and at times outrageous. Of course he hadn't been on one of the slave boats, so why was he saying he had?

Too theatrical, people said, and winced. Some began to imitate and make fun of him. I didn't understand at first what was happening. Then it dawned on me that Baldwin's exaggerated use of the word *I* had increased the backlash against him.

I did not see him after I moved away from the city. I did not want to see him as his reputation deteriorated and he himself became the object of dismissal and harsh criticism. I was stricken to see his books get less and less attention, to find that he had been left in library dust as the literary bandwagon rolled on. I knew he would understand exactly what was happening and was helpless to stop the slide into oblivion. Even the death notices talked about how out of the mainstream he had become. Do we conspire in our own downfall?

Like David Smith, Baldwin had a special affinity for children. Once, when we were walking down Second Avenue, I said, Watch Allison while I run in and pick up the laundry. Baldwin said, Are you crazy?

In those days, black and white people going down the street together were an object not only of disbelief but often of verbal abuse, which could rapidly escalate into physical violence. It had never occurred to me that his standing in the street with my flaxen-haired daughter holding his hand could be dangerous.

Then, at that moment, I saw him as a stranger would see him. He didn't look like anyone famous. He looked like an ugly, powerless little black man who had no business holding the hand of this beautiful little white girl. I knew in that moment I only understood a fraction of all the hatred and contempt he had experienced in the past and would go on experiencing in the future because of the color of his skin. Nothing he could write, none of the lectures he gave around the country, none of his appearances on television, nor any of the essays in national newsmagazines were of any help to him standing in front of a Laundromat on Second Avenue where he was just another despised black man. It was the first time I realized how limited the power of writers was, my first indication that perhaps being a great writer had no cosmic significance at all.

I'm better than they are, James Baldwin had said, and they know it. It might well have been David Smith speaking that first day I met David and I saw Jeannie in the kitchen with her two small girls hanging onto her, marginalized by David in the same way James Baldwin and I had been marginalized at the Staten Island literary conference.

But Jeannie was no longer Jeannie when I moved to Bolton. She was gone gone gone, and usually not to be mentioned. I think that he missed her and the girls and he didn't know how to get them back, that probably it was too late to do that. He didn't know he couldn't bring her back by still trying to bully her. That was one of the few things I did know about his private life. Oh, I knew he went to New York and liked to go to Five Spot and listen to Monk. I knew he went to Bennington to see friends whose names I could never remember. I had a vague notion he was teaching a course there or had taught a course or was going to teach one. I never gave much thought to his comings and goings, because my own life was in such chaos that it was all I could do to keep track of all the things that were mixed-up in mine. It wasn't as if I had to know all those things about David. They weren't essential to my life the way Luis and *Los Vientos* had been.

That time in my life was such a blur that actions fused together so that it was difficult to distinguish one from the other—I don't even remember getting the third cat—and I couldn't concentrate on what should have been important because the trivial demands seemed to take up an enormous amount of my days. I find I have mixed things up in ways that seem inconceivable. I thought I was in Spain when actually I was back in the States. I even imagined I could hear the cricket singing in its bamboo cage. Sometimes I drank a lot, muddling my mind ever more. David thought (perhaps) that he could detour my mind by hectoring it to learn more about contemporary music.

"You absolutely cannot expect to consider yourself an intelligent human being if you don't know anything about jazz."

"But, David, I don't like jazz. Most writers don't. They aren't too fond of country music either, except maybe Patsy Cline. They like symphonies and operas and some chamber music. Jazz offends some inner ear they need for dialogue, it—"

"Just listen to this. *Just listen.*" David was tramping about his jumbled living room, jabbing the air with his cigar.

Once, at his house in the midst of a great cacophony of drums and brass and god knows what, he leaned over and thrust the small statue of *The Puritan* that I so admired at me. "Here, you like it so much, take it. It's for both you and your daughter. She's a real connoisseur, that daughter of yours. I don't care she's only four years old."

As I took the small piece of sculpture, it was as if a veil were being lifted. He was *not* just an interesting neighbor who made my life easier in the Adirondacks. He loved my daughter, he liked *me*, and at that moment, he cut quite an impressive figure, tramping around his living room with the big cigar stuck in his mouth. In back of him, great dark shadows of his sculpture were outlined by a rising moon in the gathering twilight.

He was huge. He was unbelievably strong. He was *famous*. He was *rich*. What's not to like about someone being rich and famous and incredibly strong?

What's not to like is that he was Hephaestus, and the ancient Greeks have shown us that any mortal who gets involved with the gods does not end up well.

Then he said something to me that changed everything. He said, stopping to agonize over his sketch pad, "Do you ever get away from it?" Understanding too well that "It" was our work, I said simply, "No."

There are lines of demarcation that, once crossed, there is no going back. What David was saying was, We are alike. It is important to hang onto people who share the same inside spaces that you do. You haven't seen that before. Can you see it now? I would have said, Yes, I see it, and I don't know what to do about it. I think you are capable of slaying dragons, but I'm not. Are you saying you'll slay the dragons for me?

Once in a while David and I would forego for a day the crushing pursuit of the elusive visions inside our heads and go R-E-L-A-X. Let's take the skiing. At age fifty-something, David decided he wanted to do the slopes. Of course, on only the best skis. HEAD had considerable trouble running up a pair of skis for a man with the size of his feet, but months later, the longest pair of slats I had ever seen in my life arrived and David wanted to go to Gore Mountain to test them. I was looking at the length of the skis and thinking that no one could have managed them, no matter how many years of experience on the snow, and he had never been on a ski slope in his life. The only place to start was on the beginner's rope tow with my daughter and the other children, a giant of a man amidst all those children. I didn't know how to tell him that he would have to start out on a device that only children used.

"Allison is just learning," I said. "You could try this tow line she uses that is real easy. She can show you how it works."

She had got her first pair of skis for Christmas and did well until she became frightened of the rope tow. She'd caught her mitten in the gears at the end that made a loop for the rope to go back down. If the kid operating the machine hadn't had the presence of mind to throw the switch and turn everything off, I dread to think what might have happened to her hand.

Later, I was told the kid who was in charge of the rope tow had had problems like that before and that often he had to scoop up children who got to the top and didn't know how to get off. He would snap off the power that propelled the tow and literally hoist a child into the snow, letting the line bunch up and children run into each other and start falling every which way.

I was consumed with guilt. She should never have been wearing mittens. She should have had on thick leather gloves with fingers, but I was short of money and it had never occurred to me that the mitten wouldn't do. All I knew was that a rope tow was easy to maneuver. You just put your hands on the thick rope and let it pull you up. David could do that.

But would he?

I said to my daughter, "When we get to Gore, ask David to help you go up the rope tow. Tell him you're afraid to go by yourself. You know I won't be able to get him on unless he thinks you need help."

As David moved to the rope-tow line, the kids stared at him as if he were a Japanese movie monster. David ignored them. He had his skis on. He was going to go skiing. He was going to help a child who said she needed him to get her up.

But he didn't know how to manage the rope tow. He stood watching it go up the slightly slanted hill wondering, I suppose, if it would support his weight. The kid at the top who was in charge, all of seventeen, if that, looked down and hollered at David to take hold of the goddamn rope.

"You go first," my daughter said. "I'll follow after and, if I need help, I'll grab hold of you."

David took hold of the thick rope and began his ascent, bent over and wobbling from side to side as he slowly went inch by inch up the hill. When he got to the top and didn't let go of the rope, the kid took both of David's hands and threw them off the rope. David skidded to one side and fell down. He looked like a small, lumpy Adirondack mountain. My daughter had been thrown off with him. She pushed herself up using her ski poles and looked down at him with an expression I had no trouble interpreting at all: another dangerous adult. But she had a good heart, this daughter of mine. She didn't desert him.

David was floundering around, trying to find some traction so that he could pull himself up, but his skis were so long that he couldn't maneuver them parallel to the ground. The kid shut the tow down, some of the kids tumbling about, others standing placidly upright, their hands clamped on the rope, waiting for the tow to start up again.

The kid who managed the tow line went over and tried to get his hands under David so that he could pull him up. The two of them wrestled about in the snow until David finally got a ski pole anchored and hoisted himself up, his arms askew, his snow hat hanging to one side of his head.

My daughter took his hand. He looked down at her, and I could see she was talking to him. Then she tried to help him over to the hill. David bobbled along, trying to keep his balance. My daughter took her two small gloved hands and pressed them against his legs, steadying him. When they got to the crest of the hill, my daughter struck the snow with her ski poles, pushed with all her might, and took off. The hill had a very gentle slope. It only took her a couple of minutes to get to the bottom. When she finally came to a stop, she turned and looked up the hill. David was still standing at the top.

She hollered something to him, and he waved one of his ski poles. Before he could stop himself, he began to slide sideways down the hill. He veered first one way, then the other. Children flew like large, brightly colored balloons out of his way. Balloons, I thought. Perhaps everything in our lives is connected by images, the images preserved in memory waiting to appear when they were apt.

When David finally came to the bottom, he didn't know how to stop, so he grabbed hold of some child in front of him and hung on. The child let out a scream, and David let go and fell over. Some fathers who had been instructing their children came over and began trying to pull him to his feet. I could see them saying something to him, and I could tell by their faces that their remarks weren't kind.

My daughter had already started schussing over to the tow to get away from us. I skied over to David and tried to apologize to the men. David was hollering into my face that he was never going to get on that rope tow again. "I was the only adult! How could you have put me on something where I was the only grown up amidst nothing but little kids?"

"You had to start on the beginners' slope. You don't know how to ski. When you get the basics, you can use the T-bar. You should probably take a lesson. There are a lot of kids around who are good skiers and could show you how to do the turns and how to stop when you want to."

"No," the kind of *no* that means if you ever mention that idea again, I will make you good and sorry.

We stood side by side watching my daughter coming down on her second run. "You know how to ski. You could teach me."

"I don't ski that well—"

"I don't need to try anything fancy. Just start with the basics."

I didn't want to do it, but I couldn't see any alternative. "It's a question of balance and of how you shift your weight. Like this," I said and stood straight and pushed my poles and then shifted my body slightly to the right and turned. "I can do that," he said with absolute assurance. But when he tried to lean to the left, it was like releasing a ton of bricks all at once and his skis went flying out from under him and he smashed down into the snow.

It took several fathers to help me get him back on his feet. "Let's not try to do the turns right now," I said. "Let's just see if you can push yourself along in a straight line. You just put one ski in front of the other and push yourself along with your poles. Don't push too hard—David, you're pushing too hard."

All his life, his big feet had carried him well on good solid ground, but now, without any warning, he was asking them to learn some new form of transportation and they rebelled. Feet walked. They didn't ski.

He fell down three times on the way to the T-bar. I was sweating from the effort to get him back up, and my heart was torn with despair. I didn't want to ride up on the T-bar with him, but I couldn't ask someone else to do that. People were getting on really fast, and I could feel David tensing up beside me. I turned to the kid behind me and said, "This is his first time on this lift. Could you give me a hand?"

The kid grabbed hold of him on one side, and I had the other. "Slow this damn thing down," the kid said to the boy who was running the T-bar. "This old man ain't never been on one of these before, and he don't know what he's doing."

I had never heard anything worse said to a fifty-some-odd-year-old man who prided himself on his prowess with the world.

The kid pushed David on, and I slipped in beside him. We began to ascend. David was gripping so hard that I thought he might snap the bar. I was trying to figure out how to get him off. The kid was right behind me. He kept giving David pieces of advice about what to do when we got to the top and David had to get off.

David didn't get off. The kid grabbed hold of him and pushed him so hard that David skidded under the bar and fell to one side. The kid was furious with me. "Why'd you bring this guy up here? He can't ski for squat."

"He wanted to come," I said lamely.

I stood in the clear, bright air and looked at people trying to get past us. We were a hazard to every skier getting off the T-bar, but there was no moving David. He was frozen in place. The kid pulled his poles into place and left us to our fate. An old man like that wanted to kill himself, let him do it on his own.

I was trying to turn David around so that if I were to get him to his feet he would be facing the right direction when two members of the ski patrol arrived. "Heard there was some trouble up here. Is this guy hurt?"

"No, he's not hurt. He just needs to get up."

They put their hands together in some kind of Red Cross maneuver and raised him like a flag going up a pole.

"Maybe we could give you some help getting him down. The stretcher's right over there. We could put him on it and—"

"I'm perfectly fine," David said with great dignity. "I just got a little turned around. I'll be fine now."

"You sure? It wouldn't be any trouble to—"

"I—am—perfectly—fine."

"Okay, as long as you're sure." They didn't look convinced.

David stood on his skis, pressing his weight down so hard that they sank in the snow. He wasn't going to go down on a stretcher, and he couldn't go back down on the T-bar. That was not an option. People could come up on the T-bar, but they couldn't go back down, because the bar rose about thirty feet into the air on its way down.

David inched his way to the edge of where the actual slope began. Bright, happy-looking people were zigzagging through the fresh, powdery snow. A small boy whizzed past us. Two giggling girls flipped their hair back and schussed recklessly straight down, picking up dazzling speed as they went.

I heard David take a sharp breath. "Give me a push, will you, K-Kiddo?"

I didn't know what else to do, so I gave him a shove and off he went, flaying his arms with his ski poles right and left, careering from side to side and almost falling, but somehow balancing himself enough to cross into a bevy of skiers on their way down. Someone shouted, "Out of control skier on the slope!" Skiers hastily swished to sides of the slope and crouched near trees, hoping they would be protected from him.

Someone gave a high-pitched scream, and I saw this lump fly up into the air and then land, skis stuck straight up in the air. David lay still, his eyes wide open. Snow was blowing over him like a shroud. His hands were wiggling back and forth under big thick gloves. "My god, girl, what if I'd broken my arm?" he demanded when I reached his side. "How would I be able to *work*?"

The most ignominious act a skier can resort to is to have to *walk* down the slope carrying his skis. This requires an acknowledgment that he has taken on more than he can do.

Why would anyone get on a slope that was far too difficult to ski?

Because it's David Smith, I wanted to shout, watching him walk dejectedly down the side of the slope carrying skis that went at least six feet over his head, and David Smith thinks he can conquer anything.

And you? Do you still think he can conquer *any*thing?

I had been inching my way toward feeling that there was nothing in the world—except perhaps his Mercedes car—that could transform David from one the gods had morphed into what looked like a normal human being, but at that moment I was looking at a large man who had been overwhelmed by a pair of skis. He did not look like even a slayer of ants.

After the ski debacle, David no doubt decided he had lost face with me, and the truth was he had. He was not invincible, which must have shown in my face. He apparently decided he could make up for the disaster on the ski slopes by showing me what a man of the world he could be. We were to drive to Glens Falls to dinner and a movie, a perfectly straightforward expedition for normal people; but we were planners and plotters against normality, born losers out in a white, cold December night trying to make the Mercedes and ourselves behave as other people and machines did.

A blizzard was beginning, the flakes so thick that the Mercedes windshield wiper couldn't keep up with them. The car kept trying to run off the road. Why hadn't we taken the truck? In the truck, I always felt safe. It was the Mercedes that was rigged for death. That car had more malfunctions and evil ideas than any instrument of industrialization I have ever encountered. David loved it. It was his badge of honor, his award of achievement.

The Mercedes was ill-equipped to give David back the love he expected. For one thing, the Germans had not put together a car to lie about idly for weeks and then start off in thirty-five-below-zero weather. Thus would begin one of those sessions in which David and the car pitted themselves against one another.

The pattern had commenced from the first day David bought the car. Having purchased a Mercedes, what to do but show it off? That first trip ought to have been forewarning enough. Up to David's good neighbors the Hermans he went to dazzle Evans, Frances, and young Katharine. Spinning along in triumph, he neglected the proper angle of a curve. The glorious chariot went in the ditch and had to be pulled out by a tractor, the Hermans witnesses to his disgrace. I'm sure he bypassed the Hermans for a while until he hoped they had forgotten his humiliation. He always wanted things to go right (who doesn't?), but when they didn't he never seemed to shoulder any of the responsibility. With the Mercedes, he blamed the Germans. Some kraut had probably done something to make it misbehave because of losing the war.

Continuing mishaps identified the Mercedes with disaster: batteries that gasped and went dead, a dashboard whose lights went up in a blue shower of sparks and burned out vital electrical equipment. This was a car that was constantly relaying the message, **DANGER. BEWARE.** I dreaded riding in it, trembling on the handsome red leather upholstery in anticipation of another brush with death.

David Smith was in his good suit. I have forgotten my own attire, his far more memorable than mine; though, in thinking back, I might have had on the great dress before the moths ruined it. What else did I have that was decent? I was always dead broke, and of course I was carrying a purse that probably weighed almost as much as I did. David's black suit, huge, shimmering green and dead under certain slants of light; a silk shirt, custom made; a strange tie with some identifying logo, Countess Mara perhaps, Countess Mara ties being de rigueur for the rich at that time, and a "good" (translate that to mean Brooks Brothers or Abercrombie & Fitch) overcoat. With this covering of elegance, he had also put on gentleman's manners, elbowing me along awkwardly to the car, shouting back to the babysitter that we shouldn't be too late, seizing the door and flinging it open magnanimously, hoisting me onto the car seat as if I were made of porcelain, fussing about getting me "comfortable," though the purse was something of a hindrance, and I must admit, I was struck absolutely dumb (a difficult deed to achieve) by David Smith in the role of Man About Town. I saw him as The Forger at the Fire, which is far removed from Beau Brummell.

We were two people who ate and talked and drank all at the same time, arguing, accusing, interrupting, expostulating, demanding each other's attention. We had never, never, in all the time we'd known one another, been "nice," and all this elegant attention made me feel as if I couldn't find my proper place in this Adirondack moment into which the gods had thrust me. David, on the other hand, gave an impression of swimming straight for his element. It was baffling, but I accepted that he knew what he was doing. What else was I to do against such belief?

We commenced toward Glens Falls, famous from 1945 on as having been chosen by *Life* magazine as Hometown, U.S.A. Glens Falls is an odd town. It got its name because of a bet. Originally, in 1763, it was named Wings Falls after Abraham Wing, but Wing lost a bet to Colonel Johanness Glen in 1788, and the town's name was altered. Somewhere the apostrophe was lost, which has always bothered me, more and more after I took on teaching English at the local community college, so that I had from the first moment I laid eyes on the town had a prejudice against it.

The town had prospered from logging—there are large mansions still scattered all over the center of the town, though many have been made into museums (besides the Hyde, we have the Chapman and the World's Awareness of Children's Museum), or turned into bed & breakfasts because Glens Falls had fallen on hard times. Surrounding suburban malls murdered the mercantile heart of the town, where galleries and antique stores go in and out of business at a dizzying rate of speed.

Development houses and condo communities sprouted past the old city limits, and the people who lived there began to feel that since their houses were newer, they were better than those of the people who actually lived inside the lines of Glens Falls, some twelve to thirteen thousand people who were mostly working and middle class, the lumber barons long since having moved on or gone into other financially rewarding endeavors. The newer-houses people wanted a more aristocratic name, so the town split into Glens Falls and Queensbury, a name presumably reflecting upward mobility. Bolton Landing was a jumble of everything, as if someone had tossed houses and shops, garages, and a diner into the air, and they had all landed helter-skelter.

David was humming off key as he conducted his kraut car toward a moment of majesty. He was going to show me how a really first-class night on the town should be run. It was all there, I am sure, inside his head, the whole perfection of the plan laid out before we even began the long, faltering drive, the Mercedes blinking and coughing, hunching itself up, springing for snow banks.

At the restaurant, David grandly ordered lobster thermidor and (he pointed out) an impeccable white wine of absolutely correct vintage. He talked vineyards and labels happily. Oh, it was going to be such a memorable occasion!

Neither the lobster nor the proper bottle of wine was on hand, the waitress informed us. I thought to have scallops. *Not nearly fancy enough,* I could see David thinking. Seizing the menu from my hand, David ordered—I've forgotten what; it was scallops I got. He got something (at least he thought) wrongly turned out. Thus began one of those restaurant scenes where things go forth from the kitchen to the table and from the table back to the kitchen. I couldn't eat. He didn't. It was all wrong wrong wrong. The lobster thermidor and the right wine life should provide at certain times—the right time in the right place.

Looking back, I'm not sure this whole evening wasn't the result of my having mentioned in passing that I had once heard Segovia play in the Alcázar gardens of Seville at midnight, that there had been champagne laid out on a long table with a beautiful white linen tablecloth. When a train whistled, Segovia stopped playing and waited the whistle out, then began to play again. That was, I remember saying, one of the perfect nights of my life. I never said who I'd gone to the Alcázar gardens with—that would have been too much. How could David ever compete with someone who had and owned land equal in size to the state of Maryland? Take my word for it, competition was a better nomenclature for him than Roland. This night was supposed to be his proof that no one could better him for producing memorable evenings.

There was no time, with all the trips of food back and forth, to tarry at the table for an after-dinner drink. David got up, outraged, slammed some money down, and marched for the door in such a snit that when he grabbed the doorknob, it came off in his hand. "Give it to me," I said. I took it to the waitress and rolled my eyes.

We made a dash for the movie, *Dr. Strangelove*, which was supposedly the reason for this whole expedition, but *Dr. Strangelove* had gone off the bill the night before. We were left with a bad Western. Not just mediocre, but utterly, unbearably unforgettable, where the Indians were all white men in bad makeup who said *How* a lot.

At the movie, David squirmed in a seat fashioned to suit a normal man. He struggled for an inch of space for his long legs, his huge coat, for elbow room for arms thickened from wrestling with enormous pieces of steel. I, meanwhile, was tussling with my purse, which wouldn't fit under the movie seat. The man in back of David tapped him on the shoulder and asked him if he would mind scrunching down a little so that he didn't obliterate the screen. Short of decapitation, I could see no way for him to do that. "We'll move," David said in such a loud voice that people turned around and looked at us. He dragged his coat across the faces of the people sitting in our row as we stumbled across their feet to make our departure. "See if there are some seats in the back."

I couldn't see a thing in the dark, but I went dutifully toward a red EXIT sign that indicated there might be enough light to see the back row of the theater. We crawled over two people and sat down. David bunched up his coat and tried to put it on a small ledge in back of us. It kept flopping down and hitting me on the head. He would jerk it back and throw it around for a while and then look at the screen. Once, trying to catch the coat before it came down on me, his elbow hit me in the eye. He didn't even ask me if I was all right. At this point, I don't think he cared, or maybe he would have liked me to be whacked so hard that I got a concussion and then died and there would be no witnesses left to testify to the debacle of this evening.

I looked at fake Indians quirking their horses toward an undermanned circle of valiant U.S. cavalry and tried not to notice when David put one of his big hands on my arm. I had no idea what that was supposed to signify—maybe that we were companions in a disaster comparable to the *Titanic,* but he was looking out for me. I needn't worry. He'd find me a lifeboat.

Nothing would do when the movie (that palace of cinematic dreams has since been razed) was over but that we have a drink at the "best" spot in town, which David had decided was the Queensbury Hotel. Besides, it was conveniently across the street. The Queensbury has undergone so many changes and renovations since that time that I can't remember the décor or even if it was in the same room the bar is in now; what I do remember is David sitting down and stretching out to relieve his aching muscles and promptly appearing to inhabit the whole room.

The waitress had no idea what to do with him. I don't think she'd ever seen such a large man, and his vast size obviously made her nervous and inattentive.

"Coffee and brandy—what kind of brandy have you got?—and I want some cube sugar, too."

She just stared at him, immobilized.

The third time David gave her the order, he shouted it. The rest of the people in the room gaped at us as if they were spectators looking at performers in a circus. On a dais, the man who was playing twenty-year-old show tunes stopped playing. I could see David was getting ready to make a scene. What had happened to his *By god, this is going to be an evening to remember?*

The waitress finally rattled off the names of some of the brands of brandy the hotel had, and then she made the mistake of saying, "I don't think we have any cube sugar, sir, but I can bring you regular sugar."

"What do you mean you don't have any cube sugar? This is a hotel, isn't it?"

"Yes, sir, but I don't think we have cube sugar—"

"I want cube sugar!" He turned to me. "I have this thing I want to show you with brandy and coffee and cube sugar."

"Where you put brandy on the sugar and then put the sugar in your mouth and drink the coffee through that?"

"Oh," David said, "you know that, do you?"

"From Spain."

The worst thing I could have said to him at that point.

When we left the Queensbury, it was about midnight on one of those steely, still, frigid nights where the simple sounds your shoes make come out like squeals of suffering. A faint blue glow hung over everything. We got in the car, crushed with cold. David put the key in the ignition and went to turn the engine on. The key remained locked, *frozen, goddamn it.* I just sat there, paralyzed with cold and the belief that the world was in ruins and the babysitter must be out of her mind by now. I had said we'd be back about midnight. David said "not too late," which for David could meant any time before dawn.

"What are you doing?" I finally managed to get out.

"What the hell does it look like I'm doing? I'm pounding the goddamn son-of-a-bitch steering wheel."

After the steering wheel had been taught what to expect if it kept disobeying his orders, David got out and lumbered around the chassis beating the fenders, kicking the wheels, hammering on the hood. The low ache of tin vibrated in the cold; David's fierce voice carried everywhere. One thing no one could ever say about David was that he cultivated caution until he had lost the power to feel intensely. He stomped back to the car, opened the door, got in, and fiddled with the key. It remained locked. Corporal punishment had taught the Mercedes nothing.

We sat side by side, shivering, until at last he slumped over, a big man badly beaten, and said, "Let's get out the goddamn manual."

David was a man I was used to seeing work easily and knowingly around the most intricate, complicated pieces of machinery; a man who moved gracefully and serenely through masses of steel and iron; a man who every day of his life twisted and turned metal and made it do what *he* wanted. In that bitter, bitter cold, by flashlight, we poured over diagrams, read off lists of standard and extra equipment, studied graphs of performance tests, and looked at meaningless drawings of internal combustion systems. There was nothing at all about anything so basic as a key that wouldn't turn in the ignition lock. Maybe it's the carburetor, I said, remembering the *Blotto.*

"Look in the index of that goddamn manual and see if it has anything about a carburetor."

I flicked the pages and then shook my head. "Let me try," I said.

"Do anything you goddamn want. It's not going to work. It doesn't *want* to work."

I took my purse and whacked the key. The Germans apparently had not fashioned anything up to competing with my purse, for when I threw my purse on the floor, and leaned over, and twisted the key, it turned quite easily and fell into place.

We drove home without one single word passing between us. At my cottage, David leaned across me and opened the door. I could get out and up to the house on my own. The spectacle of David as Beau Brummell was finished, kaput. "Send the babysitter out, and I'll take her home," he said in a menacing voice.

I see that night as another line that had been crossed in our relationship. What had come before had been possibilities. I had taken to thinking of the ski debacle as an anomaly. I had fallen into the habit of looking at him with eyes full of admiration, and now I had seen him again in a bad light. A man doesn't like a woman to be witness to the fact that he can't carry out a simple maneuver like a romantic evening on the town.

Since I'm sure *he* had planned everything to be perfect, the way it had been spoiled had to be my fault. I didn't know how to facilitate Great Plans. The next time I saw him, we went back to being what I thought of as ourselves, workers who at the end of an exhausting day often phoned one another to come down (or up) for a drink or dinner or an argument to relieve the tedium of an Adirondack winter evening, as if for him that night in Glens Falls had never taken place. Yet every once in a while, I would see his eyes narrow as he looked at me. I knew he was sizing me up as someone who could not be trusted To Make Things Go.

He was right. I had lost the ability to shape events that would give back prodigious pleasure. I'm not just sure when—probably at the end of my second marriage. I had had hopes going into that, not large ones, I admit, but the flickerings of anticipation that I could make a life with a husband and children as part of a community in the country of my birth. I believe I gave up that hope when my agent called me one day and said that my second husband—who I now always think of as Buzz Cut—had just come into his office to get the name of the man I was ghostwriting a book for. He wanted to go behind your back, my agent said, and try to get money out of the guy for one of those whacky schemes he has. It's the worst kind of violation of trust. I could hear echoes of Shakespearean grandeur fluting into the phone from when my agent had learned English. My agent told me he had said to Buzz Cut, Don't you ever come back to my office again.

Buzz Cut came home that night and never mentioned he had been to my agent's office. I waited that evening for some mention of the incident. I would probably still be waiting if I hadn't accused him of deceit. A row, fists, screams—the apartment superintendent even arrived. There was an overturned chair and a smashed plant, but I had said everything was all right. Those were the days when it was still within a husband's prerogatives to beat his wife and children without anyone interfering except to keep the noise down because it was disturbing the neighbors.

I would look at David and think, Did you beat your wives? I didn't want to think of David like that. When that thought came into my head, I immediately tried to suppress it by talking about his work. That was a safe place to go. I remember once saying to him that I didn't think he should paint his sculptures, that the ones that weren't painted looked better. "It's my sculpture. I can paint it if I want."

"Orange and black, David? That's like something out of Halloween."

"You don't like *any* of them painted. You're against painting any of them."

"Because they look *better* when you leave the paint off."

"That's a"—sarcasm he could hardly breathe through—"a woman's point of view."

I have never learned the lesson that it is extremely hazardous to question any decision a man has made.


David took great pleasure in banging around his kitchen, which was too small for a man of his size. He was a fabulous cook, but no good at cleaning up or for those moments when things went wrong. He threw the disasters out the back door and started all over, snarling, sweating, downing brandy. He hated women fiddling (his word) around good food. They turned it frou-frou; the whole goddamn world was made treacherous by women. Men made better food than women. They did *everything* better. "Well, maybe not crayoning," he hastened to say to my daughter one evening in an apologetic voice. Sometimes he bent over her and took a crayon and made some strange scribble on the drawing she had been working on and she looked up and nodded, tucking her lips together in appreciation.

Sometimes when things weren't working out on her paper, she would come and stand by him, silent, until he noticed her, and then she would say, holding her picture up, "You show me what's wrong." I can remember the two of them bent intently over the paper, trying out various colors, one on top of another, until they both laughed and one of them said, "Yes, that's it."

During the spring thaw, I came upon David beside the back door shoveling up an enormous mess of broken crockery, old rusted pans, bent tableware. Belligerent before I had a chance even to ask, he explained, "I got tired of doing the goddamn dishes, so I just chucked them out. The goddamn snow covered them. But now—"

Now it was spring and clean-up time.

Spring was a frenzied time of activity for David. He liked to put outdoor things right. (Needless to say, not indoors, which required dusting, sweeping, and vacuuming.) The garden, for instance—he had a mammoth garden beautifully laid out, lovingly tended. All summer long, he carried armfuls of vegetables to friends; they augmented the baskets of wine and the lobsters he brought back from Albany, or the fish fresh from the lake ("Rik, the fish man says to tell you he's here"), or a beautiful roast he just couldn't resist buying but that was too big for one man on his own to eat, plus the Sunday *Times*, books and magazines, always something; he never came empty-handed. The givers: do they do it trying to show love or to find love?

Spring also meant there was the horse to deal with. My job, it turned out, was to tame Jo-Jo so that when David's two daughters arrived for their summer holiday, the animal would be placid and obedient.

"Now, listen, this horse has got some bad habits."

"I should say it does. Do you know what that horse did when I went out to get it? It ran at me with its teeth bared."

"The thing is, he needs some disciplining."

"He tried to bite me, David. Horses have big, sharp teeth. I don't think that's the kind of animal you should have around young girls."

"It's just a bad habit. Now, the thing is," he paused. "The thing is, you just get on him and teach him some manners."

"You get on him first."

"I'm way too big for him. I'd stove him in."

"Not that horse. He looks to me like he could carry—"

"I thought you loved animals. What about all those cats you've got? Would you sit on one of them? Well, if I got on this horse, it'd be just like your sitting on one of your cats."

"He tried to *bite* me, David. He ran right at me with those awful teeth—"

"Put the saddle on. Here, I'll put the saddle on. Just try him. It won't hurt just to try him, will it?"

The minute I climbed into the saddle, Jo-Jo took off down the field in front of the house and galloped in and out of all those wickedly sharp sculptures, stopping to buck, then crow hopping, plunging sideways, sitting down, rearing up. Over all my screaming and Jo-Jo's heavy breathing, the clatter of hooves and the rattle of steel as we rushed by, I could hear David roaring, "Hang on, *just hang on.* He's going to settle down. He's bound to settle down."

Jo-Jo stopped dead, planted his front feet squarely on the ground, and lowered his head. I sailed fifteen feet over his mane, barely missing an outstretched steel lance. While I lay stunned on the ground, Jo-Jo came at me with that menacing mouthful of teeth. Oh, god, I thought, and shut my eyes.

"Ah—ha—you goddamn no-good gelding—git—*git*—**git!**"

There was horse hair all over me as David picked me up. "Why didn't you hang on? You would have had him if you'd only hung on."

"He's ruined my good Kauffman pants. Look, they're full of horse hair and they're torn—"

"Oh, pants. You can always get another pair of pants. You might have hurt your hands. Pants are nothing. Hands you write with!"

David could be outrageous, angry, muddle-headed, incompetent with the Mercedes, and wrong about painting his sculpture, but also generous, clever, full of the juices of life. He was never, never small or petty. At least with me. So I am his defender, the way for a time he was mine when I was full of unhappiness and despair.

Everybody says that the last year of his life, he was only making the motions to get from day to day, but I didn't see him then; I was someone who wasn't even on the same planet so far as he was concerned. He was outraged because I said I was getting married again (a *terrible* error, which David should have tried to talk me out of, but he only stormed off without a word when I told him, not even looking back). He was finished with me as a pet project. I had chosen someone else over him.

That someone turned out to have been fashioned by the gods out of the same mold that made people like Ted Hughes, but I had been hoodwinked, the way Sylvia Plath and Assia Wevill were by Ted Hughes, by the passion of the moment. What women can't seem to see is that that kind of passion is extinguished quickly, and what remains is only acrid smoke, soot, cinders. *But, Sylvia, Assia, no man is worth sticking your head into a gas oven over. What were you thinking?*

I am looking for a life, I would have said to David if he had asked me what the hell I thought I was doing and had waited long enough to listen.

That was true, but instead I made bad marriages. You can become quite adept at it with practice. You even get a lot of attention, because you give your friends a lot to talk about. Maybe it's a need to hold center stage. Probably it's just that I have a short romantic attention span. Seekers don't really want to find Shangri-La. They want to *look* for it, not find it. Once you find love, what do you with it but wear it out? After all, how many happy marriages do you see around you?

Don't give me one example (which you probably only know from outside appearances). Give me ten. Give me ten happy marriages you know.

David was right. Put your faith in work.

At least he thought that up to the last year of his life.

In the last year of his life, perhaps he had discovered work was not always enough, and he had no more pet projects to occupy him when the day came to a close. He lived in that small, cement-brick house with himself as his only companion, except for the brief periods in summer when his daughters arrived. It is wise to remember that the force of a determined will cannot always be counted on to create the life one wants. When creative energies wear down, they are like the useless remains of a dead fire. David was finding, I think, that often when you get what you want, you no longer want it; the time for wanting it has passed. He had a Mercedes. He had a big bank account. He was at the top of museum lists. But it had all come too late. Even that grand hotel the Plaza was failing him. When he left behind his dirty shirts and rumpled suit, he expected the staff to send the suit to the dry cleaner and the shirts to be laundered and starched so that when he appeared again they would be hanging neat, clean, perfectly pressed anticipating his arrival. But the Plaza misplaced one of David's enormous shirts or hung his suit in someone else's closet. I can't remember which, maybe both. Letters, telephone calls, frustration, the Plaza polite but mystified. While I was still on his preferred list, he would come back from New York and tramp around my cottage in his oversized boots, make me listen to lists of grievances he had drawn up against that great hotel, and stamp out in a rage if I dared even smile. All I could ever think was what a perplexity he must have been to the Plaza.

That last year of his life, people said he hardly ever made scenes. People say he clung to his two girls when they came to be with him and tried to act the same as he had always been, but once, making cookies for the girls, he put salt in for the sugar and sugar in for the salt. That says it all for someone like me, a lover of symbols.

I think he retained all his life real love for his two former wives. They angered and exasperated him, or at least one did, and the other I don't think he ever really understood, but still he cared for both of them. He was the sort of man who can't take love back. Bonds for David meant forever, even when he was angry or not speaking to you or threatening you over the phone. The real part of what he felt he had locked into another one of his compartments. With the door slammed shut, where he didn't have to deal with Forster's law of **Only Connect**, where he was in enclosed in a self-made, concrete-block prison.

It was distressing for me to hear stories of how depressed and withdrawn he had become, how he seemed to have given up on the world. I carried only good memories of David, those days when he was still filled with joy and the vibrancy of someone still in love with life, when he was a vast concentration of rebellion beating against the imprisonment of the limitations of his own body and mind, when he was like a man raging against his designated fate. He was not immortal like Hephaestus. Like the rest of us, he was doomed to die.

On a May morning a little before seven, the phone rang. It was Frances Herman. "Have you got the radio on?"

"No—"

"David's been killed. In a car crash."

"It's the Mercedes," I said. "I never trusted that car."

"No, it was the truck."

Danger comes from the direction you least expect. When the truck—the truck that I had always trusted—left the road, David had been flung against its overhead metal struts. That huge head of so many unprecedented images had been smashed against those thick metal reinforcements, the truck itself scarcely damaged. Later it was sold, someone said, nearly as good as new. I'm sure the new owner wasn't told that a man who could do anything with metal was put to death by it, that the skull that had had so many visions had been broken into bits of bone by it.

David's death took place just four days before my birthday, in May of 1965, and eleven days before the little boy who would one day be given his silver dollar was born. That's years and years ago, decades actually, and yet I still feel that it is utterly and absolutely impossible that David does not come up on the porch of the new place where I am now living and rattle the house. Did he not shake everything he touched? It's too late, I feel, the *Times* vindicating his belief in himself after he's dead. He wanted to hear he was America's greatest artist while he was alive. When I think of David, I do not go in peace. *He* never went in peace. Nothing became him so well as the manner in which he shook the places he lived, the world which he challenged.

"I don't know why you want to *paint* it."

"It's mine, isn't it? I can paint it if I want, can't I?"

No, not any more, you can't; no, not ever again. The fire is out, the forge is dead.

The flames of that imagination burn on in those mammoth behemoths of metal that David thrust upon the world with his message, one no one had ever decoded before and that nobody is ever likely to encrypt again. Even those people who only went to the roof of the Met for the view must have been astonished by what they saw. Who did those? they would ask.

David Smith did those, with his huge hands and the fire inside him working with the fire from the forge where he made what he saw inside his head into those pieces you are looking at now and will never forget.

**DAVID SMITH.** It's really not such a hard name to remember.

My daughter Allison and I as we looked at the time,
Lake George in background

The Tudor cottage Roy Bongartz and Cee in an upstairs window

David Smith in his forge

## DOROTHY DEHNER:
## Sixty Years of Art

Retrospective show of Dorothy Dehner at The Hyde
Collection, Glens Falls, New York, in 1973

James Baldwin

The Puritan,
(presently on loan to the Hyde Collection, Glens Falls, New York)

My daughter on the day we went to Gore Mountain with David

Sculpture Group, Bolton Landing, c. 1963.
Photograph by David Smith.
Note in the background Jo-Jo, grazing happily.

David Smith with Dida's Circle on a Fungus, 1961,
Bolton Landing, photograph by David Smith

# AIR

Develop a state of mind like water, for in the water many things are thrown, clean and unclean, and the water is not troubled or repelled or disgusted. And so too with fire, which burns all things, clean and unclean, and with air, which blows upon them all, and with space, which is nowhere established.
(from a discourse by the Buddha
(Amitav Ghosh, *The Glass Palace*, 343)

It is 1990, and the daughter who had hung onto David Smith's leg as they went up the rope tow at Gore Mountain is now grown and receiving her Doctor of Veterinary Medicine diploma from Tufts' veterinary school.

I need to do something to show my daughter how proud I am of her. I tell her I'll take her on a trip as a graduation present. I expect her to pick London or Paris, but she says she wants to go on safari in Africa. You've been twice, she says, and I've always envied you seeing all those wonderful animals. I want to see them, too. I want to see Karen Blixen's house, I want to see Denys Finch Hatton's grave, and most of all I want to meet the African prince.

I don't think he was a prince. I think he was more like a big chief.

You always call him The Black Prince.

That was true. It was the way I thought of him. He had popped up beside me out of the sand and scrub of Amboseli, but what was bothering me more than finding a seven- foot-tall African Masai warrior of royal blood for my daughter was my bank account, which might have entitled me to write a book called *Down and Out in the Adirondacks*. So I did what most people do who have a house—I took out a home equity loan. I wonder if those home-equity people have any idea where some of the money they fork over goes.

Yes, I have a house, actually a farm with sixty acres of land, mostly scruffy, bad pines that someone planted for reasons no one can understand because they are absolutely useless; they wouldn't even work as Christmas trees. But the house is lovely, just the way it was when it was built in the late seventeen hundreds (except for a front screened-in porch that was added on sometime), not tinkered with and made cutesy and photographable for some women's house-and-gardens magazine.

I have given up trying to make my living by writing novels and been reduced to ghostwriting work for people who answer ads that scream **ANYONE CAN WRITE**. There may be a kernel of truth in this. The cliché in publishing is that everyone has a novel about coming of age, which roughly speaking means passing from adolescence to adulthood, but the people who ran those ads were not interested in finding that kind of novel. They were interested in money.

Someone sends in a manuscript—short story, poetry, memoir, novel—and the **ANYONE CAN WRITE** people send back a letter saying that the manuscript showed "great promise," but that in its present form it needed some professional polishing. For money, of course. The amount depended on the length. When a check came in, the material was farmed out to poor peons like me who toiled in the vineyards of bad literature. We worked over the manuscript for about a fourth (I calculated) of the fee the writer had sent into **ANYONE CAN WRITE**.

No matter how low I sank in the literary ranks, I could never meet the bills. I would like to say that I sold out, but that implies large stacks of greenbacks in return for handing over my integrity. What I did was capitulate, because I was a woman with two small children and no husband and I needed a steady income, which did not come from freelance writing.

*Two* children? How did that happen? Well, it happened because I have had three-and-a-half husbands. In chronological order, the parade of men through my life (who stayed any length of time) would go like this: my first husband, the boat-husband; then Luis; then my second husband, Buzz Cut; followed by David Smith; then the third spouse,

The One Who Couldn't Leave the Bottle Alone; and finally the last husband, The One We Don't Talk About, who only counts as a half because I got that marriage annulled.

The last "husband" put on such a bizarre performance before the judge that the judge took me into his private chamber and said, What were you thinking? What, indeed?

I might have said that I had developed a talent for bad marriages. It takes time and practice, like turning out a perfect soufflé or a masterful *Boeuf Bourguigonne*, but above all, it sprang from a belief in faith over fact. I knew I did not do well at the altar, and yet I kept trying, thinking I might get it right once. The father of my son had the allure of presenting a challenge: it was obvious somebody had to save him; he was doing such a poor job himself.

It took me four years to face the fact that adults have to rescue themselves. Then one day, it came to me that it would be far easier to be responsible for one adult and two children rather than two adults and two children. Simple mathematics.

I found a job teaching in a community college thirty miles away, which was a long commute, especially in the winter through sleet and snow. The college's president only gave me three credits for each book I had written, arguing that a book was only the equivalent of taking one advanced course toward a PhD. Five books only added up to fifteen credits, and I needed thirty credits to come in as an assistant instructor. The president instructed me that community colleges were *teaching* colleges, not research or publishing institutions, and therefore I would have to start as an instructor. I looked at him and said, How many credits do you get if you win a Pulitzer or the Nobel prize for Literature? I'd have to think about that, he said, and he was serious. Administrators are not renowned for having a sense of humor.

Since I was the newest instructor, that meant taking the teaching time slots no one else wanted. I was assigned two MRS night classes (Mature Returning Students), mostly women who were in the same position I was: single mothers with children they had to support. MRS seemed to be the appropriate name for the course. These MRS women were going to school at night so that they could get an education and (they hoped) a better job.

The MRS classes met once a week at seven o'clock and got out at ten, so I was doing a lot of night driving through a lot of bad weather, often arriving home well after midnight and getting up at six to make sure my daughter and son had breakfast and were ready for the seven-thirty bus to school. Sometimes, when I tried to carve a little time of my own on weekends so that I could write for myself, I would think of Spain as something I had dreamed, something that had never really existed.

I constantly worried about the kind of mother I was. I did not bake cookies with a big happy smile. I did not get down on the floor and play blocks with my children as often as I should. I did not find fulfillment in pushing a child endlessly back and forth on a swing. I was always leaving to teach classes or trying to reduce great stacks of papers that needed grading or trying to catch up with the laundry and cleaning. It's true that I read to them, that I bought them bicycles, taught them to ski and swim, watched anxiously over their safety, but those things did not seem to fulfill the qualifications of A Good Mother. You're doing the best you can, I would tell myself.

It's not good enough, I would answer back. When the children were young, I tried to compensate by collecting an assortment of animals— dogs and cats, and even a fighting cock that my brother gave me as a birthday present. It liked to roost in trees and took great pleasure in attacking people. I bought a pony for my daughter and, after she outgrew the pony, horses, one for her, one for me. I bred my mare, and we had a colt. One day, I acquired a burro I rescued from abuse; then I bought another, better, horse for my daughter. In the end, we had a total of six large equine animals whose stalls had to be mucked out every day and who all (except the burro) had to be curried and exercised daily. My starting time for a day had now moved back to four-thirty. If there was snow or sleet and I was teaching a night class, I sometimes took four or five hours to get home and was lucky to make it by midnight. I found a girl down the road who babysat for those night-time hours. She was often fast asleep on the couch when I finally got home. If I was in bed by one, I was lucky.

From the time my daughter was five, she worked in the barn. She developed into a very accomplished equestrian, but my son hated the horses. He seemed to hate everything I tried to interest him in. Sometimes when he looked at me, his eyes seemed to be sizing me up to figure out just how much he hated me. He saw his father on weekends, and he went to camp for a couple of weeks in the summer. Later, he accused me of trying to get rid of him by making him spend weekends with his father and in the summer go to camp.

I didn't know you didn't like camp.

You never asked.

And you didn't want to go to your father's?

He drank all the time.

Why didn't you tell me?

You knew that. That's why you kicked him out.

I could see it was too late to say I'm sorry. Saying I'm sorry doesn't wipe out the major errors you make with the people you are supposed to love, no matter that everyone quotes that famous line, *Being in love means never having to say you're sorry.*

I wasted thousands of hard-earned dollars from taking extra teaching assignments in order to pay an endless parade of shrinks to make my son at least like me. He told them what they wanted to hear, and they would say, Oh, he's coming along fine, when he was really planning some new malediction. Now all anyone has to do to get a rise out of me is say Oedipus complex, but the truth is that all the hopes I had held for my son liking me were not going to take place. He felt I had failed him, and he would never forgive me.

What had made his hostility so intense? I hadn't treated him any differently than my daughter, but his hatred had the intensity of a fire that never dies down. Roy Bongartz finally said to me, Well, you've certainly tried everything I've ever heard of for these kinds of kids. Which one would you say worked? None, I admitted. Where do you go from here? Roy asked. There was no answer because there was no place to go. No place to go: that would make a good title for a book. Not one I would want to write, however.

My daughter says my son and I are like oil and water. I say we don't breathe in air the same way. Mine goes through one kind of filter, and his enters an entirely different track. The oxygen that goes to our brains delivers different messages. I often wondered what the children that Luis and I might have had would have been like. Then I say, I would never have had this daughter, who is so clever and responsible, who has never failed me, and has always tried to make my life better. Maybe that was the tradeoff.

My son was gone, ran away in the middle of the night, and I had not heard from him for two years. I imagined him dead or in jail. Every time the phone rang, I would say *Hello,* waiting for the bad news. Where are you? I would think. Was I so terrible that you never want to see me again?

The answer was obvious. I concentrated on finding a cheap safari to Africa, where I thought I could share with my daughter that unique feeling of going back to the origins of man—actually woman, because our blood DNA is tested against that first woman, not the man, which is an uplifting piece of knowledge for the women of the world.

On our safari, we would travel through the veldt during the day in an open bus, and at night we would we pitch our own tents and eat food cooked over an open campfire by men whose dishes would have made the five-stars chefs of Europe envious. Often the zebras and wildebeests were no more than fifteen feet away from our campfire. At night, I heard that odd coughing sound lions make, and the nocturnal air carried predator cries of capture and extinction.

While I was growing up, I would never in a million years have believed I would one day go to England and France and Spain, let alone Africa. But by the 1980s, millions of people got on planes and went to exotic locations as if they were going shopping at Wal*Mart. The first tour I took to East Africa was called "In the footsteps of Theodore Roosevelt." I wasn't quite sure about where Teddy Roosevelt had gone, but the itinerary sounded too promising for the price to pass up. I was sure it would help me find the Africa of Ernest Hemingway and Karen Blixen, both of whom held mythic places in my mind (never mind that Hemingway had no idea what went on with women; he had loved Spain, and that was enough for me). At that time, my daughter was in her first year of college, and my son was in one of those places to kick "substance abuse," as they politely called it, meaning he was more or less incarcerated to wean him off narcotic and alcohol addictions (he had both). I was rapidly divesting myself of what seemed to be endless animals so that I was a comparatively free woman.

My first experience with Africa came almost immediately after

I climbed into the van that was to transport us from the airport to Nairobi, the capital of Kenya. I braced my hands against the dashboard, because it was obvious I had put my life in the hands of one of those drivers who don't really know how a car worked. We careered around the airport for a while—the driver seemed unsure which way we should go to get out—and then suddenly we left the lights and confusion behind and emerged into dead darkness.

All around me, the black African night pressed against the windows of the van and overhead there were more stars than I had ever seen in my life. Ahead, on the horizon, a tangle of lights from the skyscrapers in Nairobi silhouetted a city that seemed to recede farther and farther away as we drove toward it. We had only two small headlights in the deep blackness to pick our way through an endless emptiness.

Suddenly, I saw two huge orange-and-black knees racing in front of the windshield, then a long body, a longer neck, and finally a flyswatter tail. A giraffe had crossed in front of us, as if to say, You are in the Rift Valley, the backbone of Africa, with all its exotic animals, plants, people, flowers, its brilliantly colored birds, the Great Rift Valley, a 3,700 mile continental fault system that ran from the Red Sea to Mozambique.

Someone said—I wish I could remember where I had read this—that when people came to Africa, they immediately had a sense of connection because the very air was filled with the breath of that ancient past. You breathed that air in and were transported back, millions of years before, to the time a small, hairy creature timidly ventured to stand up in the tall grass for the first time so that it could see all around, looking out for danger and hungrily scanning the view of a new kind of world. Animal scents were mixed in that air, and the scent of wild grasses and the acidic smell from the roots of acacia trees, which stood on the horizon like fans opening against the brilliant purple-blue sky. This place had produced our first true Eve, an apelike creature—humans and chimps have a genetic blueprint that is 96 percent identical—a creature barely four feet tall, exceedingly hairy but with a slightly larger, rounder skull, and a jaw and teeth noticeably smaller than those of a similar race, *homo erectus*, that had existed before her. Only 275,000 years had passed since this woman started the entire line of *homo sapiens sapiens* from which we "moderns" have all evolved, no more than the quick blink of an eye in the history of the planet.

The stars throbbed with such energy and seemed so close that I felt as if I could reach out the window and clutch a handful. In that moment, it was easy to believe, as I had been told, that we were all made of the same ingredients as the stars, and every breath we expel goes out into the universe and is never lost, no matter how many times it is divided and redivided into the trillions of particles that make up the air.

My lungs were being filled with the same air that small, stunted African creature who had scarcely begun to learn the rudiments of speech had inhaled as it found the courage to push itself upright and look about. What that mitochondrial Eve (for I like to think it was a woman, not a man, who made that enormous transition to getting around on two feet instead of four) saw I would be seeing in the days ahead. I would be breathing the same air she had inhaled, listening to the same noises, taking in the same smells, the breath of human beings' first home. Even now, every breath I inhale has some infinitesimal part of the breaths Luis has taken in and given out. We were joined in a way no one could ever separate.

On the Teddy Roosevelt trip, we were put up at the New Stanley Hotel. I loved the New Stanley, even though it was not as elegant as the Norfolk, which was just outside of town and was the first place Isak Dinesen stayed when she arrived in Africa to marry her Danish count. She was in love with his twin bother, but though he was willing to bed her, he was not interested in marrying her. He left that to his brother, who needed her family's money to start a business in Africa. She wanted a title, so they made maybe a bad bargain when they joined their lives together.

The New Stanley has a big mulberry tree in front of a scattering of tables and chairs, the Thorn Tree Café, with bulletin boards around the thorn tree where people leave messages. It is said that if you sit outdoors at the Thorn Tree Café long enough, you will see anyone who ever passes through Africa. It is also said that some people put messages up for themselves just so they can see their names on the bulletin board.

On my first trip to Africa, there were of course no messages for me on those bulletin boards. That would have to wait until my daughter and I came to Africa and went our separate ways for a few hours—the center of Nairobi was still safe enough then, in 1990, to go anywhere you wanted, even alone, without being mugged or having a pickpocket relieve you of your valuables. Nowadays, I am told, you are not even safe at high noon traveling in groups. Gangs of boys crowd around the tourists and relieve them of their Western treasures.

When my daughter and I left messages on the Thorn Tree bulletin board, we wrote each other's names in conspicuously large letters. I always wrote **DR.** Allison Branson on her envelope. It thrilled me to do that and also to be seen taking a message for myself off the Thorn Tree bulletin board and feeling sure most of the people watching me were feeling disproportionately deprived because they would never have the pleasure of seeing an envelope with their name on it pinned to one of the sides of the board.

It was on the Teddy Roosevelt trip that I met The Black Prince. The members of our Teddy Roosevelt tour left the New Stanley hotel and were being transported for hours by jeeps to the Amboseli elephant sanctuary, and the trip was not pleasant. I have never seen such bad roads.

Amboseli was famous for its great herds of elephants. Cynthia Moss has spent over twenty years of her life tracking one herd, charting the lifelong relationships these elephants developed with one another. She distinguished them by markings and gave them names, recorded their matings, births, struggles against drought and poachers, and the impact of tourists on their territory, as well as the massive encroachments on their lands as the population of Kenya exploded.

I had a copy of Cynthia Moss's book *Elephant Memories* with me and, as the "In the Footsteps of Theodore Roosevelt" went out on its runs at Amboseli, I would try to identify some of the elephants from the pictures and descriptions in the book.

On our way to the lodge where we were to stay, we saw young boys tending cows in the same orange swatch of cloth Masai have been wearing even since cloth was invented. Our guide also pointed out slim, willowy warriors, their muscles rippling as they moved, racing across the plain at an even pace, never tiring, their long spears held lightly by their sides. They moved with great speed and determination. It was said they could run all day without stopping and never tire. It was said that they had courage that never failed them, and for that, if for nothing more, I admired them immensely. I knew what a small reservoir of courage I had, and that too often, I didn't even call on that. I admired them most because they had refused to bow to Western ways.

Meanwhile, the Kikuyu guide was stressing how fragile the ecology was—my words. He said something like bad things happen to land from tourists and Masai cattle, and that the area was rapidly deteriorating even more because tourists tipped their drivers to get closer to the elephants, though there was a law that said the existing roads were supposed to be the only paths that vehicles could use in the park. People didn't pay attention, he said, looking around. People gave big tips to the driver to go off the road closer to some animal they wanted to photograph. He looked around at us as if advising us, No big tip, nix the good pix.

We could have the afternoon to rest and get ready for our initial game run at four. Night runs had once been part of the itinerary, but they were now prohibited for reasons that were vague to me. It probably had something to do with the growing danger from poachers and other criminals who by 1985 had found tourists easy prey for thefts and, in a couple of cases, murder.

Those who had been in Africa all their lives said the great Rift Valley had been spoiled by the tourist trade using it as a dumping ground for anything those sightseers wanted to discard—gum wrappers, film boxes, Kleenex, leftover food, Coke bottles, you name it. If it could be thrown out the window, it ended up on the game park grounds. "You should have seen it when it was unspoiled, fifty, sixty years ago."

When I went out on the veranda of the lodge, all I saw for miles around was sand and a few scrubby-looking trees. I had seen some huts about a half a mile from the lodge as we drove in and had asked the guide what they were. "They make stuff for you tourists," he said.

*You never know what you'll find if you don't look.* That might be labeled Commandment One, I thought about the world in general. After lunch, I set off to see what the huts had. It was unbelievably hot, the air so still that the heat seemed to have sucked up all the oxygen and left the living scrambling for breath. I was panting as I walked along, lugging my purse, which felt as if it weighed a thousand pounds, my eyes fiercely fastened on the ground on the lookout for snakes. There are really deadly snakes in Africa, and I am afraid of any kind of snake, I don't care how harmless it's supposed to be. Snakes are the reason paradise was poisoned.

I had everything vital to my existence in Africa stuffed into my purse—comb and brush, a bag of makeup, toothbrush, small toothpaste, floss, deodorant, camera, extra rolls of film, passport, money (both American and Kenyan), travelers checks, Kleenex, nail file, small double compact mirror (regular and magnified), cigarettes (smoker to the end no matter how many times I've tried to quit), lighter, bug spray, two paperbacks (one a travel guide and the other reading material), a map of Africa, my vouchers for each section of the trip, sunglasses, reading glasses, a flask with brandy (*never* go without one of these; you don't know what you're going to encounter that will require something to bolster your courage. This might be filed for a traveler under Commandment Two, though the new airline regulations mean you have to take small bottles instead of a flask), a fistful of dollar bills so that if you ran out of the small bills of the local currency, you would still have tip money, a bathing suit (*always* take a bathing suit; you never know when you're going to be stranded, and the hotel where you finally end up may have a swimming pool—sort of a Commandment Three), an extra change of underwear in a plastic bag, medications (including tranquilizers, which can double as sleeping tablets), breath mints (a necessity when you wake up on the plane after a long trip), and The Indispensable Notebook for entering every single expense of the day, every impression, every place visited, overheard conversations, lyric lines, the numbers on the film you took pix of and a description (brief) of what the pix were, a list of people you needed to buy presents for, and these days credit cards and your cell phone.

Empty a woman's purse and you know who she is. Purses never lie.

Finally I stopped, trying to do something about my stricken lungs, when I felt an electric shock in the air and jerked my head up to see a seven-foot tall Masai beside me. In back of him was a kid maybe thirteen or fourteen. I had been walking through an open landscape in which there was not one tree or bush to conceal anything. For a moment I thought I might be hallucinating, one of the first signs that a heatstroke was coming on.

"You ought not be out here by yourself," the Masai said in perfect Oxford English. "It is dangerous in Africa to go out into the open alone. You never know when an animal might be near." (Call that a Masai commandment, which I appropriated as Commandment Five.)

I looked around. As far as the eye could see, there was nothing but sand and scrub. "How did you just appear out of nowhere?"

"An animal can do that even better than I can."

Even by Masai standards, this man was Brobdingnagian. He was wearing the typical orange toga-like garment of the *maroni*, a Masai designation given to warriors who have fulfilled the initial rite of passage to manhood by killing a lion using only a spear or their own hands. Though this practice had been outlawed, it remained a part of *ilmoran* (warriors) initiation. The Serengeti is thousands of miles of open land. How were the park rangers going to stop some boy from killing his lion so that he can be elevated to warriorhood? It was obvious the kid had not yet crossed that line; he had on only a simple, orange, tattered toga.

My *moroni* (I am a quick appropriator) was carrying a spear at least a foot and a half taller than the man, as tall or taller perhaps than the mast on the *Blotto*. His ears had been stretched from infancy and hung down, with huge holes between the top and bottom of the lobes. He wore long, beaded earrings, copper and beaded neck loops, and copper and beaded arm bands. Masai warriors part their hair into small sections and then braid each with cotton or wool strands to augment the lengths. Then they dye the long plaits a musky orange with a mixture of ocher and wax; the longer and shinier the plaits are, the more beautiful in their eyes. The warriors also rub their bodies with that intense ocherous color, and in the sun they look polished and beautiful as a golden statue. What would David Smith have made of him?

When it is time for a Masai warrior to take his place as an elder in the tribe, all his hair is shaven off, sort of like the bullfighter when he cuts the *coleta*. The fun's over. The excitement, too. All you're to do now is sit around and mouth wise words. There is nothing the young disparage so much as erudite instructions. No, I think. This is a Western point of view.

The man beside me had a handsome Nilotic face. He had inherited the slightly slanted eyes and straight slender nose of that race and the

Caucasian lips and high forehead. He also had the biggest feet I had ever seen—much bigger than David Smith's, and those had been *big*—and he was wearing sandals made out of rubber car tires that said Goodyear on the sides.

The young boy stood back respectfully, one leg bent under him, so that he looked like a large orange stork waiting for some command from the man beside me. I looked around; there should have been cattle with them, since the Masai believe that god had allotted them all the cattle in the world. If they came upon someone else's cattle, they felt free to appropriate them. The cattle belonged to them by divine right.

Cattle were their status symbol, the more the better. They also provided the main staple of their diet, cow blood mixed with milk, though warriors sometimes only drank the blood, believing it gave them added strength. (If my boat-husband had drunk cow blood, would he have overcome the enemy engine on the *Blotto*?) If you mix cow's blood with milk and add some of the animal's urine and let the mixture set for a day, you get a kind of cheese that is easy to carry. To get the blood, the Masai insert a small tube attached to a dart into the neck of the cow and extract the blood into a calabash or, sometimes, a cowhide bag. When they had the amount of blood they wanted, they inserted a plug into the animals' neck so that it would be easier in the future to get to the vein or artery they had pierced.

There were no cattle in sight. Then again, this man didn't look like a cow herder, no matter how many cows his god thought a man like that should have. A man who looked like that should own every cow in the world. (Even Luis's brave bulls back in Los Veintos? Oh, lord, that's a hard one to answer. They would have made a pair, he and Luis.)

"What is it you are doing out here by yourself?"

I might have said, What is it *you* are doing, popping up out of the ground and scaring me half to death? Being polite—after all, this was his land I was trespassing on—I said, "I was on my way up to those huts to see what they had to sell."

"By yourself?"

Did he see anyone else around? "The rest of them went to have a nap. They were tired after the drive from Nairobi."

We seemed to have come to an impasse, there in the middle of the escarpments of the Amboseli plains. The land looked much like the scrappy land around *Los Vientos*. I had the spooky feeling I was sliding back in time.

"I'll go with you," he said in a voice that made it plain that I had absolutely no say in the matter. I didn't care. I was happy walking in the sandy Serengeti with a man who towered over me and gave off the same sense of kinetic energy I had felt when I was next to Luis.

Of course there's the kid (walking three feet behind us in respect), which makes three, but for all intents and purposes, we were what I would consider a twosome.

I did not ask him how he spoke English so well. That's what everyone would ask. I have wanted to be original all my life. No wonder I so often felt like an outsider. At that moment, however, I ceased thinking of myself as a wanderer and decided I should be thinking of myself as a searcher, which put a more positive aspect to the whole matter. The names we give ourselves, even in secret, have a good deal to do with how we feel about ourselves. I was feeling very chipper at that moment, side by side with an exotic creature I was sure very few women in the world had ever encountered, to say nothing of the boy, or as I thought of him, The Subaltern.

"You should not be out without water, either." I was receiving the usual male reprimands for all my deficiencies, a role a man assumes the minute he has some woman under his authority.

"But not just any water," I said back, with considerable cheek, considering the circumstances.

He stopped and looked at me and frowned, a solemn, dignified seven-foot-tall Masai with the world's most beautiful teeth. "Let's go see what those huts have for this American," he said, giving me a look of dominion.

I had trouble keeping up with him, his long legs striding along, eating up space as if it didn't even exist. When we got to the shacks, a group of men ran out and began to gallop around hollering. An old man came out and put his two hands together but left his palms open to the sky. He bowed his head, and his head stayed bowed until the man beside me said something.

The old man looked up and pointed. We walked toward the first hut. Within ten feet of it, I was overwhelmed by a stench so strong that I almost gagged. Hundreds of people who had not bathed for long periods of time had come and stayed in that small room and left their scent behind. The air held past remembrances of fecal matter, both animal and human, urine, dung, disease, sweat, musk, air that came from an Africa I had never pictured, whose odor sickened me to the point where I was starting to retch.

The Masai took my arm and turned me around. "We'll wait over there and let them bring out what they want to show you. It's very hot inside these huts." There were no trees in sight, but there was a sun-bleached white stump left over from a tree that had been part of some long-ago, long-lost forest. All around us swirled sand and gravel, and over us burned a sun so intense that when I sat down, I immediately jumped back up because the log was sizzling hot.

Men were running back and forth, putting things in front of us. My Masai suddenly thrust his spear against the ground where it vibrated for a moment and then came to rest. He said something. A man went back to one of the huts, came out with a piece of dirty cloth, and gravely spread it out on the stump. I sat down.

"You are thirsty." A statement, not a question. "You cannot drink the water here, and they would have nothing bottled. I am very sorry." Meanwhile men were bringing gourds with water. I didn't know what to do. "Pour some over your hands and put your wet hands against your face. That will help."

The men kept chattering and trying to get the extraordinary creature beside me to take some kind of dried food that looked like straw. They were insisting, and finally he bowed his head, put out his hand, and said something they seemed to understand—some reason I suppose why he couldn't eat, as if eating would go against his religion. I was of little interest to these men, even though I was a tourist, and all tourists had monies, and certainly a great many of these men must have had nieces and nephews, probably the majority of them imaginative ones, who needed monies for someone's education. Please, Big Mama, for my son, my nephew, my niece, please, Big Mama. The Big Mama, which was said in English, I had been told by the Kikuyu guide, was a nomenclature of respect adopted by all tribes, even the Kikuyu who were certainly, he implied, the most educated and civilized tribe in all of Africa. What the guide would have called the man beside me, I had no idea. A big chief, I thought, but that designation didn't seem nearly appropriate enough. A Black Prince.

"Have you anything in particular you would like to look at?"

"Well, I'm interested in masks."

"Is there a reason for that?"

Was there? Not that I knew. The idea of a mask had just come to me as something appropriate to the time and place. Or perhaps it was the quick current from the subchambers of my mind that suddenly called up the faces of my Aunt Ruth and my Aunt Florence, and I said, "A lot of them remind me of my family."

"You do not look anything like any of those masks. Perhaps then you are adopted?"

"Oh, if only that were the explanation, but I'm afraid not."

"Then you are running away?" A question this time, not a statement. "Looking for your place," he said, and this time it was a statement.

"All my life."

"You think then there is a particular place for everyone?"

"It's a puzzle I've been trying to solve, that everyone has a special place where he or she belongs, but now I'm not so sure. What do you think?"

This should have been a very odd conversation for me to be having in the middle of the Serengeti plains with a Masai warrior I had not known more than ten minutes, but actually I felt quite comfortable waiting to hear what he had to say on the matter.

He stood there, heavy with thought, searching the recesses of his mind for an answer. "I have had the same problem," he said at last. "Do you think there might not be an answer?"

"Oh, lord," I said, "I hope not."

A ragged line of merchants (if they could be called that) paraded toward us. "We will look at the masks they have and see if they have any that remind you of your relatives and some that may even remind me of mine." I got a glimpse of those extraordinary white teeth in what might have been a smile. I wanted to say, Who would ever have dreamed someone like you could be funny? No, funny is the wrong word. Ironic, that would be it.

With his two big hands, he examined the items that were being thrust before him. He had ceased to pay attention to me. He kept shaking his head and saying something, and the man who was showing him a mask or a piece of jewelry, some large bowl or a basket, would seem to agree and retreat to look for something else, going backward, never taking his eyes off that giant figure and all the time making what sounded like apologies.

He was picky as hell. Finally he handed two masks over to me. "Old," he said. "Not terribly old, but worth having."

I had no idea how much I should be paying for such objects, and bringing up money is always a touchy subject, especially with someone you've just met. "I think they're very nice. How much do you think I should give him?"

"We will arrange that when you've chosen everything you want. Do you have a ceiling?"

"I beg your pardon."

"How much do you want to spend altogether?"

I really didn't know. I was just starting out on my tour, and I had limited funds—when didn't I have limited funds?—but it was obvious I was never going to get advice as authoritative as this, so I thought I should go with it. "What would be your ballpark figure?"

"Ballpark figure?"

"When we get all done, you should tell me how much you think I should be spending, and I'll see if I can spare it."

"We should make a ceiling. Otherwise I will be setting things aside that we might have to turn back, and that would not be good."

"No, I certainly don't want to do anything that would seem rude. Let's say fifty to seventy-five dollars, but I'd rather it were closer to fifty. Do they want Kenyan or American money?"

"American would be better." I could understand that. This was at a time when America was at the height of its power, before all our frailties and financial shenanigans surfaced, a period when people thought we were gilded with gold, and though we did a great deal of harm where we went, we did it with the best of intentions.

I broiled in that sun for more than two hours. It occurred to me that if I didn't get back to the lodge and people discovered I was missing, there would be a great deal of consternation, but I was fascinated by the way this man examined each object carefully, even the shabbiest ones. He was giving respect to each offering so as not to demean any of the men's merchandise. Finally he put aside two masks, an enormous basket that I wondered how I would ever be able to carry back to the States but that was so intricately woven and beautiful my heart was set on it the minute I saw it, and last a necklace made out of old woven strings and metal beads that looked like bird shot. I had no interest in it at all.

"This is very rare," he said, dropping the necklace into my lap. There were two side strands to go around the neck, with a raggedy piece of string to fit over a metal bead on the opposite side so that you could fasten the strings around your neck. Three strings hung down the center, each carrying different sizes and amounts of beads. There seemed to be no pattern to the way the beads had been arranged or how many had been put on each of the woven strings. The strings were dirty, and the metal beads looked as if they weren't even worth the effort of throwing away.

"It is a bride's necklace," he said. "You hardly ever see them anymore." He was waiting, I could see, for me to exclaim over how wonderful this treasure was, but I was just puzzled. Why would I ever wear it?

My Masai took hold of the necklace and held it up to my neck. Then, very gently, he put it around my neck and fastened it. He looked at me as if he were trying to see my soul, and then he shook his head up and down, yes, that would do. I wore the necklace well. He was satisfied with his work.

"A man comes to the woman he wants. He brings a string like this of beads. Each bead represents an amount of cows he will give to have her as his wife, and he offers the necklace to the woman. If she takes it, she goes with him, but if she won't take it, he hasn't offered enough cows. He can either look for another woman, or he can go back and decide she's worth more cows. This bride's piece has three strings and many beads. This was for a woman worth a great many cows."

I paid less than thirty dollars for two masks, the basket, and the bridal necklace. "A little gift of appreciation as well," my Masai said. I was looking down at the bills I had left in my hand. What was not too much and not too little? He looked over, took some dollar bills out of my hand, and distributed them. The men went into raptures of joy.

"Now," he said, "I will walk you back to the lodge."

The boy stork, who had stood the entire time without moving a muscle, put his foot down and fell into line behind us. We were walking side by side, and I finally asked the question I had been wanting to ask all along. "Where did you learn your English—I mean, it's kind of a surprise to be out in the middle of Amboseli and hear someone speaking Oxford English." I did not, out of politeness, say black or Masai or native or African.

"Cambridge."

That was it?

"I went to school there. I came back and went to work in Nairobi, but I didn't like living in the city. I decided that I wanted to be with my own people and do what I could to help them." Pause. "I did not find living with Westerners what I thought it would be." Westerners I took to be a polite way of saying white.

"But you put yourself out for me—you spent *hours*—"

"When I first saw you, I just wanted to warn you about being out alone and then," he looked down at his enormous feet, "and then I saw—you had a look on your face—as if you were really lost, not just here in the Amboseli—and I thought, You mustn't just leave her out here. You must go with her. Maybe you will find out why she has that look."

We stood there in the midst of all that space and there was nothing but an airless expanse of light. We had come together, we *were* together for that moment, and then we would part and never see each other again. But I had the bridal necklace. For some reason I did not understand, I was a woman worth a great many cows in this man's eyes.

We began to walk again. He had slowed his pace so that we went together, side by side, toward the lodge. I needed to think of a way to thank this extraordinary man for all he had done. Did the Masai drink? I was sure they brewed some kind of potent beer in their *shambalas*. Maybe tea would be better. "Won't you come in and have a drink or tea or something? I really don't know how I can thank you."

Employees from the lodge began pouring out, shouting, waving their hands. The Masai beside me stood stock still with the spear straight by his side, not moving a muscle, still as a figure in a bas relief, just the way the boy had been still as a statue all the time he had been waiting for us while the bargaining was going on. It must be something they were taught from the time they were very young. In the midst of the pandemonium—the workers from the lodge had surrounded us and were dancing up and down and yelling—the manager and our Kikuyu guide ran out. They were both beside themselves. My Masai stood tall and silent, watching impassively, but behind the dark measuring eyes I saw a glint of profound contempt.

"Goodbye," he said. "Thank you for the invitation, but I never go into these places." He said the word *places* as if it they had been put under some ancient curse and, as soon as I went in, I would be under that evil spell as well.

I still had the bridal necklace on. I had carried the masks in the big basket, which was slung over one arm. I took my free hand and held it out. I wasn't sure whether he would take it, if I might already be contaminated. Without hesitation, he gripped my white hand in his huge black one. "I wish you a good life ahead," he said.

I could see he didn't think this was going to be true. And I could see he thought he wasn't going to have one, either.

If we could, I thought, we should go away and find a place where there were no other people. We would never have to deal with the world again; we would live apart, but not so far apart that we didn't know we were close by each other. We would never lie to one another, we would never betray one another, we would honor every commitment we made to each other.

I thought for a moment I heard the sound of hoof beats, but when I looked out on the endless scrub of Africa, all I saw was a small group of Masai warriors running soundlessly on the rim of the horizon into the unknown. The hoof beats were only inside my head, a memory from the past of all that had been taken away. Vanished into thin air.

The Masai and I stood with our hands clasped together so long that I wondered what the people around us thought. It was as if we were lovers parting for the last time. Then he let go of my hand, and

I watched as he and the boy walked toward the horizon, two black smudges against the African air. The hotel manager kept tugging at my arm, and I kept pulling away from him. I didn't want anything to interfere with my concentration as I watched those two figures grow smaller and smaller. They would soon merge into the air and be gone. In the end, everything disappears into thin air.

There is a dove in Africa that sings a song you can never forget,

> *My mother died*
> *My father died,*
> *My brother died,*
> *My sister died,*
> *They all died died died*

I would hear that bird singing from planted greenery that encircled the lodge. That is my Masai's song, I would think. Whenever I hear it, I will remember my Masai the way when I hear a cricket I am suddenly back in Spain and Luis has been returned to me. Leaving a land you love, leaving someone you love, forecasts what death must be like. Our real role in the world, my friend Jane Nelson once told me, is to see one another into the grave.

The older we get, the more we lose. At the end, it is not successes we count up, but losses. There is no way to replace them. But you have memories. Those are what the total of your life is about, the memories you take out and string like beads on a necklace, invisible though it may be, you know it's there. It is possible to put your hand up and touch a bead and say to yourself silently, That was the day I was with my Masai at Amboseli. That was the day Luis and I went out in the Land Rover and left everyone else behind. That was the day Luis's mother came to see me. That was the day I had my daughter, and no one knew where her father was; off drinking, it turned out. Never mind, he's gone. Has been for years, as if he had never existed, except that I have his child.

That daughter was back home, but she was also here in the Amboseli, as strong as any memory I had ever had.

I am remembering the day she won the trophy for jumping at Bennington. She made her palomino Sandy jump the last fence that had been raised to an unreasonable height. Allison and another girl were the last two left in the competition. The other girl went first. Her horse balked, and she retired across the ring to see if my daughter could get her horse over.

Allison was on Sandy, who had a placid disposition and did not like to jump, but my daughter's good jumper was lame. Sandy did everything else well enough, but she did not like jumping. Allison wanted to jump though and the first fences had not been too forbidding. This last jump, however, was another story. It was way too high. I knew that. Allison knew it, and certainly Sandy did; but my daughter cantered Sandy down and turned her into the jump, and then she dug her knees in. Sandy started over the hurdle. Halfway across Sandy seemed to stop, suspended, right in the middle of the jump. I thought they would both crash down, my daughter with the horse on top of her.

You could hear people's breath being sucked in. I wanted to look away, but I couldn't. Then Allison dug the ends of her heels in harder, and Sandy went over. Everyone exploded in applause. There wasn't a person in the whole arena who didn't realize that it was the rider's determination and courage that had driven that horse over the jump. That was both a good and a bad memory. Some memories are mixed that way. Why is it that there seem to be so many more bad memories than good?

The hotel manager began berating me. "Do you realize who that was?" It was a rhetorical question. Of course I didn't know who that was. "He go away, to England, stay there, go to famous school, come back and lib in Nairobi, then come back here and be the one Masai go to when they wan help, have a fight, git in trouble." He looked at me as if he couldn't understand how I, of all people, should have been with such a great chief.

"Look at what you have around your neck," he said in exasperation. "Very rare, very, very rare. You want sell?"

I shook my head.

"So then go to room. I send fruit."

"That's all right. I'm just thirsty."

"Git Big Mama Coke, git Big Mama bottle water, git the Big Mama fruit," he shouted at his staff, his face locked into determination. "You must wear that," he pointed to the necklace, "all time you here. Big insult you don't. Peoples know you hab it," I had no idea how this would be true, but I took his word for it, "and they be—" He shook his hands in front of him and wobbled his head back and forth, indicating great agitation. "If you no wear dat, there be big badness for you with peoples."

A huge basket of fruit came almost as soon as I got back to the room. Six Cokes, bottled water. Flowers—beautiful, exotic flowers. When I went to the dining room, the manager came over to see if I had the necklace on. The guide, who had stopped making such a big fuss about the fact he was a Kikuyu, made a point of paying an extravagant amount of attention to me. When we went for the game run, he insisted I sit beside him, the best seat in the van, and when he was pointing out something, he spoke to me as if I were the only person in the van.

None of the "boys" who worked at the lodges would take any tips. They would shake their heads vigorously, no, they didn't want my monies, pointing to the string necklace. If they took money, they seemed to be saying, they would be committing a breach of etiquette they would never be forgiven.

So I wore the necklace—actually, I got so I never took it off. That way, I wouldn't have to remember to put it back on. Once, when I came out to the van without it, the guide made such a terrible fuss that I had to go back in and put it on again.

Here in Africa, I am special, not because of anything I have done, but because I have known someone who is. That is one of the clues to success I have not absorbed before, that success is often the result of knowing someone of consequence—not what you have done, but who you know.

I see something else: it is often luck that confers this entry to entitlements. Luck is better than hard work. I remember Roy Bongartz once telling me that, but I hadn't listened closely enough to absorb the ramifications of what he said. I think I remember him saying as well that I didn't have what you call good luck. I had odd luck.

The other members of our tour were not enthralled by all this attention I was receiving. For the rest of the trip, at every lodge, somehow the word had gone ahead and I was singled out. I tried to make things better by sharing fruit and flowers, but it was no good, especially since as soon as the fruit in my room was gone, another basket would arrive. The last day of the trip, one of the women came up to me in high dudgeon. "I want you to know we're all sick to death of you wearing those filthy pieces of string around your neck and encouraging Africans in their voodoo."

"Voodoo? I think you have the wrong continent," I said, which was about the worst comment I could have made. It implied she was stupid as well as jealous. Worse, at that moment, a big British man, all sunburned and blotchy with drink, came bustling up to me and said in the commanding voice of one who is used to being obeyed, "I'll buy that off you," pointing to the necklace. "I'll give you a good price for it. Name your price and I'll—"

I fled to the van that was to take us to the airport and out of Africa.

*I want to see the animals. I want to see Karen Blixen's house, I want to see Denys Finch Hatton's grave, and I want to meet an African prince.* My daughter should have added, And I need to meet Wallace.

Wallace was a treasure I had found the first time I was in Nairobi. He was outside the New Stanley Hotel standing in front of his cab. There was a whole line of cabs and drivers, most of them shouting and plucking at my sleeve to get my attention, but Wallace just stood by his cab and waited. He was too proud to entreat. I shook off all the others and walked over to Wallace, and he gave me one of those big African smiles, gleaming white teeth in his beautiful black African face.

Wallace and I were made for one another. There was something in both of us that loved a quest. I would hear about some place I wanted to go, tell Wallace no one knew where it was, and he would find out where it was. I would be filled with admiration that he had found it and that we would both go and not tell anyone else what we had discovered. He spoke passable English, which was a help, because one of the "boys" who carried my luggage up the first time I was at the New Stanley said to me, after he fussed opening and closing the closet door, the bathroom door, turning on the lights, turning off lights, pointing to the bed, opening the blinds at the window, and checking that the water thermos was full, Of course you are also entitled to a free Masai. That couldn't have been what he meant, I thought, though strange countries had strange customs. After some time, I thought what he was trying to say was, And of course you are also entitled to a free massage.

Wallace was always on time. He always carried spare bottled water in case I ran out. If the trip turned out to be a long one, he would stop the car and get out for a cucumber or an orange, anything that could be peeled. He would carefully prepare two equal portions, gravely hand me one of the halves, and eat the other himself. Wallace's hands, I discovered, were skilled in ways I would never have dreamed of: he could fix the car when it refused to start; he took me to ColPro to find the right clothes to wear on safari; he could hoist huge boxes that must have weighed sixty or seventy pounds; he could turn a small piece of fruit delicately around as he stripped the skin away in one long, curled peeling

Luis's hands were earth hands. David's hands had been fashioned to turn into reality large monuments that had once only been visions that had no dimensions in real space at all. Wallace's hands were the hands of a man who believed that labor and honor went together. He believed in preserving his dignity, even if he were poor. He waited for customers to come to him; he did not run alongside a possible fare and plead, Take my cab, you take my cab, Big Mama. He had been born black in a poor country to people who had little means, but he had fashioned for himself a path to self-respect. Do not degrade yourself. Do not make money the measure of a man's worth. Do not ever try to take advantage of someone else. Above all, use what little you have and make it into something worthwhile in your own eyes. I believe I would identify this as Commandment Six.

I knew he never overcharged me—as a matter of fact, I often thought he undercharged me. I would have left my money, my passport, my travelers checks—even *my purse*—with him and never given it a minute's thought. I often did. He was like the British after World War II, the war that destroyed their empire but left them still full of a sense of honor that made their sacrifice worthwhile. They could stand proud amidst the ruins.

I didn't rest or relax in the time we had when the tour group came back and forth to Nairobi; I went with Wallace on expeditions. The first was to the Karen Blixen house, which was not difficult to locate since everyone in Nairobi knew who the Baroness Blixen was. She was a legend in her adopted land even before, under the name she chose to write under, Isak Dinesen, she published *Out of Africa*, which had later been made into a film with Meryl Streep playing the part of the baroness. Yes, I had come to Africa to see the animals, but I wanted more than anything to see Karen Blixen's house. I make lists. The top five things to see. The top five things to avoid. The top five presents to bring back. At the top of my list for things to see in Kenya was Karen Blixen's house. Second was Denys Finch Hatton's grave.

Karen Blixen's coffee plantation had once been quite a distance from Nairobi, but with the population expansion and the migration of hundreds of thousands of Africans to Nairobi, it now stood in the midst of a suburb at the outskirts of the city, appropriately called Karen. Later her house became the first National Monument of Kenya.

The first time Wallace drove me out to the house, there was very little furniture, but I remembered clearly the bedroom that was almost completely intact with her own things. I remembered seeing Denys Finch Hatton's bookcases with his initials on them in the living room. The house was just being opened to the public, and there was no one else about except an extremely obliging man who took me into the middle of the almost completely vacant living room—except for the initialed bookcases—and told me to stand still and wait. He disappeared, and a moment later the music from the movie *Out of Africa* flooded the room. It was a very emotional moment for me, because I felt connected to Karen Blixen, who had lost both her adopted country and the one man she truly loved.

Karen Blixen was a woman of losses: She lost her husband to endless infidelities (Bror Blixen was oddly the basis for Hemingway's portraits of great white hunters in his short stories and novels). She lost her coffee plantation to fire. She first lost her lover because he was unable to make the commitment she wanted (some would have said demanded). She went bankrupt and lost the farm to which she had given her life. And just before she left to go home to Denmark, she lost the love of her life; he didn't just desert her. Denys Finch Hatton's small plane crashed as it took off from Voi, and he and the boy with him died instantly.

I knew that Denys Finch Hatton was buried up in the Ngong Hills in back of the coffee plantation that Karen Blixen had lived in while she was in Africa, but even the curator of her house didn't know where the grave was. I said to him, Karen Blixen had a long pole with a white flag put up at Denys Finch Hatton's grave so that she could stand in her garden and look up and see a flutter of white and know that Denys Finch Hatton was there. I would count this as having done my homework, but the curator gave me that look of one who is dealing with a difficult woman he wished would go away.

While I was at Amboseli that first time getting the bridal necklace, Wallace had been asking around, and when the group came back, he found me and said, *Oh, the Big Mama gonna marry.* He pointed to the necklace. I shook my head emphatically that I was not getting married, but Wallace was already laughing. He had been having a little fun with me. Then he said, I think I know where the grave you look for be.

We had some trouble finding the right road up into the hills because it was hardly a road at all, really little more than a dirt path, that bumped along until it petered out. We got out and walked. We found the obelisk about a quarter of a mile up the hill. Denys's brother Toby had had a brass plaque attached with two lines from Coleridge's poem "The Rime of the Ancient Mariner" that Denys had loved:

*He prayeth well, who loveth well*
*Both man and bird and beast*

Around the grave, there was a circle of whitewashed stone that Karen Blixen had taken from her drive and brought up day by day to outline the grave. No one there remembered Karen Blixen or knew how the stones had got there or who the person in the grave was or why it was so important that I, an American white woman, would come thousands of miles to see it. Certainly they did not know that Karen Blixen had written *Out of Africa*, a work so admired by Ernest Hemingway that the year he was awarded the Nobel Prize for Literature he had said she deserved the award more than he did.

One of Karen Blixen's favorite toasts—rose-lipped maidens and lightfoot lads—came from an A.E. Housman poem she was very fond of because Denys had quoted it so often while he was alive.

*With rue my heart is laden*
*For golden friends I had*
*For many a rose-lipped maiden*
*And many a lightfoot lad.*

It was the toast she gave just before she left Africa, when a man came out of the bar at the Norfolk Hotel, which had refused her a drink her first day in Nairobi. Women were not allowed in that males-only bar, and now one of its members did the unthinkable: he invited her in. All the men stood up as she was given her drink, for all I know the only woman who was ever allowed to invade their bar. She raised her glass and said, Rose-lipped maidens, lightfooted lads.

I never knew Wallace's last name. I would send postcards to the New Stanley Hotel with the name Wallace printed in capitals on it and presume he would get them because everyone there seemed to know him. I would say "Wallace" to the hotel help, and they would say in pidgin English, He's out with a fare right now, or He hasn't come by yet, or He's around the corner getting a coffee. I never once said "Wallace" and someone at the hotel said *Who?*

When I came through emigration with my daughter, the man looking at my passport said my visa had expired. I said, It is good for six months. I just got it. No, it no good. Maybe we fix this up someway. He looked at me expectantly. He meant, Give me some monies, and we can make this problem go away. I want to see your supervisor, I said. Maybe I make mistake month with day. Let me look again. He stamped the entry date, looking at me with hatred.

How would the little bit of the money I could have given him as a bribe make any difference to me while it might have been able to make a lot of difference to him? Four billion people in the world live on less than a dollar a day. I spend more than that on a coffee at Starbucks, but the truth is that the man looked like a shifty shyster. I didn't have any sympathy for him, and I didn't believe he was one of the four billion who live on a dollar a day, and he was not going to get one red cent out of me. Really it had nothing to do with principle. It had to do with my memories of Buzz Cut and how he tried to make me give him all the money I made—What do *you* need a bank account for? he would sneer, as if I were such a moron about monetary matters that I would be threatening the world economy by possessing any cold cash on my own (shades of my boat-husband, of wives who never learn to drive or learn how to write checks). When, in the end, I resisted and kept money in an account that he couldn't get his hands on, he disappeared. The gods be praised, nobody knew where.

He had been such a sweet talker that I had failed to remember that all successful swindlers take you to Niagara Falls with their waterfall of words so that they can give you a fiscal hosing down. Thinking about my daughter's father was not an uplifting experience. I think instead of my daughter, who, like Wallace, believes that words are cheap but actions reveal the real person you are, both of whom believe (I tell myself) that bribery was the opposite of honor. I wanted to stand on the side of honor (Commandment Seven) the way my daughter and Wallace did.

Very early in our relationship, Wallace had taught me the basic element of righteous behavior when he would stand respectfully in front of some policeman who had pulled us over (Westerner in the back, good prey, that) and listen to the policeman talk about some infraction of tangled Kenyan law that Wallace had committed. Wallace didn't argue. He would just stand, dignified and silent, his lips pressed together, waiting. Argument, he seemed to be saying silently, was useless. He was taking a stand; remaining stationary but resolute beside his cab, jamming up traffic, horns blowing, people shouting, Wallace standing, not arguing, just silent and resolute, until some bureaucratic god of redemption appeared and said to the crooked policeman, Let this man go his way, find someone else to harass. In other words, bribe people who will give you money, not trouble.

The first time one of these episodes took place, I said to Wallace, Weren't you afraid he might take us to jail? I did not say, I don't want to be in a Kenyan jail.

If you no be with me, I would no be pulled over. I didn't do nothing. Maybe the policeman thought he scare you, you give him monies. But me, he don't care nothing about me. It was good, though, you in cab so he don't beat me with that stick he carry. They like using that stick, even if you pay them some monies to make them go away. I am sorry you see peoples like this. Once people have—what is the English word?—honors.

Honor, I said. Honors are like medals they give you because you did something brave. Honor is—I stopped. What kind of definition did I have to give him? The only word I knew that explained all its ramifications was Spanish, *pundunor.* Your word is your bond, you do what you think is right, not what is easier or more profitable. Honor is—is—a recognition of the fact there are right ways to behave and wrong ways and that you try to try to live up to the right ways. Oh, dammit, I don't know how to define honor. You have this feeling. It tells you how you should act.

There are a lot of feelings, and different people have different kinds of feelings. Hemingway struggled all his life to know the difference between right and wrong. He came up with a lame explanation, that when you did the right thing, you felt right afterwards. But that's post mortem; it evades the real answer. You have to know before, not after, what you should do. Maybe he should have said that you build up a series of rules for yourself by understanding after you have done something whether you felt you acted in the right way. If you didn't feel you had, you knew you hadn't done what you should have. In that way, you build a code of honor that tells you how to act beforehand.

Men for centuries have been working on answers to that question. Choose the ones that apply to you. Learn as you go along. One of the reasons you get old is to learn. I'll remind myself of that when I'm old and hobbled and flounder around for words. I know the answer to what honor is, I'll say. Who do you think will want to hear what I have to say?

Wallace isn't old, and he knows what honor is. Ask him.

But pick a better place, a better time.


I had planned to arrive with my daughter two days before our tour started so that she could see the Blixen house and Finch Hatton's grave before we started our tour because they were not on our itinerary. I had sent a card to Wallace telling him to meet us at the airport and giving him the flight number, the airline, and the time of our arrival. We were something like four hours late, but there was Wallace waiting for us as we got through customs. I was so glad to see him, I wanted to throw my arms around him, but he would have been mortified. Our bags didn't come, I said after I introduced my daughter. Did you get any of the cards I sent you?

Yes, he said with his big toothy smile, I receive cards you send.

I had lots of things I thought Wallace might want in my duffel—cigarettes, a Timex watch, some American tee shirts, shaving gear and soap, small presents for his four children. I went on and on, trying to explain, because I didn't want him to think I had come empty-handed. My daughter was with the station master trying to fill out a form that was in such inexact English that the questions were impossible to understand, but she had the air of one who has just been assigned the title of doctor and was making a far better impression than I would have. Also, she was blonde. Being blonde anywhere, but especially in Africa, goes a long way for women. Just to be sure, I had put the string necklace around her neck.

She came back and said the man she was supposed to speak to wasn't there, but the man she had spoken to couldn't seem to comprehend that *both* our bags had been lost. She had got, she felt, nowhere. Never mind, I said, Wallace will fix it, and Wallace said, Yes, Big Mama, I think I can do dat. You wait here, Big Mama. I not be long.

Wallace has clout, I thought, and a great sense of satisfaction came over me because a person like Wallace, who I so much admired, liked me. We are judged, it is said, by our friends. Our enemies as well, but who wants to think about that?

When Wallace drove us from the airport into Nairobi, I kept looking for a giraffe—actually, any African animal would do—because I wanted my daughter to have the same kind of transcendental experience I had had the first time I arrived in Kenya. For mile after mile, we saw nothing but the crushed wrecks of cars abandoned to the endless stretches of scratchy land that ran right up to the skyscrapers that were so incongruous in the middle of the African desert. She seemed happy, my daughter, looking out the window at all that barren ground. I wanted to say, It looks just like the land around *Los Vientos*, but I had

311

told my daughter almost nothing about Luis or *Los Vientos*. She would never have existed if I had stayed in Spain with Luis, not something I thought appropriate to bring to her attention.

"Wallace," I said, "let me book us in at the New Stanley. You can get some other fares while we put our things in our room. We're going to ColPro to get Allison some clothes—"

"I figure you hire me by the day, Big Mama. It work out cheaper that way. You pay by the hour and you go all day, you get cheated for your money. You rest some, and then I go with you to ColPro so you can put your things in the car. Then we go on where you want."

"I want to go to the safari park outside town because I know there are rhinos there, and you can never be sure you'll see one in the bush."

"You never sure you see leopards neither."

That was true. I had not seen a leopard on the Teddy Roosevelt tour. They were getting scarce, the way the cheetahs were. Cheetahs had become so inbred that their immune systems couldn't fight off the regular diseases of the plains. In ten years, twenty years at the most, there would probably be no more cheetahs in the Serengeti, something a new Veterinary Doctor of Medicine would not like to hear. Animals can't vote or carry guns, so they have little way to protect themselves. I'm sure if they could, they would rush to Wal*Mart and buy guns and ammunition. The only two things Wal*Mart is willing to order for you are guns and ammunition. You cannot order camping equipment or toys or pool cues— nothing but lethal weapons.

"From park I take you to an African restaurant I know—not the Carnivore—dat be for later, tomorrow maybe. A *real* Africa restaurant you like."

Most things change from the way you remember them, but Wallace was just the same. ColPro was just the same. I could hear the happiness in my daughter's voice as she called out from the booth where she was trying on clothes, and since she was happy, I was happy

When she came out, she pirouetted about and said, "Well, what do you think?"

"I think you look ready for Africa."

But in the eight years I had been away from Africa, I could see every thing had deteriorated. The streets were worse—broken cement, huge potholes, gangs of kids hanging around and looking menacing. The people looked poorer and seemed depressed. The stores looked shoddier. It was as if everything in the country was going downhill.

Everything about Spain would have changed too. *Los Vientos* would have been full of expensive things in (I hoped) bad taste that Luis's wife had ordered from some awful place like Harrods's. If it had changed, I wanted it to have changed for the worse. I couldn't stand the idea of Luis's wife making it better. I would never have changed it, never. Except maybe for the wagon-wheel table, but I might even have come to like that in time. Time has great powers we often don't recognize until it's too late. Call that Observation, not Commandment, Eight.

I have my promise to myself not to get in touch with Luis. Years have gone by, and no matter what the temptation, I have resisted. Perhaps my doing "good" hadn't really been doing good at all, but was only some fascist leftover, Catholic patrol inside my brain keeping me from reaching for a pen or the phone. Good should be spontaneous, shouldn't it? Not imposed with reluctance and anger. I was angry, I was terribly angry with the world for being the way it was, with all its endless, baffling rules, which I always seemed to learn too late to help me straighten out the mistakes I'd made and set the wrongs to right.

You should be happy, I told myself. You are in Africa with your daughter, whose face had just lit up with delight as she sees her first real African animal, a warthog with two babies trailing after, the warthog's tail straight in the air like the mast on the *Blotto*.

The game park outside Nairobi has a scruffy, artificial air about it, as if the animals had learned their constrictions and trudged about those confines with listless resignation. Wallace's African restaurant was crowded, tumultuous, and had a long line of people waiting to be served. We best go to the Carnivore, he said with obvious disappointment. The Carnivore is listed in all the guide books. It is what I would describe as Westernized, with tables of tourists consuming all the various kinds of wild game available in Africa (well, I'm not sure about giraffe). Waiters circulate with great platters of different meats, and you take whatever you want. I liked—I have no idea why—the crocodile meat best. It never occurred to me until later that I had taken a newly minted doctor whose life's work was to save animals to a restaurant that served their meat, which someone had to have slaughtered so that it could be put on her plate.

I was wearing the bridal necklace, but nobody came up and asked me if I wanted to sell it. No one even seemed to bother looking at it. I had been counting on the necklace to get me the same kind of recognition I had received before. A sense of entitlement is not the right way to look at the world, but this I can tell you: I loved all that attention and preferential treatment. Roy Bongartz would not have been proud of me. He believed shallowness was a major sin. He was one of those people who always took the high road. I was one of those people who too often took short cuts and back alleys.

My daughter perked up the next day when Wallace drove us out to Karen Blixen's Mbogani house, with its long lawns and sweeping views of the Ngong hills, which Karen Blixon had loved so much and which became a curse for her. The soil there was too acidic to grow coffee, and she lost all her money trying to bring the plantation to profit during her seventeen-year stay in Kenya. Finally she could no longer borrow from her family and had to sell the farm to repay her debts. The Nairobi developer who bought the seven-hundred-acre estate offered Karen Blixen a parcel of land and her house. "I would rather live in the middle of the Sahara," she told him, "than on twenty acres in the suburb of 'Karen.'"

The house was now almost fully furnished with items people had donated. These are not Karen Blixen's, the guide informed us, but they come from the same time period when she lived in the house. This was a different man than the one who had played music for me while I stood in the midst of the living room looking at the initials DFH on Denys Finch Hatton's bookcases. There were a lot of people browsing around and no music at all. It would have been more dramatic, I thought, if there was the music, but the guide had other matters on his mind. He went into rapture when we came to the bedroom, which still had the muted, lemony look I remembered from my first visit. The guide pointed to the mosquito netting draped over the bed that he said made it look like a royal resting place. Then the guide threw out his arms, taking in the whole expanse of the room. "Oh, it be so beautiful," he cried. "It be too beautiful for us to know how to say how beautiful it be. Think of that lovely woman who lived here. She lay on that beautiful bed." He pointed dramatically to the bed. "It make your heart want to remember forever, that beautiful woman lying on that beautiful bed. Don't you see her there, that beautiful woman on that beautiful bed? Oh, I hope you see it! We should be thanking god for such a beautiful moment."

My daughter looked at me and said, "Do you see it, Big Mama, do you see that beautiful woman lying there on that beautiful bed?"

"I see that beautiful woman lying on that beautiful bed with a beautiful man. Do you think we should tell this guy about Denys Finch Hatton?"

"I think we should ditch this guy and wander around on our own and then go to Denys's grave. I don't think we need to go to the gift shop they've put up, do you?"

Denys Finch Hatton's grave had tourist buses all around it. There was a little stand that sold bottled water and Cokes, and the man on whose land Denys was buried was charging people to see the grave, something Karen Blixen would never have imagined when she had written, "The grave was a thousand feet higher than my house, the air was different here, as clear as a glass of water; light sweet winds lifted your hair when you took off your hat; over the peaks of the hills, the clouds came wandering from the East, drew their live shadow over the wide undulating land, and were dissolved and disappeared over the Rift Valley."

The air is always different in special places, but this was no longer a special place. Like my daughter, I wanted to leave Nairobi and get to Amboseli and find the Masai prince. I wondered if he would recognize me.

Yes, I thought, he will.

We went in a zebra-painted van to the same lodge, but it had a new manager. I had been away so long, eight years, that I didn't recognize any of the "boys," nor did any of them remember me.

315

The elephants were still there, but now there were too many elephants for the amount of land they had been squeezed into. Every tree seemed stripped bare, broken and dying. Soon, Cynthia Wood would have to make choices about which elephants were to be shot—culling the herd, they call it antiseptically—so that the elephants that were left would have enough food. Even then, in a short time those elephants would have killed off what was left of the trees and brush and need to be culled again. An air of disaster hung over the preserve, as if it were in its dying days.

The tin huts up the road from the lodge had been tarted up for the tourists. When I tried to describe The Black Prince—putting my arm up in the air and saying, Very tall, and then trying to look wise and saying, A great chief—nobody seemed to know who I was talking about. By this time, everything about people who had come to buy things had poured out of that lodge and up into those tin huts. The men in the huts probably never wanted to see any more of these foreigners, but they needed big monies for the education of their (mostly non-existent) children; that was how they made their living, selling tacky representations (mostly made in China) instead of the beautiful baskets and extraordinary masks I had seen with The Black Prince. The huts had been fumigated and had shelves with dozens of duplicate copies of the same masks and heads sold on every street corner in towns where tourists who went to Africa crowded.

I was afraid my daughter would think The Black Prince existed only in my imagination, but I had the necklace, which the shopkeepers looked at impatiently and then turned away, not one of them making a bid on it. The tin huts have joined The Age of Vulgarization, which is now global, conceived, run, and ruined by "innovative enterprise."

My daughter was looking around in bewilderment. She couldn't picture the huts as they had once been. She only had my word they had been that way. I am a storyteller by choice, if not often by trade, and could quite probably have made up the whole episode. It had the right romantic ring—the lost maiden in distress in the midst of great danger rescued by the (black) prince. It's my mother's chimera, my daughter probably concluded, since we never found The Black Prince. We never even got a clue as to where he might be. He had disappeared into thin air, an air full of dark prophesies of what was to come to Africa in the years ahead—corruption, financial manipulations to benefit those in power (Zaire's Mobutu was said to have stashed as much as two billion dollars he had wheedled out of the World Bank into Swiss accounts), civil wars that never ended, genocide, famines, female mutilations, rape and amputations, AIDS, sexual slavery for both young boys and girls, mass murders. No one had dreamed in those hopeful years that followed the end of colonialism and the countries took on their own independence that they would be worse off than they had been under the Europeans.

I had tried to go back to humans' first home again, and you can't go home again, not even to adopted homes. That's a universal commandment, so I guess if the last commandment wasn't a real commandment but only a comment, we could call this the real Commandment Eight.

Since we were traveling much of the time so near the equator, day and night were equally divided, and when the sun came up, it rose in a riot of orange and yellow over long, deserted stretches of land with acacia trees and zebras and wildebeests silhouetted against the sky; when night was ready to take over, the sun sank so fast that it was there one minute and gone the next. Then the night noises began: a lion coughing, zebras barking, occasionally a trumpeting from elephants, and other sounds I did not recognize, though I knew the hyenas and jackals came out at night and the leopards prowled. My daughter and I would sit on a log and watch the sun go down. We were silent, tied to our own thoughts. They belonged only to ourselves and a night slitted with thousands of glittering stars.

There is no sky on earth, I think, that has as many stars as an equator sky. Twice we got up near dawn to see the Southern Cross, which for me turned out to be a big disappointment. Its formation of stars looked more like a kite than a cross. During the day, we could see Mount Kilimanjaro, at 19,341 feet above sea level Africa's tallest mountain, which was actually in Tanzania; it was the mountain Hemingway had cared about so much, which my daughter would one day climb, with its cap of snow and the long purple shadows it cast across the plains.

Because of global warming, the snows are all vanishing. One day soon, there will be no snow at all on the mountain. Hemingway's famous short story "The Snows of Kilimanjaro," where a leopard is found at the height of the mountain buried in snow, will make no sense at all. I see this as a parable of what is happening to the world at large.

We saw the sun come up every day because we got up in the dark to be ready to go on our morning game run at six. I piled one sweater on top of another and wore a bush jacket, and I was so cold that I still had to borrow something more from my daughter, who all her life has seemed more sensible and better prepared than I. There was strong tea and a basket of biscuits on a table set up near a blazing fire. We huddled around its warmth and swallowed the scalding tea and jammed biscuits in our pockets for later on in the morning. We would be gone four hours and ravenous by the time we got back to camp. Never go anywhere without food should be Commandment Nine.

Gradually, as the sun moved overhead, the day heated up until even in short sleeves, if there was not a breeze, I would sweat and steam. We wore hats against that sun and dark glasses. The dark glasses were a nuisance because I had to keep taking them off to use my binoculars. Some people are excellent spotters. I was mediocre and always felt ridiculously proud if I spotted anything at all. My daughter was spectacular as a spotter. She could find a lion against all that golden landscape as if it had been outlined in black.

My daughter spotted a leopard up in a tree (I finally saw a leopard) and could even hear baboons before we saw them. She did everything better than I did. I hoped this would extend to love as well, but I had reached the point where I had come to believe love was a taste of Eden, where the world was suddenly as it should be, but that moment was brief. The snake came, and you were always cast out.

After the morning game run, we usually returned to camp and wolfed down a combination of breakfast and lunch. Sometimes we picnicked by a pool where there were forty or fifty hippos splashing around. The Greeks had called them river horses. You rarely see them out of the water during the day because their skin is so sensitive that they get badly sunburned if they stay out in the open too long. Then their bodies fester. They leave the water at night to browse.

The guide gave us a printed list of rules about how to behave if the hippos came near camp:

DO NOT TRY TO TAKE PICTURES OF THE HIPPOS.
DO NOT SHINE FLASHLIGHTS INTO THE HIPPOS' EYES.
DO NOT TRY TO FEED THE HIPPOS.
DO NOT CHASE THE HIPPOS.
DO NOT SING AND DANCE AMONG THE HIPPOS.
DO NOT HIT THE HIPPOS ON THE HEAD WITH STICKS.

Hippos kill more people than any other animal in Africa, the guide said. I found this difficult to believe. Not only did hippos look playful and often even placid in their pools, but crocodiles were always leaping out of their hiding places and snatching a child and pulling it under in less than a second. The crocodiles had underwater lockers where they stashed their food. They liked everything ripe. They built up an inventory, like capitalists, but they had not evolved into retail distribution. They have small rudimentary brains and cannot stick out their tongues, so they would make poor entrepreneurs.

Cape buffalo were said to be the most dangerous game on the plains because they would run you down and not just spike you on a horn the way the bulls in the rings in Spain did; they would hook you first and then throw you to the ground and stamp on you until all the bones in your body were crushed.

Rhinos were feared by hunters almost as much as Cape buffalo. Rhinos were usually camouflaged in the brush and came out so fast that there wasn't time to fire a gun (guides were allowed to carry firearms when on walking safaris). Rhinos have extremely poor eyesight, but when they sight an enemy, they cannot be deterred. They will charge at fifty to sixty miles an hour, and they weigh well over a ton.

Even the giraffes, my favorite of all the animals, can kill you with a kick from one of their long, strong legs. But on the whole, giraffes were the most endearing of all the African animals. The females would gather all their young around a tree or shrub and surround them in a place where they could browse with a circle of "aunties" to protect them.

Most people want to see lions, especially a lioness with cubs, but I wanted to see wild dogs because they have nearly been exterminated by farmers and are almost never encountered anymore in Africa. They were considered the worst predators on the plains and would come into a ranch and devastate a herd of livestock. A pack of wild dogs will gather around a cow and sort it out from the herd and tear it apart in less than five minutes.

Wild dogs have a horrific smell, but they—like jackals and hyenas— are wonderful parents and serve, along with the vultures, the hyenas, and jackals as vacuum cleaners of Kenya's Great Rift Valley, that six-thousand-mile crack in the earth that runs from Lebanon to central Mozambique and neatly divides Kenya into two distinct parts.

One early dark morning when we were just setting out, there was suddenly an overpowering odor that flooded the van. The driver slammed on the brakes and yelled, "Wild dogs!" All around us, black and white spotted dogs were running so fast that they had come and gone almost before I could put a real impression of them into my mind. Their smell hung on, in the van, in our clothes, in our hair, and on our hands. Suddenly I was taken back to the *Blotto* and the smell of the sea. The desert at moments seemed like water surrounding us on all sides, and I was filled with the presentiment of death.

Death is ever present on the air of the Serengeti. Animals and humans live with it minute by minute and thus become inured to it; like them, I quite soon became used to it myself. Yes, used to it. The first time I saw one animal run down another and kill it, I felt my heart leap up in my throat and my lungs slam shut. The second time, I was a little less distressed. In no time at all, death became a matter of course, something taken for granted.

Even the marker at the edge of the Ngorongoro Gorge in memory of Michael Brzimek didn't get the emotional acknowledgment it deserved.

Michael Grzimek was killed when he was just twenty-five. He was flying a small plane across the Ngorongoro Crater. A griffon-vulture hit the right wing of Michael Grzimek's plane and bent the wing in; that in turn blocked the rudder cables. The airplane went into a spin and struck the earth with such force that Michael was killed instantly.

We were sitting, my daughter and I, in the crusty dead grasses in front of Michael Grzimek's grave. My daughter turned her head toward the vast emptiness that is Africa in front of us. I had no idea at all what she was thinking.

D.H. Lawrence thought to be alive was to feel as if you were on fire. David lost the feeling of fire, I thought. He no longer could smell in the air that sweetness that is always there when your heart is finally filled with grace, as mine was at that moment. The sky suddenly filled with the wings of doves over the green shrubs that struggled to survive at Michael Grzimek's grave. I thought, Michael Grzimek is home.

If you know where you belong, you will be all right. It might be the place you began your journey, where you were born and your family had lived for generations. It might be in your own country; it might be in another country. But there is a place, just as there might possibly be a person, that was meant for you, and if you were foolish enough not to realize you had found either—and they often came together—then your life would never fit into the mold that was meant for it. You would become a wanderer. Like The Black Prince. Like me. Like Ulysses. Everything turns out to be a Greek myth in one way or another

The gods don't want us to be happy, I say to my daughter. They want us to have a taste, but they don't want us to own the real thing, not for long. It's as if they like punishments, those gods, I say to my daughter.

Which gods? she asks, puzzled.

Whichever ones you choose.

> *My mother died*
> *My father died,*
> *My brother died,*
> *My sister died,*
> *They all died died died*

My daughter grabs hold of my hand. I'm so glad you brought me, she says. I will never forget these days, Karen Blixen's house and Denys Finch Hatton's grave, the Serengeti, the animals, even the smell of the wild dogs.

She thinks she'll remember them all, but she won't. Fragments of a few will come back to her, but we can't choose what we remember. Which part inside us makes those choices of what to remember and what to forget? Or to value some small part over so many seemingly more important ones? Are we many people bundled there inside, some not even recognized? There is one who bullies the rest aside, and its name is The Chooser. How does The Chooser decide which memories to select?

My daughter says, I will always remember us sitting here at the grave looking out over Africa. Look, out there in the distance. A whole herd is moving. I can't tell whether they're zebra or Cape buffalo. It doesn't matter. They're what I came to see, animals moving across the Serengeti.

She presses my hand lightly. Our blood seems to mingle and our hearts to beat together. She *is* my blood, and she will go on after I am gone, carrying me as a part of her. I will be somehow still living.

You need many things to live. You need air. You need water—after all, two-thirds of the earth is water, and human beings have bodies made up of sixty percent water, but they need air even more than water. It is my contention that they need the air of a particular place that makes them know they have finally found a small space where they feel they belong.

At that moment, this is where we belong, my daughter and I. In my mind, a small creature is pushing herself up to stand and look out on the great plain. I know it is a woman, like my daughter, like myself, transported by a blur of some great herd of animals running on the horizon. Her genes are still in mine, in my daughter. We three are connected, will always be connected. Perhaps The Chooser started with her.

Thomas Hobbes characterized life as "solitary, poor, nasty, brutish, and short." That is one view, easy enough to accept. I prefer Freya Stark's way of looking at the world. It would be pleasant, she says, "to look back on a life that has never given its soul for money, its time to a purpose not believed in, its body to anything but love."

Time has not beat us, I tell Luis. We have remained young and beautiful to each other. We have never grown old and ugly. We are always at that moment when you rode up at a gallop and leapt off your horse and took hold of my hand and I knew you loved me and you knew I loved you. You have had me always as you had me then. You could never have had me that way in real life. It is the two of us, you and I, who have beaten time. But, Luis, I say, even memories die the moment the air leaves our bodies, and then our history, yours and mine, will have vanished without any trace left.

How do you know that? Luis asks me, and of course I do not know that. Nobody does.

We are wanderers in a world where we are supposed to find answers that suit our needs and aspirations and to try to rectify the wrongs that were done before us. That custodianship, I think of there in the midst of the Serengeti, is Commandment Ten, and my heart is calmed for a moment and at peace with itself.

With my daughter, now Dr. Allison Branson, who has just graduated

The Sixty Acres farm house

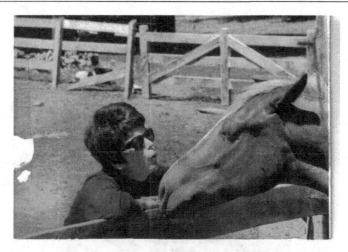

With my Tennessee Walking horse colt

Giraffes crossing the road at twilight

My daughter writing a message for the
bulletin board of the Thorn Tree Café

Elephants at Amboseli

Masai warriors

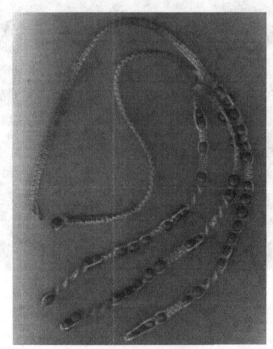

The bridal necklace

The van. I'm in the hat

Wallace with me in Africa

Karen Blixen's house

Allison in her ColPro clothes

Spotting lions in the grass

Michael Grzimek memorial 12.4.1934—10.1.1959

There is a bronze plaque that Michael's father had composed.

HE GAVE ALL HE POSSESSED
INCLUDING HIS LIFE
FOR THE WILD ANIMALS OF AFRICA

# Acknowledgments

Cover by Larry Dudley of The Hudson Press

I would like to take this opportunity to thank the following people who encouraged and kept me going on this book. I am using alphabetical order; they all equally helped in one way or another.

Linda Barber
Allison Branson
Carrie Buckman
Janet Jacobson
Roger Longo
Judy and Paul Madison
Jane Armstrong Nelson
Paul Pines
Ron Pisano
Anne Wycherley

And in remembrance of

Mary Allison, for whom my daughter was named
Roy Bongartz
Richard Carrott
Barthold Fles
Wesley Hare
He who was Luis of *Los Vientos*
Beverly Jacobson
Elinor Price
David Smith
Helen Taylor
Richard Tierrnan

All the animals of the Serengeti that have been slaughtered

And certainly I would never have got through the formatting if not for Amy McHargue.

Most of the pictures in this book I took myself years ago with an old-fashioned camera, now, alas, defunct. I want to thank the following for permissions to use their materials: Dorothy Dehner. Sixty Years of Art. Oct. 16–Nov. 28, 1993. Charles R. Wood Gallery, The Hyde Collection, Glens Falls, New York.

Nor would I have been able to use the poem and the pictures of David Smith with Dida's Fungus and Sculpture Group, Bolton Landing, without the permission of Copyright: The Estate of David Smith/Licensed y VAGA, New York, made possible by the cooperation of Rebecca and Candida Smith and the help of Susan Cooke, who had the authority to give permission from the David Smith estate. Michael Brensen, who is presently writing the definitive biography of David Smith, was also a great help.

I want to thank Susan Sherman as well for permission to use the lines from her poem "The Color of the Heart."

An earlier version of much of the material in "Fire" appeared as a chapbook, *David Smith, I Remember,* that was published in 1984 by The Loft Press. The picture of David Smith in his studio was lent by Alan Cederstrom at that time for the cover.